4

This book may be recalled before the above date.

Closing the Asylum

THE MENTAL PATIENT IN MODERN SOCIETY

Peter Barham

Second Edition

PENGUIN BOOKS

PENGUIN BOOKS

Published by the Penguin Group
Penguin Books Ltd, 27 Wrights Lane, London w8 5TZ, England
Penguin Books USA Inc., 375 Hudson Street, New York, New York 10014, USA
Penguin Books Australia Ltd, Ringwood, Victoria, Australia
Penguin Books Canada Ltd, 10 Alcorn Avenue, Toronto, Ontario, Canada M4V 3B2
Penguin Books (NZ) Ltd, 182–190 Wairau Road, Auckland 10, New Zealand

Penguin Books Ltd, Registered Offices: Harmondsworth, Middlesex, England

First published 1992
Second edition 1997
10 9 8 7 6 5 4 3 2 1

Filmset in 10/12pt Monophoto Times
Printed in England by Clays Ltd, St Ives plc

1001403520

0140265805

Contents

Acknowledgements

I am grateful for discussions with numerous people, and also to audiences in various places who have heard me talk on these themes, during the period that this book was brewing and finally written. I should especially like to express my gratitude to those users of mental health services who have taken part in the projects in which my colleagues and I have been engaged over the past few years and to the bodies which have supported this work, in particular the Joseph Rowntree Foundation. For various forms of advice, support and practical assistance my special thanks to: Peter Campbell, Martina Gartner, Geoff Griffiths, Dr Wouter Hardeman, Robert Hayward, Christopher Heginbotham, Dr Maurice Hindle, Dr Jennie Metaxa, Dr John Orley, Professor Geoffrey Pearson, Huw Lloyd Richards, Dr Graham Thornicroft, Dr David Towell and Irving Velody. Dr Roy Porter also commented most helpfully on an earlier draft. Lastly, my thanks to Ravi Mirchandani for his patience. Needless to say, I alone am responsible for what I have written.

Figures 1 and 2, on pp. 18 and 19, are reproduced from *The Provision of Mental Health Services in Britain: The Way Ahead*, edited by Greg Wilkinson and Hugh Freeman, The Royal College of Psychiatrists, 1986; figures 3 and 4, on p. 137 are reproduced by permission of King Edward's Hospital Fund for London, and are taken from *Contracting for Community Care: Strategies for Progress*, by C. Hawker and P. Ritchie, King's Fund, 1990.

Preface to the Second Edition

In preparing this new edition I have resisted the urge to tinker with the text. This book was written by a somewhat younger self, and whilst there is undoubtedly a need for a different and better book on the subject, the argument here holds together, I believe, and there is nothing in it with which I wildly disagree. Instead, I have added a new chapter in which I try to draw attention to some of the changing configurations in the landscape of the asylum, and to the alarms and debates that have gone on over the past six years or so. As will become evident, I hope, our sense of the history of the asylum has been complicating, as much as our awareness of the current scene.

It is, perhaps, useful to stress again that this book does not aim to present a comprehensive account of community mental health care or anything of that kind. It tries to put the displacement of the mental patient in contemporary society in a wider historical perspective, and to uncover the lineaments of ethical questions about the bonds between people with mental illness and their fellow human beings that are generally hidden beneath the surface of debate. How strong are these bonds, what holds them together, what happens when they break, why bother about them anyway, and so forth? It does not presume to offer any answers, but it is intended to be a resource for those who, in one way or another, are led to think about these issues. The new material is by no means exhaustive, but I have provided quite extensive notes and references. I hope some may continue to find it useful.

For encouragement, advice, and practical assistance in preparing this edition I am grateful to: Peter Campbell, Robert Hayward, Michael Neve, Geoffrey Pearson, Emma Phillips, Alastair Rolfe, Henry Rollin, David Wright, John Yates, and Robert Young. Inevitably, all the eccentricities and shortcomings are my own.

Introduction

'One of the stately homes of England,' Joseph, a long-term inmate of one of the old Victorian asylums, remarked to me one morning some years ago. That was not always how Joseph characterized his residence; more commonly it was a 'rubbish tip, a dirty, scruffy, rotten hole', though sometimes he also pondered whether it might not be a 'farm' or a 'college': 'We thought it was a college when we first got here. Next we thought it was a farm. Then we thought it was a hospital. Then we thought it was a farm again.'[1] From the point of view of the hospital staff, Joseph's altercations over where he now found himself placed were so many signs of the internal confusion and disorder that had brought him to the asylum, but we do not have to search very deeply into the history of these institutions, and the images that have been given of them, to recognize in Joseph's musings an understandable uncertainty as to what society has been trying to do with people like him. Since Joseph made his pronouncements, those with rather more power than him have authorized the closure of a large number of the Victorian asylums and the process of institutional dismantlement is set to continue over the coming decade. 'For the last forty years,' wrote Edgar Sheppard, professor of psychological medicine at King's College, London, in 1872, 'it has been the persistent effort of our legislators, under the coordinated stimulus of science and philanthropy (chiefly administered by our own noble profession), to bring under observation the loose and scattered madness of the country, and provide for its subjects fitting homes and refuges.'[2] For the past thirty years our contemporary legislators have been animated by rather different conceptions of what are to count as fitting homes and refuges for people like Joseph, and execution upon the Victorian legacy is now being carried out in earnest.

But what is the project of closing the asylum or, in that ungainly term, deinstitutionalization all about? By which perception of the institution is the project mostly powered, the idea of it as a stately home or as a rotten hole? In Britain deinstitutionalization has been proceeding by stealth for some time but, as has been rightly pointed out, it is 'less the expression of a single process and a coherent philosophy than the outcome of a number of trends that have different objectives, emphases and intellectual foundations'.[3] At issue in this conflictual design is the question of how societies like our own are to dispose (with all the ambiguities of that word) of people like Joseph. The aim of this short book is to identify and explore some of the conflicts and ambiguities in the contemporary project of closing the asylum. We shall, of course, want to consider the part played in these developments by science and philanthropy, and not least by the noble profession of psychiatry.

In Joseph's usage, the 'stately home' was, of course, ironic, but Edgar Sheppard deployed a similar image with a rather different intent in an indignant outburst against those who had dared to question the benefits of asylum regimes:

I will venture to say that there is no class of persons in the United Kingdom so well cared for as the insane. The best sites in the country are selected for their palaces, within which a cubic space per lung is measured for them ... The fat kine of our fields are laid under contribution for them; the corn and wine is stored for them; clothing of the warmest and supervision of the best are provided for them. Every sort of indulgence within reasonable bounds is theirs. Though a large number of them are of the most degraded type, and have made themselves what they are by their own vice and wickedness, they are equally (if not altogether wisely) sustained and sheltered. They are rained upon by sympathy and sunshined by kindness. They are fenced about with every sort of protection which the legislature can devise. Magistrates, guardians, commissioners, friends inspect them, visit them, record their grievances, register their scratches, encourage their complaints, tabulate their ailments.[4]

Notions of lavish provision have not been lost upon contemporary administrators appalled at the spiralling costs of maintaining these gargantuan institutions. The history of the asylum is one of the displacement of scale. What were intended by early Victorian reformers as small country houses to provide refuge for not much more than one hundred inmates had been transformed by the end of the century into sprawling 'stately homes' that behind their elegant façades reproduced the worst conditions of urban over-crowding. Even as recently as the late 1960s there were almost two thousand inmates in Joseph's asylum. But the house party, it is said, is now over. The estate has fallen on hard times and can no longer afford to entertain its guests in the manner to which they had been accustomed; they must now leave and find their own ways back to the city.

But what is imaged as a reduction of scale in one dimension, is represented as a recovery in another. In an ironic reversal, the mental patients are to be dispatched from the urban mob in the rural asylums back to the actual cities to live, not, it is said, in institutions but with their own families or in small homes. That, at least, is the official view of it. In reality, many of Joseph's confeder-ates have discovered that there are other dirty, scruffy, rotten holes besides the asylum. Joseph would certainly have been impressed by the remark of one contemporary observer that 'the chronically mentally ill patient has had his locus of living and care transferred from a single lousy institution to multiple wretched ones'.[5]

In his address to the annual conference of the National Associa-tion of Mental Health in 1960, Enoch Powell, then Minister of Health, sounded the death knell for the asylum pastoral and fore-cast 'the elimination of by far the greater part of this country's mental hospitals as they stand today'. This was, of course, the famous 'water-tower' speech: 'There they stand, isolated, majestic, imperious, brooded over by the gigantic water-tower and chimney combined, rising unmistakable and daunting out of the country-side – the asylums which our forefathers built with such immense solidity.'

Powell did not underestimate the rigours of the campaign on which he was now embarked: 'This is a colossal undertaking, not so much in the physical provision which it involves as in the sheer inertia of mind and matter which it requires to be overcome. Do not for a moment underestimate their power of resistance to our assault . . .' Yet he urged his troops onward with the declaration that 'if we err, it is our duty to err on the side of ruthlessness. For the great majority of these establishments, there is no appropriate future use.'[6]

Powell's forecast was unduly optimistic and though large

numbers of long-stay patients have been discharged from mental hospitals over the past three decades, until quite recently not a single hospital had closed. In the last few years, however, the commitment to scaling down and closing many of the mental hospitals has been adopted in earnest in government policy and the idea that the Victorian asylum should be closed has now come fully into its own. A vigorous debate has ensued, largely prompted by the discovery that while the government is keenly committed to the scaling down and closure of institutions, it is apparently rather less committed to providing the means whereby alternative forms of service could be mounted in their stead. The whole thrust of the policy of 'community care' has to a considerable extent been brought into disrepute as a cover for an elaborate cost-cutting exercise. 'The pace of removal of hospital facilities for mental illness,' a Parliamentary Select Committee reported, 'has far outrun the provision of services in the community to replace them. It is only now that many people are waking up to the legacy of a policy of hospital run-down which began over twenty years ago.'[7] Critics had hoped that the pace of hospital closure would be slowed but the government has provided renewed endorsement of the denunciation of the mental hospitals. A health minister borrowed from Powell's address to round on his critics: 'No one reading today's comments on mental health issues can possibly doubt the wisdom of his warning that those institutions, and the people and the natural conservatism within them, have fought a vigorous rearguard action'; and in 1991 the government Green Paper *Health of the Nation* envisaged the closure of many of the remaining ninety mental hospitals by the year 2000 as 'relics of an out-moded pattern of care'.[8]

Vigorous though the debate has been, the preoccupation with the mechanics of hospital closure, and with the creation of new administrative structures for service provision that have followed in the wake of the Griffiths Report on community care, has meant that the terms of debate have been unduly narrowed and a number of crucial underlying issues have in consequence either been forgotten or have surfaced in an obscure form. If the proponents of current policies have sometimes been fanciful and misleading in their proclamations and lead some to suppose that they do not have the best interests of the mentally ill at heart, then it is equally apparent that among a significant faction of the critics there are growing doubts about the fitness of many people with mental illness to be considered integral members of the community. Not far below the surface of what is being said from different positions, we can feel the pulse of a number of fundamental questions that have to do with the basis on which people with a history of mental illness are to be permitted to participate in the life of our society.

The aim of this book is to widen the scope of the discussion, to envisage the central problem not simply as an administrative or managerial one but as one that implicates the terms on which people with mental illness are to be accepted in social life; through the prism of the debate about the closure of the asylum we need to identify the nature of the challenge that confronts mental health policy. The book is perhaps best described as an attempt to put questions to the contemporary debate about deinstitutionalization from a particular corner, one that is above all preoccupied with what it means to be a mentally ill person in our society and with the social and historical roots of the obstacles and constraints that still impinge upon the lives of people with mental illness.

As a historian has written, we have inherited from the last century 'a deep disposition to see madness as essentially Other'.[9] Despite the intentions of mental hospital reformers in the present century, and the numerous variations in hospital regimes that have emerged, the mental hospitals have always been overcast by the heavy burden of stigma that has attached to them. The legacy of the Victorian asylum is, in an important sense, the abolition of the *person* who suffers from mental illness. In place of the person we have been given mental patients, their identities permanently spoiled, exiled in the space of their illness on the margins of society. Recent histories of psychiatry have helped us to see that the history of madness cannot be grasped without a prior understanding of the history of reason or rationality:

... a bird's-eye view of the history of psychiatry shows that profound developments have contributed over the centuries to 'constructing' the mentally sick person as a type, fit for treatment or at least incarceration. Society has progressively defined itself as rational and normal, and by doing so has sanctioned the stigmatizing and exclusion of 'outsiders' and 'aliens'. And the particular device of the walled and locked asylum – which after all ended up housing far larger populations than did prisons – backed by the medical specialty of institutional psychiatry ... underscored the differentness, the uniqueness, of those thus 'alienated' or 'excluded' ...[10]

Contrary to the progressive, scientific self-image of modern societies, the consequences of the growth of rationalization have not untypically been dehumanizing and at times resulted in a severance from a properly ethical understanding of human predicaments. The question to pose today, therefore, is whether we are in a position to resolve the historical problem of the marginalized and excluded mental patient, and posit an understanding of rationality through which the severed dialogue between reason and madness might be renewed. From this point of view, the project of deinstitutionalization might be conceived as pre-eminently an ethical project, concerned to provide a systematic revaluation of mentally disturbed people and their place in social life. Or is it more likely, we shall need to ask, that policies of deinstitutionalization are fated to find themselves in thrall to the same conflicts and pressures in modern societies that have kept the mad apart and underlined their 'differentness'? A group of users of mental health services asked recently that they be given some hope, by which they meant some hope for a more promising kind of life in our society. Essentially, I am concerned in this book to tease out why this is such a difficult request to satisfy.

In attempting to give an account of the roots and conflicts of deinstitutionalization I have focused mainly on the British experience, but in order to provide a less parochial perspective, intellectually as much as geographically, I have at points drawn on other experiences. The book does not try to provide answers as much as to let some air into what has generally been a rather sealed discussion, and I make no claim to give a comprehensive account either of the history of mental health policy or of contemporary innovations. Neither, in the space available to me, have I attempted to embrace the entire spectrum of mental health problems in our society. As has been argued recently, social policies of deinstitutionalization have resulted in a marked diversification of experience among different social groups, not least ethnic minorities, in their encounter with mental illness and the traditions and institutions of psychiatry.[11] In what follows the discussion of people with a history of mental illness will largely refer to people with long-term mental illness, in particular schizophrenia. What I have to say here may, perhaps, hold some general relevance but clearly the discussion of gender differences, for example, or the mental disorders of the elderly, would introduce additional considerations.[12]

The plan of the book is as follows. In Chapter 1 I explore the troubled history of deinstitutionalization in Britain and in Chapter 2 I try to engage some of the significant questions in an encounter with the experiences of former mental patients. Chapter 3 explores the roots of contemporary problems in the rise of the late-nineteenth-century asylum and the consequent dehumanization of the mental patient, and Chapter 4 looks at how the legacy of the asylum has been perpetuated in the present century, in particular the legacy of a public psychiatry which had become the science of regulating paupers. Chapter 5 examines in more detail the conflicts and ambiguities of contemporary policies of deinstitutionalization, the curious mixture of desolation and hope which they have to offer, and Chapter 6 summarizes some of the issues and asks whether hopes for more promising prospects for people with mental illness can be realized.

1 Exodus

Behind the Palatial Façades

The asylum is by no means a singular phenomenon and the history of modern societies shows wide variations not only in the circumstances and timing of the construction of asylums but also in the form and style of asylum regimes. Joseph would doubtless be appalled to learn that there are today, perhaps not in Britain but certainly in other parts of Europe, far worse rubbish tips or 'dirty, scruffy, rotten holes' than the one in which he had the misfortune to pass several decades of his life as a career mental patient. Nevertheless, despite the variations, the creation of proliferating systems of asylum regimes in which an expanding population of mentally disturbed persons are excluded from society, and the concomitant degradation and humiliation of the status of mental patient, is a uniquely modern phenomenon. Yet if asylums are typical products of modern societies, so also are the alarms and scandals that have arisen around them. The asylum has always been a problematic and unpredictable creation and has never settled placidly into the social landscape for any length of time. Mental hospitals, as asylums were subsequently styled, have for long been in trouble and continue to be so.[1]

Much in keeping with Joseph's perceptions of the dissonance between the palatial façades and what lay behind them is the description by a visitor in 1857 to Colney Hatch Lunatic Asylum on the outskirts of London (now, though not for much longer, Friern Hospital), which opened in 1851 as Europe's largest and most modern institution:

The enormous sum of money expended upon Colney Hatch ... prepares us for the almost palatial character of its elevation ... the whole aspect of the exterior leads the visitor to expect an interior of commensurate pretensions. He no sooner crosses the threshold, however, than the scene changes. As he passes along the corridor, which runs from end to end of the building, he is oppressed with the gloom; the little light admitted by the loopholed windows is absorbed by the inky asphalt paving, and, coupled with the low vaulting of the ceiling, gives a stifling feeling and a sense of detention as in a prison. The staircases scarcely equal those of a workhouse . . . In the wards a similar state of things exists . . . of human interest they possess nothing. Upwards of a quarter of a million has been squandered principally upon the exterior of this building; but not a sixpence can be spared to adorn the walls within with picture, bust, or even the commonest cottage decoration . . . There is no more touching sight than to notice the manner in which the female lunatics have endeavoured to diversify the monotonous appearance of their cell-like sleeping rooms with rag dolls, bits of shell, porcelain, or bright cloth.[2]

And the Lunacy Commissioners themselves observed only a few years later that

It would be difficult to instance more perfect examples of what the wards of an asylum for the insane should not be, than are presented here by what are called the refractory wards, especially those in the basement of each division, constructed originally so as to exclude the light from those portions of the corridor where it is most required. The gloom is unrelieved by comforts of furniture of the commonest description; the seats, notwithstanding the many paralysed and feeble persons, are fixed wooden settees in the windows, or long unbacked benches on either side of the dining-tables . . . to the inquiry why none of the male inmates in all basement wards, excepting two persons, had knives and forks to eat their dinners with, reply was made, that the men were all of them too dangerous to be trusted . . .[3]

Over the past thirty years or so a number of critical observers, most notably perhaps the sociologist Erving Goffman, have documented the degradations and ironies of asylum regimes, and these have doubtless helped to inform the image that is now commonly held of the asylum.[4] It would, however, be a mistake to suppose that the genre of asylum criticism lacked a history. In Britain in the second half of the nineteenth century a small but vocal group of Victorian psychiatrists inveighed against the tendencies of the burgeoning institutions of the period to produce 'asylum-made lunatics', and their critiques were at least as trenchant as those of their contemporary counterparts. Yet, as historians have shown, the mood of the times was unreceptive to these onslaughts and almost another century was to pass before the concept of 'asylum-made lunatics' acquired any significant political leverage.[5]

The Changing Relationship between Mental Hospital and Society

It is commonly assumed that very little changed in mental hospitals in Britain before the late 1950s and early 1960s. The significant indicators of psychiatric and legislative innovation are usually taken to include the introduction of the major tranquillizers in the mid-1950s, the Mental Health Act of 1959 and the increasing adoption of social and industrial therapies. To the extent that mental hospitals continued to possess a primarily custodial function until this time the assumption is accurate enough, but at the same time it obscures recognition of the extent to which marked shifts in patterns of admission, and in the use that was made of mental hospitals, had begun much earlier, well before the extensive adoption of the new methods of treatment.

In a detailed study of the operation of a large mental hospital in the London area from 1957 to 1972, Elizabeth Bott has provided a revealing historical analysis of changes in the use made of the hospital since it opened in 1905. Through to the mid-1930s there was little to remark on about the patterns of admission except for a continuous increase in the population of the hospital. But from the mid-1930s on the picture becomes more complicated and, as Bott relates, 'a new population apparently started coming into the hospital, a population who left hospital more readily as well as coming in more readily'.[6] First admissions started to increase in the 1930s, remained stationary during the war and then rose rapidly in the decade 1945–55. There was also a marked change in the age pattern of admissions and, particularly in the period 1945–55, an increasing number of old people (over sixty-five) were admitted to the hospital, a large proportion of them women.

These trends were doubtless stimulated to a large extent by developments within psychiatry and in mental health legislation. So, for example, the Mental Treatment Act of 1930 provided for the creation of out-patient clinics and for 'voluntary' admissions to mental hospitals. Similarly the physical treatments of the 1940s, such as ECT, which was introduced into the hospital Bott studied in 1944, insulin therapy, introduced in 1947, and transorbital lobotomies, introduced between 1947 and 1950, appeared to promise a more optimistic approach to the relief of mental disorders. From the 1930s on, the gap between psychiatry and general medicine narrowed and family doctors were able to communicate 'to patients and relatives a belief that madness might now be curable'.[7] From this point of view, the shifts in patterns of admission testify to a gradual change in the relationship between mental hospital and society, in which the stigma of the asylum was to some degree moderated and the boundary between mental hospital and society became more permeable.

But Bott is at the same time right to suggest that the changes in the use that was made of the mental hospital between 1935 and 1955 cannot entirely be accounted for by the formal innovations of the period. The prevailing psychiatric wisdom has been that the increase in admissions was caused by the introduction of physical and social treatments, in particular tranquillizers, but these were not extensively adopted until the late 1950s, by which time, in the case of the hospital Bott studied, the rate of first admissions had already slowed down. A more likely explanation is that, particularly in the decade following the Second World War, the loosening of familial ties and networks made families less able to cope with disturbed members and more willing to have recourse to professional help. To this extent, it seems plausible that 'the spurt of therapeutic inventiveness inside the hospital in the late 1950s and early 1960s was more a response to the increased number of admissions than a cause of them'.[8]

By the late 1950s, then, there had developed a somewhat more favourable relationship between the mental hospital and the wider society, and the following account instances the kind of profile which the mental hospital was now trying to establish in the public imagination. It borrows from an older tradition of asylum pastoral, certainly, but with a decidedly progressive intent. In the late eighteenth century, we learn, Woodford comprised a scatter of stately homes just north of London, each in its own imposing grounds, one of which was Claybury Hall. In Woodford today is to be found 'the great hospital of Claybury in whose park-like grounds the old house of Claybury Hall still stands, and if a Woodfordian of the days of George III could be dropped by a time machine in Claybury grounds today he would recognize his surroundings at once'. In the hospital archive

... there is a wonderful book prepared by Humphry Repton, the landscape gardener, who in that year of 1791 came down at the request of the owner of Claybury Hall to compile a book of suggestions for the improvement of the grounds. His delightful sketches show the layout which he found when he arrived and that which he proposed by way of amendment. Our Georgian visitor would, however, see more extensive alterations than those envisaged by Repton. A hospital which accommodates over 2,000 patients and 200 resident staff is more like a small town than a hospital, and Claybury Hall is now only a small part of the network of buildings which form the home of such a large number of people.

So runs the preface to a prospectus published in 1958 proclaiming the merits of Claybury Mental Hospital as a progressive and growing community. Originally the Claybury Lunatic Asylum, brought under the responsibility of the newly constituted London County Council, it opened for business on 16 May 1893, the reception order for the first patient arriving at 8.45 a.m. The 'sad thing about those early days', the prospectus continues,

is that all mental patients were treated as dangerous persons who must be restrained in case they did harm to others, or at any rate to themselves. In the attitude towards the patients there has been a gradual, but nevertheless radical, change in the last fifty years. Of course this is true of much of our era. Road and air transport, television, atomic power, whether for good or ill, have utterly changed our world in the same period. But these differences are all physical ones, and the difference between a lunatic asylum and a mental hospital is far more significant, for it is the sign of a spiritual growth in the hearts and minds of men.

The mental hospital ward 'is no longer the rather grim and fearful place of the past. Increasingly an atmosphere of freedom, normality and helpfulness prevails and this not only adds greatly to the patient's happiness and comfort but also to his chances of recovery'. For those who do not recover 'the modern mental hospital ward can now provide a free, happy and homely atmosphere in which to pass their lives'.

The 'Chronic Culture' of the Mental Hospital

There were indeed still many patients who passed their lives at Claybury. Though the decline in the hospital population had already begun in about 1952, before the introduction of chlorpromazine, in the late 1950s the primary function of Claybury, as of Bott's research hospital, was still to provide long-term custodial care. In Bott's hospital about three quarters of the patients were long-stay at this time and by 1972 this proportion had dropped to two thirds. Significantly, among people under sixty-five there was only a slight decline in the rate of chronic hospitalization from 1934 until the late 1960s. As Bott says, neatly summarizing the overall development from the 1930s to the 1950s, 'the old custodial function of the hospital has continued, but a new short-stay function has been added'.[9]

In the late 1950s and 1960s a number of notable changes were introduced into this, as into other, mental hospitals. The iron railings surrounding the perimeter were dismantled, many of the wards were unlocked, patients were given individualized clothing, more recreation was provided and programmes of occupational and industrial therapy were introduced. The remarkable thing about Bott's account, however, is the resilience of the 'chronic culture' of the hospital, despite the numerous changes introduced into it. It may not have been a 'grim and fearful' institution but there was not much sign of 'spiritual growth' in the hearts and minds of the keepers of those who resided there. There were, in effect, two hospitals. The Chronic Hospital was only a few minutes walk away from the Admissions Hospital but, as Bott describes it, socially and emotionally it was in another world, 'peaceful, orderly and dominated by the ethos of the nursing staff'.[10] Compared to some of the state hospitals described in the American literature, the chronic culture here was 'kindly and humane, though slow moving and often tranquil to the point of unreality'.[11]

The pervasive atmosphere of tranquillity and changelessness that Bott describes was produced by the forcible submission of the inmates to their keepers. Interestingly, we have from the same period an informative account by Denis Martin, physician superintendent of Claybury Hospital in the early 1960s, who was much influenced by the ideas of the therapeutic community pioneered by

Maxwell Jones, of the type of traditional mental hospital regime which he was attempting to reform at Claybury. In the traditional mental hospital

... the satisfactory running of the whole hospital depended upon the submission of the patients to authority with a minimum of resistance. Traditional ways developed of dealing with those who were unable to submit adequately to the life of the institution. Fifty years ago these consisted mainly of locked doors, various forms of mechanical restraint and segregation of the sexes. These were followed by the employment of heavy sedation and in more recent years by the use of electrical cerebral treatment, prolonged sleep by drugs and the operation of prefrontal leucotomy.[12]

As Martin points out, these refinements of method, and the change of definition from custody to treatment, were none the less still conducted within an authoritarian system of management, presided over by a physician superintendent, in which the submission of the inmate was mandatory. Indeed, the prime function of the regime was to provide for the efficient management of the socially excommunicated and to secure their compliance in this exercise. The system of communication in the hospital was inevitably one-way: '... the most unfortunate feature of this lack of communication and demand for submission is that the patients find themselves at the bottom of the hierarchy, and at the far end of the communication system'.[13]

Ironically, compliant patients had less chance of communicating with the doctor than truculent ones and in some wards it is quite difficult, we learn, 'for a patient to communicate directly with the doctor, unless he is physically ill or mentally quite unmanageable'.[14] If we consider

... the various aspects of the traditional system which not only impede treatment but actually foster much of the distressing symptomatology of mental illness, one problem stands out clearly above all others. Lack of channels of communication seems to be the fundamental barrier to constructive change and fosters a very formal and superficial kind of personal relationship, both amongst staff and patients.[15]

Bott highlights some analagous features in the management of the excommunicated, for example the taboo on talking to patients:

If there were two nurses on a shift, they talked to each other and not to the patients. Several students who worked temporarily on chronic wards reported that if they talked too much to patients the sister or nurse would say, 'You're supposed to talk to me!' Talking to patients is dangerous because it threatens to puncture the barrier that keeps sanity and madness in their proper places.[16]

The inmates are perceived by their keepers to inhabit an alien and potentially contaminating sphere of madness:

Nurses usually adhere to the cultural definitions of madness as something to be shunned and, even though they know that many of their patients do not typically behave in a mad way, the fact that patients have been medically defined as ill means that it is legitimate to regard all of them as mad ... Since nurses cannot get away from the madness physically, they get away from it emotionally; they develop some form of relationship that locates madness in the patient and sanity in themselves, with a barrier to prevent contamination. Such an arrangement allows the nurses to stay in the situation without feeling that their minds are being damaged. It justifies the use of control by nurses, entitles patients to care and refuge, and is a virtual guarantee that they will continue to be thought ill and therefore will not be sent outside.[17]

In common with other critics of the asylum, Bott and Martin underscore the duplicity of the medicalized mental hospital regime. The inmates are all deemed mad and incapable (and may well be formally represented as such in the psychiatric litany), yet their ability to understand and comply with what is required of them, not least their labour, are essential to the efficient management of the institution. As Martin nicely expresses it:

Most mental hospitals rely considerably upon the patients to keep their various departments going. If the patients called a general strike the hospital could be severely handicapped. The same is true of the wards and often it is a few good workers who make it possible to run a ward efficiently. These facts mean that patients become deeply involved in the economic necessity of the hospital. They are often very aware of this and may resent the hospital using them in this way. The question of work might be a clear issue if it were not for the fact that we believe, probably quite rightly, that occupation has great therapeutic value. This does, however, open the door to rationalization in the name of treatment of the needs of the hospital for patient labour.[18]

Another aspect of the duplicity is the pretence that patients are in hospital entirely for medical reasons when in actuality they are there largely for social reasons. As Bott trenchantly remarks, hospitals that attempt to use the conventional definitions of how and why patients are admitted find themselves in a dilemma, 'because these definitions land the hospital in a situation of trying to help an individual on behalf of a society which does not recognize its wish to get rid of the individual as well as to help him'.[19] The medicalization of personal and social problems has, she suggests, a debilitating effect. Patients 'have to act as if they were more ill than they really are to retain their social refuge'; and for their part, 'nurses have to engage in considerable self-deception because the care they provide for social reasons is regarded by society, including relatives, as a medical rather than a social necessity'.[20]

The Mental Hospital in a Social Process

Now, the interesting thing about Elizabeth Bott's account is not that she furnishes another round of dispiriting tales about traditional asylum regimes but that she adds a crucial twist to the story. The duplicity of the mental hospital, she suggests, is the product not of some form of psychiatric conspiracy but of the social pressures exerted on the hospital and the much-remarked-upon tendency of modern societies to ostracize the mentally ill, and treat them as non-persons, while claiming to be doing something else. We can see this clearly if we look more closely at Bott's special interest in how some people come to be stuck in hospital. Bott noted that though in common with other mental hospitals the long-stay population in the research hospital had declined in the late 1950s, the rate of chronic hospitalization by contrast had changed comparatively little between 1934 and the late 1960s. In other words, contrary as we shall see to the prevailing beliefs of the period, new long-stay patients were still being created in sizeable numbers.

Though 'illness' is certainly a factor in chronic hospitalization, and there 'may well be in a population an inherent core of people who are likely to become emotionally and mentally disabled', none the less in Bott's view the 'processes involved are not synonymous with the processes involved in chronic hospitalization'.[21] The creation of the chronic mental patient, the process of turning a mentally distressed person into an Other, a permanent hard-core case, is pre-eminently a social process. Chronic hospitalization occurs when a hospital place is available and appears to offer a more viable social place for the patient than could be found outside. In other words, people who get stuck in hospital are people for whom there is no viable place in society.

It may be instructive to ponder the corollary of these arguments. In 1960 the Minister of Health was to declare that building mental hospitals: '. . . is not like building pyramids, the erection of memorials to a remote posterity. We have to get it into our heads that a hospital is like a shell, a framework to contain certain processes, and when the processes are superseded, the shell must, most probably, be scrapped and the framework dismantled.'[22] Now what processes did the minister have in mind? On Bott's argument there are two significant processes, what we may think of as a natural process and a social process. First is the continuing incidence in a population of various groups of people inherently at risk of becoming mentally disabled; and second a social process that inclines towards the marginalization, devaluation and exclusion of mentally disturbed people. Bott's special concern is with the tenacity of this social process and the way in which it exacerbates the inherent vulnerabilities of certain groups. The 'process' that she identifies is clearly not a property of the mental hospital but of the operations of a particular kind of society. To claim that it had in some way been superseded would in effect be to claim that a revolution in social consciousness had wrought some systematic revaluation of the mentally ill and that they were now to be welcomed back into the community. For lack of such a revolution, the elimination of the socially provided option of chronic hospitalization is hardly likely to resolve the problems vulnerable people encounter in securing a viable social place for themselves.

In brief, Bott's prediction is that a programme of deinstitutionalization that fails to address the vicissitudes of people with mental illness in this wider field of social forces is likely to run into difficulties. We are likely to find that: the run-down or closure of hospitals will not significantly deplete the pool of people inherently at risk of mental disability; the social processes that degrade the life chances of such people will persist; and the deceptions and duplicities in the social treatment and management of the mentally disturbed are likely to be reproduced on new sites. Against this cautionary background we may look now at some of the optimistic beliefs of the 1960s.

The Optimism of the 1960s

Though notable reforms took place in many of the mental hospitals throughout the 1950s, the existence of the hospitals themselves was not put in question. In the early 1950s, as Kathleen Jones has reminded us, 'public debate centred on how to encourage patients to accept mental hospital care, not on how to get them out'.[23] Even as the celebratory prospectus from Claybury Hospital was being written, however, a rather different conception of 'spiritual growth' was being prepared for, and at the outset of the 1960s the 'scene was set for more strenuous efforts to deinstitutionalize patients' and the emphasis changed from the 'gradual evolution of community care to vigorous attempts at discharge'.[24] In 1960 the Minister of Health forecast the elimination of the mental hospitals, and the Mental Health Act of 1959 had already announced a shift from a specialized service based on the mental hospitals to a more diversified community service embracing a range of agencies.

To a large extent, however, the declarations of government policy in this period represented not so much a new departure as an assertive formalization of trends that were already taking place. Though the decline in the mental hospital population had started some years earlier in a number of hospitals, it first became visible in the national statistics in 1955. The high point in the population of mental hospitals in England and Wales had been achieved in 1954 with 148,100 patients and since then the numbers have declined at a relatively even rate. Statistics showed that between 1954 and 1959 there were 8,000 fewer residents in British mental hospitals and in a study which has now come to assume a seemingly iconic status for its encapsulation of the optimism of the period, and the influence – ill-judged, some would now say – that it exerted on policy-makers and planners, Tooth and Brooke drew on these figures to predict the eventual erosion of the long-stay hospital population.[25]

As others have remarked, a number of influences at the beginning of the 1960s combined to reinforce a focus on deinstitutionalization in the sense of getting people out of hospital rather than on community care and supporting them outside hospital. The literature of protest against the indignities of mental hospital regimes on the one hand, and the new-found psychiatric optimism about the major tranquillizers on the other, converged to suggest that the concept of community care did not require elaborate specification or commitment.[26] At the level of the critique of the asylum, certainly, there was an ironic affinity between those for whom liberation from the asylum meant a liberation from psychiatric conformity and those for whom psychiatric progress was now able to promise the return of the mental patient to social conformity. The critique of the asylum, many assumed, provided the key to the understanding of the problem of chronic mental illness and of the long-stay mental patient. The nineteenth-century notion of the 'asylum-made lunatic', it might be said, had at long last become genuinely authoritative. An influential body of opinion held out the promise that, assisted by powerful medicaments, former mental patients could once again become diligent citizens, able to resume their place in the community. Similarly, if patients could be quickly returned to the community after an acute stage of their illness, chronic disabilities could be prevented.

The concept of community care did not seem to require much specification simply because the character of the ex-mental-patient in the community remained to a large degree unspecified. The distinctive character of the mental patient of a previous era could, it was believed, now be erased from the script of social life and replaced by a less remarkable or distinguishable persona. Community-care facilities at this time were envisaged as transitional, stepping-stones between a brief period of hospitalization and full reintegration into the community. So, for example, the objectives of day centres were to prepare former patients for employment in the open market. A transitional period in a rehabilitation hostel or a day centre, it was believed, would accomplish the mutation of former mental patients into ordinary citizens, distinguishable from their associates only by their occasional attendances at out-patient clinics to renew their prescriptions.

Elizabeth Bott has remarked on the difficulties of professionals in this epoch in confronting the 'idea of persisting incurability or persisting occupation of facilities for long-term care',[27] and others have observed how the suggestion that 'some patients might require no less than lifelong support in some sort of sheltered, protected setting was either ignored or denied in the hopeful, therapeutic climate that prevailed'.[28] The representative concept of 'hope' entertained here was evidently not that of bringing people who were vulnerable, and in some respects different, back from the sites of exclusion into which they had been put the and finding a place for them in the community, reintegrating them as members despite their differences; it was instead the hope that such people would no longer be different, that all that made them different or peculiar would have been abolished.

Because of their evident interests in the complexities of communal relationships, and their commitment to understanding mental health problems in a communal framework, we might be tempted to suppose that the work of Denis Martin and others in the 'therapeutic community' tradition had been the guiding stars in the application of community-care policies. Ironically, however, the eclipse of the asylum and the transfer of mental patients to the community has been assisted not so much by some renewed psychiatric interest in the relations between mental patients and the environments in which they are located but by theories and practices which have played down the role of the environment in favour of a somatic understanding and physical methods of treatment.[29] Indeed, many of the most vocal enthusiasts for community-care policies were those doctors inspired by the promise of the new drug treatments. Those traditions which viewed the specialized, communal resources of the mental hospital as a therapeutic instrument were judged failures or at best dispensable. Professional consideration of social and communal relationships could conveniently be set aside for the 'technical fix' provided by the drug treatments.

'The active communal relationship,' Manfred Bleuler wrote in his magisterial study of schizophrenic disorders, 'seems to me to be the most important principle of treatment.'[30] But the weight of professional psychiatric opinion in Britain in particular was to lampoon this sort of suggestion. The irony is that the arrival of 'community care' signals the emergence of a politics which entertains the hope that the moral and communal dimensions of mental suffering need no longer be the focus of specialized attention or of elaborate public provision in the care of people with mental illness. The 'community' came to possess a null value – it was not seen as a therapeutic site or as the arena for an interrogation of the moral crisis in the relations between people with mental illness and the larger society, but just as the place to which people were to be sent back after medicine had cured them. Psychiatry, declared a Conservative Secretary of State for Social Services in 1971, 'is to join the rest of medicine ... the treatment of psychosis, neurosis and schizophrenia have been entirely changed by the drug revolution. People go into hospital with mental disorders and they are cured, and that is why we want to bring this branch of medicine into the scope of the 230 district general hospitals that are planned for England and Wales.'[31]

For a psychiatric profession anxious to divest itself of its custodial function this had for some time been an enticing prospect and, as Kathleen Jones relates, in Britain psychiatrists increasingly abandoned 'the social view of psychiatry for a strictly medical stance'.[32] The new drug treatments meant that they could now style themselves as

... experts in pharmacology rather than experts in human behaviour. Abnormal behaviour patterns could be controlled: they need not be understood. The psychiatrist could carry out his work as other doctors did – relieved of the burdens of attempting to follow the processes of disturbed minds, the strains and complexities of unfamiliar lifestyles, the pressures of unemployment, squalid housing conditions and poor nutrition. There was no need to enter the jungle of human emotions – love, hatred, pain, grief. It was a great deal less wearing, and a great deal more respectable in strictly medical terms.[33]

'Failures and Problems at the Margin'

At the turn of the 1960s it was envisaged that by 1975 the decimation of the asylum regime would have been completed, but the White Paper of that year accepted that the predictions had been optimistic. Though many long-stay patients had been discharged, not a single mental hospital had closed, and numerous unforeseen problems had arisen in the creation of community services. None the less the White Paper held firm to the philosophy of community care and integration:

We believe that the failures and problems are at the margin, and that the basic concept remains valid. We believe that the philosophy of integration rather than isolation which has been the underlying theme of development still holds good, and that for the future the main aims must continue to be the development of more locally based services and a shift in the balance between hospital and social services care.[34]

It is not, of course, what the quixotic prose of the White Paper intended to convey, but by the mid-1970s it was becoming evident enough that the failures and problems of the mental health services did indeed find themselves on the margins of society and that this issue, far from being a marginal one, was now becoming quite central. For some years research had uncovered evidence that all was not well with the current application of the philosophy of community care. Contrary to the optimism of the early 1960s, 'new' long-stay patients had begun to accumulate in a number of mental hospitals, much as Bott had found in her own study.[35] Bott also pointed out a dimension of the wider picture overlooked by Tooth and Brooke in their prediction of a continued decline in the long-stay population based on the statistics for 1954–9. Over this period there was also an increase in the number of short-stay patients, many of them, Bott suggests, the self-same discharged long-stay patients who had found their way back to the hospital. Throughout the 1960s and 1970s it also became apparent that the degradations and indignities associated with mental hospitals were not peculiar to those regimes and that they had a nasty habit of reproducing themselves in some of the newly created settings in the community. And as the ranks of the unemployed swelled, the rehabilitative ideals of the period of buoyant employment in the 1960s looked increasingly questionable.

In an influential, but scarcely representative, body of research and innovation, research workers from the Maudsley Hospital demonstrated that people with vulnerabilities could be maintained in settings in the community but only so far as they were provided with long-term supportive conditions. Along the way they discovered that the distinction between the hospitalized mental patient and the recovered patient in the community stood in need of some refinement: 'A clear-cut distinction can no longer be made among the needs of patients who are in a hospital, are obtaining care as day patients or as out-patients, or are being supported while living at home. A patient is no longer ill and in a hospital or well and out of a hospital.'[36]

Even allowing for the validity of the protests against the asylum, the idea that the historical legacy of the marginalized mental patient could be dismissed without conflict now seems unduly sanguine and there is evidently reason enough for thinking that policies of deinstitutionalization have not addressed themselves sufficiently seriously to the question of how a modern society like Britain is to provide a viable social place for varied categories of vulnerable people.[37] Recent alarms about impending mental hospital closures are therefore not so much reactions to a new policy direction as the culmination of a troubled history of policy decisions which has seemingly generated new social problems in place of those it was hoped to resolve. The disarray in the administrative and financial structures for community-care provision were confirmed by the evidence of a number of authoritative critiques such as the reports of the Audit Commission and the House of Commons Social Services Committee, as also were some of the detrimental social consequences of the current application of community-care policies.[38] For example, as has been widely reported, many people with a history of mental illness (both former long-stay patients and new patients for whom a permanent place in a hospital is no longer available) have been returned to a place which, if it has not always proved viable socially either for them or for those they live with, has none the less certainly been idealized as such by policy-makers and even clinicians. As Brigid MacCarthy has remarked, there has been a tendency to project the family as

... the place where genuine care is dispensed. This idealized model of society has meant that care is given in the community, but not by the community. The state hands the caring role over to one or two adults, usually female, at an enormous economic saving. This ideology, together with the propensity of many women to follow an ethic of caring, persuades the clinician to advocate, and potential carers to assume, demanding supportive roles as a duty. Neither party can readily question whether the patient continuing to live with the family is really the best option.[39]

Over the past thirty-five years almost 100,000 long-stay patients have been discharged from British mental hospitals but in the meantime fewer than 4,000 places have been provided in local-authority hostels, and the Department of Health has little idea as to what has happened to the vast majority of those discharged and apparently has not troubled to find out.[40] Significantly, from the standpoint of Bott's interest in the social processes that contribute to the making of a long-stay patient, research has found a high correlation between the Jarman index of deprivation based on the major socio-demographic indicators of poverty, social isolation and ethnicity, and the rate of recruitment to 'new' long-stay status (a stay of one year or more) in mental hospitals.[41]

The Closure of the Mental Hospitals

For some years now, it has been government policy to reduce the number of in-patient psychiatric beds to around 48,000. In 1985 the average number of psychiatric beds occupied each day in England and Wales was 64,800, a return to an occupancy level last witnessed in 1895; 84 per cent of the planned reduction of long-stay psychiatric beds has been achieved and now it only remains to resettle the final sixth of long-stay patients.[42] Figure 1 (overleaf) shows the decline in the number of patients resident in mental hospitals per 100,000 total population for the years 1954–81, and Figure 2 the reduction in bed occupancy for Friern and Claybury Hospitals from the late 1950s onwards.

Over the past few years, discovering which, and how many, mental hospitals are due to close has been a hazardous enterprise. Indeed in 1985 the Social Services Committee reported that there was some scepticism 'as to the likelihood that any hospital will actually close. The fact is that, more than twenty years after the 1962 Hospital Plan, no major hospital has closed . . .'[43] Since then, the National Schizophrenia Fellowship has shown itself to be a diligent sleuth in the matter and has uncovered a number of inconsistencies in government statistics. Their investigation revealed that 'it proves very difficult to get an accurate and up-to-date picture of what is going on; all published figures and information appear to be at least two years out of date and in many cases are inaccurate and therefore unreliable'.[44] Apart from inconsistencies in govern-

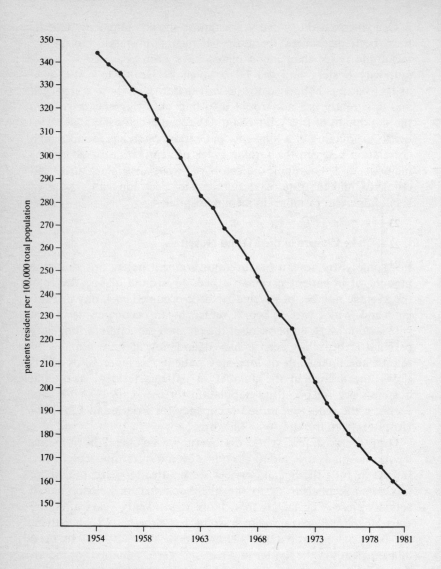

Figure 1 Patients resident in mental hospitals in England and Wales at the end of each year, 1954–1981 rate per 100,000 population

Reproduced from Wilkinson and Freeman, 1986

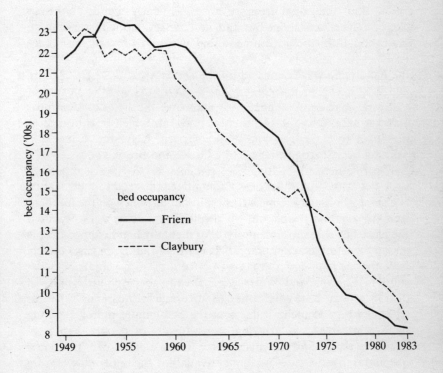

Figure 2 Bed occupancy in Friern and Claybury Hospitals

Reproduced from Wilkinson and Freeman, 1986

ment responses to Parliamentary Questions, there were also discrepancies between government pronouncements and the claims made by individual hospitals. The most blatant inconsistency was brought to light by the opposition health spokesman when he requested a list of mental hospitals for which there were no closure plans, only to find that 'it included four which had already closed at the time of the answer and two others which had closed during the time it took to carry out the survey'.[45] The Fellowship established that thirty mental hospitals (most of them small ones) had been closed between 1980 and 1989, and that thirty-eight hospitals (several of them large) had approved closure dates, most before 1995. There was also an additional group of hospitals which intended either to close or to reduce in size but had no date set. Notwithstanding an indication from the government that it would proceed more cautiously with the hospital closure programme, the data unearthed by the Fellowship was confirmed by the Secretary of State for Health, and the Green Paper *Health of the Nation* forecasts the closure of many of the remaining ninety hospitals over the next decade. In the London area, for example, mental hospitals which health authorities plan to close by 1995 include Friern, Claybury, Cane Hill, Tooting Bec, St Augustine's, Long Grove and Brookwood.

The resettlement of long-stay patients is clearly an important issue but as the Social Services Committee remarked in their report, 'The almost obsessive concentration in public policy on the mechanisms for "getting people out of hospital" has sometimes obscured the basic fact that most mentally ill or mentally handicapped people already live in the community.'[46] It is worth noting, in this connection, that as long ago as 1977 33 per cent of all psychiatric admissions in England and Wales were already to psychiatric units in district general hospitals rather than to mental hospitals.[47] People with a history of mental illness in the community number among them a sizeable, and growing, constituency of people who have never been long-stay patients and for whom a permanent place in a hospital is in most cases no longer available. The impending closure of mental hospitals thus invites consideration not merely of the fate of the older generation of long-stay patients but also of the prospects available to the younger generation of patients who throughout their illness careers have always been beneficiaries of community-care policies. As J. K. Wing has remarked recently,

'The impact of run-down and closures on care for people who are at risk of long-term disability who have never been long-stay in hospital is now as important as (perhaps more important than) the immediate impact on those who have to be moved out in order to close the hospital.'[48] Indeed, there are grounds for suggesting that the main objects of public concern at the present time are not so much discharged long-stay patients as short-stay patients with frequent admissions, the so-called 'revolving door' patients.[49]

In what follows I shall focus mainly on the experiences and concerns of this younger generation, since they are more truly harbingers of what is likely to be in store for new recruits to the psychiatric system, but it will be helpful first to look briefly at the fortunes of some of the long-stay patients who have recently been discharged from mental hospitals under sentence of closure.

The Resettlement of Long-stay Patients

Anyone who has been associated with the run-down of a hospital that is being prepared for closure knows that it is a messy and often painful process. Patients have not always been secured the 'ordinary housing' that managerial rhetoric has promised them and budgetary pressures have sometimes hastened the exodus of patients before the planning of their resettlement has been properly completed. For staff who have worked there, sometimes over decades, the closure of a hospital is akin to a bereavement and they may easily feel that the value of what they have contributed over the years has been put in question. It is still early to make a full assessment of the conduct and consequences of hospital closures but we do have some data to go on.

Of special interest is the evidence that is starting to emerge from the work of a research team based at Friern Hospital which is carrying out a long-term evaluation of the resettlement of over 900 patients in north London from both Friern and Claybury hospitals.[50] When completed it will, perhaps, provide the first systematic evaluation of the process of total closure of an asylum ever to have been undertaken. Considered as a whole, the residents of the two hospitals are a highly dependent group with many behavioural difficulties. As many as 35 per cent of them are still actively psychotic and there is little evidence of 'burn-out' among older residents. Furthermore 25 per cent of residents were found to be incontinent of urine or faeces, in some instances of both. One third of the group wanted to leave hospital, one third to stay, and the remainder were uncertain.

Each year a more disabled group of residents is being discharged and a follow-up one year after discharge has so far been completed on a group of 161 leavers, made up of two cohorts, the first a group of 44 patients discharged between September 1985 and August 1986, and the second a group of 117 discharged between September 1986 and August 1987. All of them had spent at least a year in hospital, some of them as long as sixty years, and none of them were suffering from dementia. Their age varied from eighteen to over a hundred, with an average of sixty. The primary diagnosis in 80 per cent of the cases was schizophrenia. The study group was matched with a similar group of patients likely to remain in hospital for at least another year.

Contrary to what some had feared, there were no suicides; no one was imprisoned; only three people became homeless, all of them people who had led a vagrant lifestyle before they became long-stay patients; and only four people were readmitted to hospital because they were dissatisfied with their placements in the community. At one level the pattern of life of the discharged patients did not change very much. In terms of clinical and behavioural measures, for example, there were no significant differences between the leavers and the control group at the end of the year. Similarly, there were few changes in patients' social networks and they did not appear to have established new relationships in the community. These findings doubtless reflect the histories and disabilities of this patient group, and point to the limitations on what can be achieved here, but it was at the same time evident that the residents had benefited from the transition to the community. The model of care which has been deployed is predominantly that of the 'home in the community', generally a group home with high staffing levels, and these were found to be much less restrictive than the hospital environment and the residents preferred them. On reassessment one year after leaving hospital, there was a marked increase – up from 17 to 74 per cent – in the proportion of people who were satisfied with their accommodation.

But perhaps the most interesting finding emerged in relation to discharged patients' attitudes towards their medication. At the time of the original interview about equal numbers of the leavers group and the control group said they found their medication helpful. On follow-up there was a slight increase among the hospitalized group who found their medication helpful but a dramatic decrease in the number of leavers who found it so, down from 53 to 18 per cent. Limited though they are by their histories and disabilities, these discharged mental patients have none the less within the space of a year seemingly started to develop a more independent view of themselves and demonstrated a reluctance to take medical authority for granted. If, from a medical point of view, they continue to be active patients, they have perhaps been helped to recognize that that is certainly not all that they are.

Broadly similar findings emerge from studies conducted in other hospitals. The average age of the long-stay population in Warley Hospital is 65.1 and the average length of stay 26.6 years. Only 17 per cent of the residents had spent less than five years in hospital and 57 per cent had spent more than twenty years there. Almost three quarters of them had a primary diagnosis of schizophrenia. Interviews conducted with a group of patients most likely to be moving into the community in the near future revealed that most of them wanted to move out of hospital, but understandably many of them were also worried about how they would cope both financially and psychologically. When they were asked what they liked about being in hospital, they tended to mention aspects such as the staff and the support they received, together with food, warmth and safety; their dislikes included difficulties in living with other patients, restrictions (such as set times for meals and going to bed), lack of privacy, noise (the permanent blast of radios on the wards) and the stigma of the mental hospital environment.[51]

Quite a few of the patients had friends within the hospital, but relatively few of them wanted to live with, or close to, their hospital friends after they were discharged. A large majority wanted to live with others rather than alone, but at the same time they made it clear that they wanted to live with only a few others. Over three quarters also said that they wanted to have their own bedroom. Most of them recognized that they would need practical support to live in the community, though they were sometimes uncertain as to how much support they would need. Hardly any of them thought that they would need twenty-four-hour cover. Proximity to shops was a key requirement in their community locations as also were bus stops and railway stations. Many of the residents said they wanted to embark upon an educational course when they left hospital or to find paid employment, though several were worried about the availability of desirable work opportunities.

At Springfield Hospital, which originally opened for business in 1841 as the Surrey County Pauper Lunatic Asylum, the average age and length of stay was very similar, though 54 patients had not left hospital for over forty years. As rated by hospital staff, 145 patients had expressed a clear preference for where they would like to live in the future and of these one third wanted to stay in hospital and the remaining two thirds to live independently, most of them with their family or in a flat of their own. As the researchers comment: 'It is interesting, and perhaps surprising, that a majority [of those] with a preference wished to leave hospital and indicates how important it is for individual-based planning to include the patients' views.'[52]

There appears to have been some discrepancy between residents' and staff assessments, in that the staff thought that only a very small number of residents would be able to live independently, and nearly two thirds of them were recommended for community placements with twenty-four-hour staffing. None the less the vast majority of them were 'thought capable of existing in community settings with a greater degree of independence than they enjoyed in hospital'. Furthermore, while there was evidence of socially unacceptable behaviour, and some concern about dangerous or violent behaviour, the behaviour of most people was judged to be manageable in community settings, with only a few patients posing serious problems.

Similarly encouraging findings have been reported by the team from the Personal Social Services Research Unit at the University of Kent in their evaluation of the 'Care in the Community' demonstration programme funded by the government, which consisted of twenty-eight pilot projects, eight of them for people with a history of mental illness, to explore different ways of assisting people to move from hospitals into the community.[53] Difficulties were sometimes experienced in establishing the projects, for example in acquiring the right kind of accommodation in the right place at the right time, and in the resettlement teams disagreements not infrequently arose between different professions about the nature and causes of mental illness, with criticism of the psychiatric profession for concentrating unduly on people's deficiencies and neglecting their strengths. Not everyone benefited from the move but overall the well-being of the ex-patients was greatly improved and 'it was common to find clients expressing immense satisfaction with their "new lives" in the community after ten, twenty or more years in hospital'.[54] For example:

> Integration by clients into 'ordinary' community lifestyles was not complete, but most people were regularly using shops, churches or pubs, and there was much more activity outside the confines of the place of residence than these people had enjoyed in hospital.

> Twice as many people expressed positive attitudes about activities in the community compared to their attitudes in hospital.

> Most had more choice about how they spent their time and the activities engaged in, although more generously pitched social-security benefits or the greater availability of 'real' jobs would significantly improve the situation.

> Even though it takes time for people to build up social networks, reported social contacts were greater in number in the community than in hospital.[55]

There was not much evidence of the typical failings of deinstitutionalization policies:

No hospital resident was dumped in the community to drift without supervision or support, nobody was destitute or homeless, and nobody was imprisoned. There were few readmissions to hospital, and only a subset of those was associated with mental health or extended beyond a month's duration. Mortality rates were low, and the suicide rate was less than 1 per cent in the first nine months after discharge from hospital. The burden on informal carers was very small, for the reason, sad perhaps, that few clients had family or other informal care settings to which they could move.[56]

Community care was shown to be no more expensive than hospital care, though the team issued the caution that the costs were not identical for everyone and that 'higher costs were associated with greater achievements in the promotion of client well-being'.[57]

If, broadly speaking, the resettlement process from mental hospitals appears to be proceeding relatively smoothly, the data from the Friern and Claybury study reveal that there were at the same time a number of readmissions to hospital, and it is here that there are some grounds for concern. For example, three readmissions came about as a direct result of the reassessment by the research team:

One was a middle-aged woman with manic depressive psychosis who had been placed in a flat. When visited, she was found huddled on a mattress in a cold, dark basement flat, in a state of psychotic depression. Another was a middle-aged man, with a schizo-affective psychosis. He was living in a 'board and lodging with care' scheme and was found to be grossly psychotic and at risk of harming himself and others. The last person in this category was a man who lived in a council flat and admitted to feelings of depression along with suicidal ideas. In all three instances the responsible medical team was alerted and the patients were soon readmitted.[58]

We can be grateful for the presence of the research team here, but what they do not tell us is how soon, if at all, the 'responsible medical team' would have picked up on these difficulties if the research team had not been around. The picture complicates also in relation to violence. So, for example, the 'assessment of two patients revealed behaviour which could have had serious consequences, although this behaviour had not yet come to the attention of the police'.[59] In one instance a young man suffering from schizophrenia, brain damage and alcoholism had been discharged to a hostel but had subsequently returned to his mother's flat where, from his mother's report, he was evidently behaving in a grossly psychotic manner and physically assaulting her. Again, the patient was readmitted to hospital following the assessment by the research team. While the overall picture does not exhibit a distinct pattern of violence, it is none the less clear that in a minority of cases tragedies could all too easily occur if vigilance is not exercised.

What then do we learn from the Friern and Claybury evaluation to date? Certainly, the majority of these discharged patients can be helped to cope in the community; by and large they welcome independence, they do not want to be career mental patients, nor do they need to be; in many cases the disabilities of the discharged patients are very evident but with continuing staff support they can be helped to enjoy a better life. But we learn also about the risks in this whole undertaking. Nothing has gone wrong here – no one was imprisoned, there were no horrendous acts of violence – but we are looking at a very special set of circumstances: careful monitoring by a research team; facilities to readmit patients quickly in an emergency if necessary; a willingness on the part of the hospitals to take people back if they want to return and have their placements reassessed. This is a genuine and dedicated effort to undo some of the miseries and deprivations that have been imposed upon people by long years of needless incarceration. Most notably, the programme has been especially well resourced: each patient from Friern and Claybury hospitals is leaving the hospital with a dowry of around £14,000 per annum for the remainder of his or her life (roughly the amount that it cost to keep a patient in hospital on 1983 figures), and in addition a system of double-funding has been provided to keep the hospitals open during the transition period.

This is, therefore, very much a 'showcase' undertaking. Nothing to criticize about that, but it exhibits all the features which have attracted scepticism to model programmes.[60] It ought hardly to make us sanguine about the difficulties in implementing it elsewhere. Take away some of these special provisions, and we can sense the problems that might arise; in a minority of cases there are real risks and dangers, the stubborn persistence of a mental illness that unseats people's abilities to care for themselves and makes them sometimes a danger to others. Furthermore, while the programme is succeeding, the difficulties in maintaining it are not likely to grow any lighter. Each year a progressively more disabled group of patients is being discharged into the community, with heavier demands on the staff providing the support services in the community. At present the arrangement appears to be slightly cheaper than hospital care but the position may change. Many of the patients who have already been discharged are able to cook for themselves, for example, and so this aspect of the support services can sometimes be dispensed with. But this is unlikely to be true of those who will follow after. In addition, much clearly depends on the morale in the new community homes. In a few years time, after the research team have packed their bags and interest in the Friern and Claybury resettlement programmes has waned, we cannot be altogether confident that the commitment to sustain the present quality of care will be maintained.

The Limitations of Community Provision

There are a number of examples in Britain of community mental health services that have largely been successful in replacing the mental hospital by psychiatric units in district general hospitals supported by a variety of community facilities. The best known of these are perhaps the services developed by the Worcester Development Project and by the Torbay Health Authority.[61] A recent report of ten years experience in South-Verona, Italy, has also confirmed that it is possible to deal with the full spectrum of psychiatric morbidity within a community-based alternative involving intensive and continuous care in the community and with limited back-up from the mental hospital.[62] Neither in the case of Worcester nor of South-Verona has there, for example, been any significant accumulation of new long-stay in-patients. But if these are examples of what can be achieved, it would be misleading to see them as representative or even as necessarily offering models which could be adopted elsewhere. Worcester and Torbay and also, as we shall touch on later, South-Verona, exist in national contexts that are marked by sharp variations in mental health care. These three districts are socio-demographically rather similar – largely middle-class or semi-rural populations – but as the following examples show it is plain that in inner city areas of London a sizeable group of people is not well catered for by the community-care schemes so far developed.

Discharged into Westminster

A recent survey of 215 psychiatric patients discharged into Westminster between June and December 1988 illustrates both the structural constraints within which people with mental illness have to operate when they come out of hospital, particularly in the sphere of housing, and also in equal measure the constraints that are placed upon acute mental illness services which mean that they are not able to provide more than a form of casualty service.[63] If patients are dislocated, then so too are services, in their inability to establish meaningful connections with relevant areas of people's needs.

The survey is of particular interest in that following the closure of Banstead hospital in 1986, Westminster became one of the first areas without recourse to a long-stay hospital. In common with other inner-city areas it experiences a high level of psychiatric morbidity and homelessness. The study examined the fate of people discharged from the three psychiatric units which now serve the area. The profile which emerged is, perhaps, in the inner-city context, predictable enough. The majority were single or separated/ divorced; 60 per cent of the sample had stayed less than a month in hospital; 75 per cent had had one or more previous admissions; and at least half of these had been in hospital in the previous year.

The study identified shortcomings in the provision of long-term support services, particularly in day care and employment, but the most conspicuous gap in provision was housing. Before admission, two thirds of the sample were living in various forms of independent accommodation, only 5 per cent were in supported accommodation, and over a quarter were homeless or near homeless. As the authors rightly argue, the adequacy of community mental health services must in important measure be assessed on their ability to provide appropriate housing for patients on their discharge from hospital. The key question is, to what extent are people more appropriately housed on discharge than on admission?

The findings in this respect were not encouraging. Quite a complicated pattern of movement emerged: nine people who had previously been homeless moved into supported accommodation, but eleven of those who had previously been in independent accommodation now found themselves homeless, and the overall percentage of homeless people therefore increased slightly on discharge. Furthermore the evidence suggested that the housing conditions of over a third of the sample were to varying degrees less than satisfactory in relation to their well-being, and more particularly the supply of supported accommodation only catered for a minority of those who were judged to be in need of it.

The Prospects for People with Schizophrenia

A related view of these problems emerges from a study of the fate of people with a history of schizophrenic illness resident in west Lambeth in south London.[64] The long-stay hospital which previously served the area, Tooting Bec, is in the final stages of closure but, as the authors point out, the demise of the hospital will affect only the fortunes of those patients who are still resident there, most of them in their fifties or older, for whom resettlement plans are being carefully developed. For the majority of younger patients in the locality, however, Tooting Bec, in common with other long-stay hospitals, effectively closed many years ago. Probably the largest group among those who would previously have become career mental patients are people suffering from schizophrenia, most of whom are now admitted to acute psychiatric wards for short periods only. But what alternative career prospects has the closure of the asylum permitted this group of people?

The findings of a preliminary survey of seventy-four patients discharged from three units serving the district, and followed up a year later, are disquieting. Efforts by health and social services to maintain contact with the patients over the period had been minimal; 33 per cent of them said that they had not attended outpatients or seen a psychiatrist or a community psychiatric nurse during the previous three months, and 68 per cent that they had not seen a social worker during this period; 50 per cent were neither employed nor attending day services of any kind. Not untypical was Jane's predicament:

Jane is twenty-eight. Six years ago she took an overdose; since then she has been admitted to psychiatric wards eight times. She now lives alone in a flat which has no furniture, except in the bedroom. She feels that something is wrong with her brain and that she needs a new one. She feels inadequate, has become withdrawn and feels depressed. Jane moves slowly. She does nothing at all for perhaps six hours during the average waking day. She is friendless, seeing no one. Her family, though living close by, prefer to avoid her. She rarely eats a hot meal. Her eight-year-old son has been in care for four years. Recently Jane has been feeling angry; refusing to open the door to professionals and threatening her neighbours with a bread knife. Her community psychiatric nurse was away for four months and apparently as a result Jane has missed her last depot injection.

More rare but disturbing was Colin:

Colin is thirty-seven and living in a flat which most people would consider uninhabitable. A part of the building has collapsed, every one else has moved out. During nine years of schizophrenia he has felt persecuted, hearing threatening and hostile voices. He converses openly with the radio and TV. He has become a virtual vagrant, living by petty theft and eating from dustbins. He has probably been assaulted several times, suffered abuse as 'tramps' do. He stands, talking to windows, in city streets at any time of the day or night. He is completely isolated; he has no friends, no family contact, receives no social-security benefits and no medication. He accepts his situation. He feels well, all seems normal. During a typical day he will spend his waking hours doing nothing, preoccupied with his thoughts. Following his four admissions he has not taken part in follow-up care – and has thus not been followed up.[65]

The problems here are neither a natural consequence of these patients' disabilities nor do they derive from a dearth of knowledge about what can be done to help people like these lead more satisfactory lives. As the authors are careful to point out, there is now persuasive evidence that good psychiatric treatment combined with social care can significantly improve the prospects for people with long-term mental illness. The problem is, rather, one of application. Administrative ineptitude coupled with financial constraints has produced a form of medical delivery seemingly quite dislocated from an appreciation of the patients' social circumstances and needs. Thus the authors report how

In the course of carrying out this survey we were disquieted to find that medical records are often very brief and that written post-discharge plans are infrequently included. In addition, it is unusual for there to be a clear statement that a particular patient will require long-term community care. Finding out what care is being received by any individual is difficult, and junior doctors appear to be required to make decisions about patients with little help from medical records.[66]

Neither health nor social services appeared to play any meaningful role in relation to these patients other than through hospital admission. So, for example, there did not appear to be a system through which either service might become aware of deterioration in a patient's condition unless the patient initiated contact himself. Such are the demands on community mental health services that they tend very often to be reactive rather than pro-active, and there is very little time available for preventative work. If patients miss out-patient appointments, and fail to respond to letters, they frequently find themselves discharged. The promise of a policy of community care is that it will attend to people's health needs closer to home, without displacing them from their roots in the community. But on the evidence of studies such as this it is clear that people with long-term mental illness in the community may find themselves as structurally isolated as ever they were in the asylums, and in addition their health needs may now be ignored. In equal measure they find themselves neglected, both as patients and as citizens.

The Ward Environment is Bad for your Health

We can appreciate the pressure on acute mental health services more readily if we look at a recent account of the east Lambeth service provided by the Camberwell Health Authority.[67] The authority has already lost the beds to which it previously had access in Cane Hill Hospital and by the summer of 1988 had only sixty-six acute in-patient beds, fifty-eight of these in two wards in a district general hospital. Apart from a modest increase in the community psychiatric nursing service, the loss of beds has not resulted in an increase in community provision. While the reduction in psychiatric hospital beds in central London is in line with the reduction that has taken place across the country, as the authors point out, the admission rates to psychiatric hospitals for inner London are significantly higher than for the country as a whole.

The final closure of Cane Hill Hospital is fast approaching and careful plans are being laid for the support of discharged patients in the community. Yet as the authors argue, no matter how thorough the plans, it is most unlikely that they will obviate the need in the future for short periods of hospital admission for many of these patients. Such is the pressure on beds, however, that the threshold for admission to the in-patient unit has already risen considerably and the authors worry that only the most seriously disturbed patients will be admitted.

To understand the force of these alarms, we have only to look at how the acute mental health service has deteriorated already between 1986 and 1988, even before a new influx of patients into the locality from Cane Hill. Over this period the proportion of admissions from ethnic minorities rose from 28 to 44 per cent (the majority of Afro-Caribbean origin); and the proportion of formal detentions rose from 28 to 42 per cent. In 1986 patients from ethnic minorities were no more likely to be detained under the Mental Health Act than white patients, but in 1988 58 per cent of 'black' patients were detained formally compared with only 29 per cent of 'white' patients. A previous survey had predicted that a drastic reduction in beds coupled with a failure to provide adequate community-based alternatives 'would lead to an unacceptably low standard of care for patients, who would be rapidly recycled through an untherapeutic treatment facility'.[68] The present report appears to confirm these fears and demonstrates that the failure to provide adequate facilities both inside and outside the hospital has resulted in an increase in the numbers of revolving-door patients, particularly among younger people suffering from psychosis.

But why the increase in the numbers of patients formally detained? The authors suggest that the quality of the environments on the wards has a good deal to do with it. So distressing are the ward environments, the authors suggest, that they may inadvertently provoke violence among patients as the only feasible way of attracting attention or communicating. In consequence, the most disturbed find themselves placed under detention and the less disturbed simply leave. 'It is not uncommon,' we learn, 'to recognize that a patient might benefit from hospital admission, but to feel that the environment found on such in-patient wards would not be appropriate and could even be detrimental.'[69] In other words, the implication behind this carefully argued and understated report is that the psychiatric wards of the district general hospital are not the kind of environment which a responsible doctor would want to wish upon *anyone*, let alone someone who is in a state of acute distress.

The acute mental health service has evidently been reduced to providing only a form of crisis management of the dangerous and the severely psychotic, and even here it is unable to do its job properly. In this example, as in others in inner-city areas, the breakdown in community-care provision derives not only from inadequacies in available support systems in the community but also from the depletion of acute in-patient services.[70] As is well recognized, for certain kinds of patients to survive in the community there must be the possibility of moving without too much difficulty from one part of the care system to the other. If we are to take it seriously, community care is to be viewed as a policy of inclusion which provides for the health needs of people who are to be sustained as integral members of the community. Not untypically, though, what is delivered under the banner of inclusion is actually a policy of exclusion and erosion. There is a certain irony to the recognition that the district general hospital, which has for long been promoted as the flagship of the drive away from the mental hospital, has now under some conditions come to reproduce some of the worst features of traditional mental hospital regimes.

Far from providing relief from pain, a period of respite or refuge in the proper sense of asylum, arguably these conditions of care conspire only to make matters worse. What we have here is a field of forces in which the most vulnerable members of the community, many of them from ethnic minorities, are subjected to a degrading set of pressures which can serve only to aggravate pre-existing tensions between black people and white psychiatrists.[71]

The New Pessimists

Against this background it is perhaps scarcely surprising that some observers should have been tempted to rewrite their scripts. So, for example, in 1979 Kathleen Jones described how as 'the asylums grew in size, so they increased in rigidity, and became distinct subcultures, with their own ethos, their own way of life, and their own social hierarchies'. The effect of this system, she went on to say, was to create institutionalized personalities and 'there is some justification for the view that, whatever the dangers and shortcomings of life in the community, what the community was likely to do to ex-patients could not possibly be worse than this'.[72] But then almost ten years later she tells the story rather differently. 'In the nineteenth and the first half of the twentieth century,' we learn, 'institutional care was not a problem – it was a solution. Life outside was harsh, and "asylum" held its literal meaning – a place of refuge.' In the post-war period various reforms were undertaken inside the hospitals, some patients were given 'parole' and attempts were made at 'after-care'. From the mid-1950s, however, 'this placid and mildly progressive policy was abruptly thrown into reverse. The hospitals, which had been the main centres of clinical practice and research, were decisively rejected and sometimes violently attacked in the move to the community.'[73]

The manufacture of the institutionalized personality in the 'dependency culture' of the asylum was well described in 1962 by Denis Martin. An 'important aspect of much mental illness,' Martin argued, 'is the unconscious dependence of the patient upon others.' The attraction of the benevolent authority of the mental hospital is that it regulates the entire life of the patient:

... not only is food and shelter granted but life is made materially very comfortable and satisfying in many ways. Entertainments, discussions, cinema, television, outings, sports and many other activities are provided. This helps to ensure that patients submit to authority, although it is certainly not provided with this end in view. Such material provision and the relative security of hospital life rapidly absorbs the dependence of the patient, who no longer feels the need to think for himself in anything but the most unimportant trifles. So long as he submits to authority, that same authority will be his benevolent provider for life and often is.[74]

Interestingly, some recent moves to rehabilitate the mental hospital and revive the vintage genre of asylum pastoral make no mention of institutionalized personalities and the detrimental consequences of authoritarian regimes. Thus one observer expresses doubts on

... the popular notion of a welcoming community giving sanctuary to those unfortunates who have been incarcerated against their will for many years in the semi-locked confines of the establishment asylum. In reality the hospital community has provided a sheltered sanctuary for those who do not fit into the wider community of the outside world, which by and large rejects them for their oddities and eccentricities of behaviour. The hospital community with all its resources is able to provide a varied and stimulating day, comfortable surroundings, reasonable meals, and a social programme ... In terms of quality of life, have we exchanged the womb-like security which the chronically disabled previously enjoyed, in what was a sheltered true asylum, for the uncertainties of trying to compete in the normal and somewhat rejecting larger community?[75]

A psychiatrist who has campaigned to prevent the closure of Friern Hospital claims that 'over 99 per cent of the long-stay patients' at the hospital

... are there because they chose to be and this is typical throughout England and Wales. It is more reasonable to say that patients are evicted when hospitals are compelled to close and their land and buildings sold to meet financial deficits. The traditional hospitals are spacious, with equally spacious grounds, providing occupational and industrial therapy, art, music and pottery, dieticians, religious services, organized outings, libraries, patients' clubs, subsidized boutiques and friendship networks established over years.[76]

One country in which claims for the retention of the mental hospital appear to be taken more seriously than elsewhere is Scotland, which has consistently pursued its own independent mental health policy and has never followed England and Wales in adopting a formal commitment to replace the mental hospitals by community-based services. Thus in 1985, for example, Scotland still had 319 in-patients per 100,000 population compared to 160 in England and Wales. Recently a working party concluded that in Scotland 'there remain groups of patients whose mental illness renders them either recurrently or permanently so disturbed as to make in-patient care the preferred method of treatment on humanitarian and social as much as on medical grounds'. Public comment, the report noted, 'now increasingly focuses on concern about the wisdom of wholesale mental hospital closures if the consequence is to be the accumulation on the streets of clearly disordered people who, though they may be *in* the community are not an integral part *of* the community'. The report envisaged 'the need for major reconstruction of present mental illness hospital provision and the construction of new types of in-patient facility'.[77]

These proposals have recently been extolled in a leader in the *British Medical Journal* by a professor of psychiatry from north of the border as offering a model for England to follow. The writer summarizes the consequences of community-care policies in the United States, Italy, and England and Wales: 'Slowly, however, it became apparent that all was not well. The disabilities of chronic schizophrenics did not melt away when the hospital gates closed behind them.'[78] Much the same concerns have been voiced by other parties, notably the National Schizophrenia Fellowship in their widely publicized report *Slipping through the Net*.[79] It would be misleading to represent all these critics as offering an unconditional celebration of the mental hospital. In one aspect they caution against the hasty destruction of the mental hospital system before an alternative network of services has been brought into being, in another they propose a moderated view of the kinds of support structures that will be needed for some groups of people with severe mental illness.

Framed in these terms it does not seem that there is much to cavil at here. But underlying this debate are deep uncertainties and differences of opinion over how to understand and conceptualize the problems and predicaments of people with a history of mental illness living in the community. On the view from north of the border, for example, it would appear that what should concern us most are less the consequences of a history of social failings than the failings of schizophrenics themselves. Schizophrenics are by and large damaged individuals, at risk to themselves and often enough to others, whose handicaps and peculiarities predominate over whatever they might be thought to have in common with other people. Contrary to the misplaced optimism of a previous generation of psychiatric zealots, so the argument runs, schizophrenics have in large measure shown themselves unable to square up to the tasks demanded of them in social life. They are to be thought of as *in* the community but not as an integral part *of* the community. From this point of view, what to a large extent we find in the community are neglected mental patients who are not properly recognized as such. The project of closing the asylum, and the dispersal of mental patients into the community, is accordingly best characterized as a worthy idea founded on mistaken assumptions. Sadly, but inevitably, many of these unfortunate people must be seen and dealt with, benignly but securely, in terms of their differences, as secondary sorts of people when judged by the standards of the capable majority.

The force of Elizabeth Bott's discussion of how people come to be stuck in hospital was to suggest that the vicissitudes of people with a history of mental illness in a modern society require some consideration of what we might term the politics of 'place'. These recent assessments of what has gone wrong with community-care policies nicely pre-empt discussion of the contemporary politics of place by referring the bulk of the problems to the innate deficiencies of the mentally ill themselves. Compelling though such assessments may seem in the light of the undoubted hardships experienced by many former mental patients in the community, there is, I shall argue, rather less integrity to them than might appear and we stand in need of a rather different framework in which to understand both the history of what has gone before and the critical issues of the present moment. To see why this is so we will need to approach closer to the experiences of former mental patients and attempt to look at their circumstances from their own point of view.

2 'Get Back to Your Ward'

'The Patients Who Choose Loneliness'

Some light on how we might begin to assess the challenge to mental health policy is thrown by an account of an experiment in community mental health in which failings in service delivery have seemingly been made good. In an article provocatively entitled 'The patients who choose loneliness', a journalist describes how on the advice of a health minister he took himself off to Hackney in east London to view the implementation of the 'civilized and humanitarian' policy of community care at its most successful:

We are in showpiece land. Behind a battered door on a bleak Hackney housing estate lives a schizophrenic who enjoys the best care that Britain has to offer outside a hospital.[1]

Stepping through the door:

. . . things are not quite as you would expect given the ministerial eulogy. A pathway of dirt and blackened grease fans out into the living-room, which is in semi-darkness. Threadbare drapes are hung permanently across the windows. Cigarette butts and spent matches are scattered, like seed, in every corner of the room. The air is hot and stale . . . There are no sheets or blankets on the single bed. In the kitchen, there is little sign of food; a pan of congealed fat stands on the stove and a packet of sugar is spilt across the sideboard . . . Roy lives here. He is forty-eight and for most of the past twenty-five years someone has looked after him as he has moved in and out of hospital, living in hostels and community homes, struggling to hold the line against the illness that threatened to destroy him. His wrists bear the scars of suicide attempts. Now he has a flat and is on his own.

Though he lives alone, Roy is looked after by a team from Hackney Hospital, which provides long-term support to people with mental illness living in the community. A member of the team visits him regularly and he also attends a day centre. Despite the obvious deprivations of his social situation, Roy is none the less certain of one thing: he doesn't want to be back in hospital: 'I was very pleased to get my own place. You've got your own privacy. In hospital you're ordered about. You have to get up at a certain time, you have to wash up. You can't do what you want. You have to take account of other people's preferences.'

Confronted with Roy's predicament, the journalist goes on to remark, 'you wonder what the minister was on about. Is this not the kind of neglect highlighted by those who have attacked the community-care policy for its inadequacies and campaigned to have the mental hospital closure programme slowed down?' Yet, as he rightly points out, 'the paradox is that in Roy's case the facilities *are* there according to the minister.'

Compared to the general run of newspaper articles on the discharge of mental patients to the community, the merit of this piece is that it faces up to the tensions and dilemmas in the situation. A number of observers have criticized the implementation of community-care policies with the tacit assumption that we have some idea of what it would mean for community care to work, yet here we see that in the terms the government proposes, it is working but turns out to be a rather forlorn enterprise. The government has promised that 'adequate medical and social care' will be made available for people like Roy in the community, but as the journalist asks: 'What is "adequate"? What is "care"?'

There are two notable things to be said about Roy. The first is that he is poor. As two members of the team from Hackney Hospital commented in response to the article: 'Individual poverty remains the most difficult issue in people's efforts to re-create their independence. For every one on a low income, not just for those with a mental illness, there is no possibility of good housing through home ownership. Whatever the permutation of benefits, disposable income is often so low that it takes great ingenuity to provide even the most basic food, warmth and clothing.'[2] So, for example, a recent study has shown that the concerted promotion of policies of community care by the government has been accompanied by a decrease in real income for the poorest 20 per cent of the population over the period 1979–87, and that income inequality is presently greater than at any time since the Second World War.[3]

The second thing to say about Roy is that he does not want to return to a mental hospital. Apologists for the mental hospital understandably worry that the exodus to the community may, among other things, result in the neglect of the basic health needs of discharged patients. Certainly, from a recent study of the views and experiences of patients discharged from Claybury Hospital, it is apparent that the ex-patients had found it easier to secure attention to such matters as the ailments of their teeth and feet inside hospital than outside it.[4] But from these same ex-patients, and from the studies we discussed earlier, it is equally apparent that there is rather little support for the contention that these people had specific-ally chosen to live in a mental hospital. The majority of them were only too glad to be permitted the opportunity to leave. To represent informal status as a choice is somewhat disingenuous, for as one observer has observed:

It is a rare patient indeed who comes to the hospital explicitly seeking treatment for difficulties that he acknowledges . . . If a patient comes to a mental hospital, it is because someone thinks that he is the sort of person who cannot be held responsible for his behaviour and needs to be control-led and removed from his customary social place. 'Removals' was the word that used to be used to describe the process of getting patients out of their homes and into the hospital, and it still defines the essential features of the process with commendable exactness.[5]

One way to read Roy's experience is to suggest that the discussion of mental hospital closures needs to be concerned with rather more than the shortcomings in the management of disabled people and to embrace also the revaluation of the status of people with mental illness in our society. If, as critics of the asylum have alleged, the history of the asylum is in large part the story of how people with mental illness have been marginalized and excommunicated from social life, the question arises of how such people can feasibly be brought back on to the map and new channels of communication with them opened. From this point of view the significant challenge is to the legacy of mental patienthood and the constraints on membership that confront people with a history of mental illness in the community. As a group of users of mental health services put it recently:

The problem with community care is not just about management. It is about misery, poverty and a style of mental health service that offers no real choice about the type of support available ... The kind of service provided by mental health professionals is not the only, or necessarily even the main, issue that determines the quality of people's lives in the community ...[6]

The vulnerabilities of people like Roy are evident enough but the vocabulary of disabilities can readily be invoked as an instrument to foreclose understanding. Once we have netted someone like Roy within the encompassing image of a 'chronic schizophrenic', the social deprivations he happens to suffer appear regrettable but largely irrelevant to the authoritative pronouncements we make about him. In the language in which he describes Roy, the journalist betrays a representative uncertainty as to whether Roy is to be described in the kind of terms that we use to depict people whom we identify as fellow human beings or in the vocabulary of psychiatric difference, as a 'mental patient' or a 'schizophrenic'. And behind this uncertainty lies, among other things, the question of whether people like Roy are capable of entertaining a coherent view of their situations and making choices about what they think is best for them, or whether it should not be left to others, like the professor from north of the border, to determine how to dispose of them.

New Partners in the Debate

Despite the rhetoric of community care, and pronouncements about the benefits that it will bring to former mental patients in the community, surprisingly little has been done to explore the experiences of such people and draw them directly into the debate about mental health policy. It is of some importance that effort be made here for, as Kathleen Jones has remarked, 'As the length of stay in hospital becomes shorter, and patterns of community-care diversify, the value of a service-oriented view of the course of a patient's illness steadily diminishes.' Typically, the patient 'becomes visible for a few days or weeks, gets treated or caseworked, and goes away again'. What, Jones asks, 'happens in the periods of official invisibility'?[7]

In collecting evidence on the state of community care for the mentally ill and handicapped, the members of the Social Services

Committee were barraged by submissions from professionals and other concerned parties, but revealed in conclusion that they had experienced 'difficulty in hearing the authentic voice of the ultimate consumers of community care'.[8] Traditionally, psychiatric knowledge has provided thick descriptions of the patient and thin descriptions of the person in which the patient is represented as a notional person but never fully described as such. Inevitably, there are those who want to maintain the rhetoric of distance and shore up established positions. But this is profoundly unsatisfactory, for what increasingly the era of community care is bringing about is a new intermingling of voices in which the authority of this or that brand of professional knowledge cannot be taken for granted.

Here are examples from some recent work in which my colleagues and I explored the trials of a group of people, most of them in their late thirties to early forties with a history of schizophrenic illness and living in the community, from their own point of view. The members of the group are perhaps not untypical of that large group of people with a history of schizophrenic illness who 'alternate for decades between acute psychotic phases and phases of improvement or recovery'.[9] The study from which several of these extracts are taken is described more fully elsewhere and my purpose here is not in any sense to provide a comprehensive account, merely to highlight some of the key issues that arise for people with long-term mental illness living in the community.[10]

Stigma

A difficulty many people encounter in attempting to strike up relationships is the stigma of mental illness. As Simon puts it:

'If I meet somebody who isn't or hasn't been in the hospital, then you don't mention that you're psychiatric and hope to God that nobody else mentions it in your family or whatever that meets them later. Because the attitude from people, some of them, they just . . . you can tell they're embarrassed and don't know what to say or anything . . . They think it's terrible. I think unless you've had somebody in your family who's had trouble, which a lot of people must have done, but some of course haven't and they have a very strange attitude towards psychiatric . . . it's taboo, you mustn't talk about it . . .'

Sarah describes how she wants to be on an equal footing with other people but if she lets it be known that she has had a mental illness she is at once made to feel 'less of a person':

'It's important to me to feel equal to other people . . . I like *pretending* to people when I go into a pub, I like doing that, I like just starting a conversation with someone and letting it flow and not saying anything. I like doing that, but if they were to get to know me really well, I'd have to tell them and then I wouldn't be on a par with them.'

An additional source of difficulty is the idea that the person with a history of mental illness never properly recovers and is somehow irrevocably 'tainted' by the illness. As Simon relates:

'They don't know what to say because it's not like a physical illness where they can say, "Oh, you have broken your leg, but it's better now", they have in their mind, "Are you going to get poorly again?" . . . People wonder "Is he really better, or is he still poorly? Is he OK with the children, is he going to beat them up, is he going to have a fit?" People get all sorts of funny ideas.'

The application of the term 'schizophrenia' often aggravates this sense of 'taint'. For example, Sarah recounts how

'You wake up every morning and you think, "Oh, God, I'm a schizophrenic!" If the doctor hadn't told me I'd just have woken up and thought, "Well I'm just going through some sort of illness and I'll probably get over it." But once you get diagnosed, you start thinking all sorts from different corners about the illness and it just gets worse and worse.'

The idea that the person is irrevocably flawed introduces special difficulties when he or she applies for a job. Simon describes it thus:

'I went after a job just recently at a local bakery and I saw a lady there who interviewed me. And as soon as I mentioned – I put it as nicely as I could – that I had had a nervous breakdown – I didn't mention schizophrenia or anything like that – and that I was well over my troubles – her face dropped and her attitude completely changed. I could tell it wasn't my imagination and of course I got the letter in the post a few days later saying "thanks, but no thanks". I could have got that kind of letter anyway but I think because I mentioned about my illness it went against me.'

Looking for New Horizons

This is how Simon perceives his situation:

'I feel that I could do a job of some sort or at least I could give it a try. It's another thing convincing an employer to give you a try of course, but I feel that I could quite probably do a job now so really I shouldn't be just sort of sitting back and doing nothing. I should be trying in some direction . . . I've actually tried applying for jobs but I've got the usual "sorry on this occasion" letters and it's obvious that with me psychiatric background and me lack of references and me lack of work experience time-scale-wise, that I can't really offer an employer what they want in the way of *recent* references. So if I can say to an employer, "Look I've done this for six months or a year and I've got this qualification", then it's possible then. But to go and say, "Well, I've got four O levels in the year zero BC and I've done very little since", well they just don't want to know, they'll take somebody else who's got the recent experience and the recent qualifications.'

On a previous occasion he

'. . . went to the Job Centre and said, "Look I want a part-time job at the very least, can you help us?", and they said, "Well, why aren't you signing on?" of course, "Are you signing on?", and I said not, and they said "Well, what's the problem?" and I told them and they said, "Oh, we usually find people from 'that place',", as they put it – the hospital – "can't cope with a job."'

For lack of an alternative Simon has now embarked on a word-processing course at the hospital rehabilitation centre. While he holds out some hope here, overall he is unimpressed by the rehabilitative claims of the centre:

'I don't think it is rehabilitation, to be honest. They *call* it that but they don't really . . . They do try and find jobs for people occasionally but people end up going there for years quite often and they don't get rehabilitated at all. I think it's just somewhere for people to go quite often. But they do do a little bit of rehabilitation, it is possible . . .'

One of Simon's main concerns is to find a satisfactory alternative to incorporation in a psychiatric system which, he feels, affords him no real prospects. Recently he has moved from a hostel to a bed-sit, only to find that he is now considerably isolated:

'Everybody seems to keep themselves to themselves. I've only ever spoken to one person and he seemed very sort of abrupt and didn't seem to want to really know. It isn't the same as the hostel where you shared communal facilities like the TV room, the laundry room and the kitchen – the main kitchen – so you do tend to mix a bit. There is one or two prefer to keep themselves to themselves but usually people tend to mix pretty well. And it's completely different when you move out of a place like that, everybody just sort of shuts the door and that's it, bars are up and you never see them. It's a shame really . . .'

Yet despite his loneliness, if he had to choose again between a place in a hostel and independent living, he would still opt for independence:

'I would choose to stay where I am because I didn't like the idea of being connected with the hospital. I know it sounds daft but I've always regarded the hospital as being like Colditz . . . the sort of place that you don't want to be, and I also have the general idea that I want to eventually break off from the whole system and be totally independent. In every other sense than that, the hostel situation were a good one, it's just the thing at the back of your mind where you sort of say, "This is part of the hospital, I'm still really in the system, and therefore I'm not really anywhere near being better," sort of thing.'

To feel part of the system, in this sense, is to feel less than a person:

'It's a bit demoralizing . . . You're sort of tied to the strings of the hospital, the apron strings of the hospital I suppose you could say, you're being treated like a child really, and you prefer to think, "Well, I'd like to be independent and this is OK temporarily but I want to move on eventually and break away from all this."'

Medication: The Battle with the Doctor

Inevitably, a major concern for many people is over the medication they have been prescribed. Of particular relevance here are the difficulties people encounter in their efforts to exert some control over the dosage that is administered to them. So, for example, Vaughan is reluctant to see himself as an invalid and after recovering from a relapse is soon eager to re-establish himself in work. He describes his experiences with psychiatrists in attempting to negotiate his concerns:

'That's the big battle, the battle with the doctors, when you're feeling better and you feel it's time to cut down your tablets. The doctor I saw said, "You're going to need injections for the rest of your life." I said I was going to look for a job and he said, "I wouldn't bother looking for a job, just get an hour or two's rest every day." I said, "That's no good, I want to get out and get a job." He said, "Oh no, I should take it easy" . . .'

Cyril is a man in his mid-fifties who since his wife died some years ago now cares single-handedly for his severely handicapped sister-in-law. Looking after his sister-in-law demands his constant attention but he has recently been put on a new drug with, it would seem, little or no effort to monitor its effects and he now feels 'doped' most of the time. He has misgivings over his relationship with the psychiatrist but feels himself powerless to change it:

'No, I'm not happy with it. Dr Perkins hasn't the time. You wait one and a quarter to one and three quarter hours, and you're in three minutes and out. "Come back in twelve weeks!" There's no explanation given why they've changed these drugs, he just rung for the nurse who brought the prescription through, he signed it, she took it back and I went, and they put it into me. They didn't say, "Right we're going to try a brand-new drug on you, we don't know the side-effects," they didn't say anything like that. I mean, I

might be a guinea-pig, I don't know. It could be a brand-new drug,
or the combination could be brand-new, mixing this drug with
what I already have in me . . . I'd like him to explain what were
happening.'

'Has he ever told you about the illness you have had?'

'No, he does the talking.'

'Have you ever asked him?'

'He doesn't reply. He's superior. When you walk in, you sit
down . . . Between you and me, he's superior to me, I'm the patient
and he's the doctor . . . *He* does the talking . . . I wish he would
spend a little bit more time and explain, explain what the side-
effects are going to be.'

In Sarah's experience of mental health professionals, people like
herself are always at risk of being patronized. In order to gain
acceptance – 'Look, my mind's as good as yours or as strong as
yours!' – they have no alternative but to fight for recognition.
Sarah is insistent that she can make her own responsible choices
about her life:

'You're having an old battle with your doctor – "I want to come
off my medication!" "Oh, if you do you'll become ill again." You
have to be really strong, you have to say, "Look maybe I won't
become ill again." Then it's a personal choice of yours but you have
to really go back to them and say, "Look, I want to come off it."
I'm going through it at the moment. While you're on medication
you're always going to be sleepy or ill or not perform like you used
to be able to perform. So that's the next stage I'm going through
with my doctors, trying to get off the medication.'

'The idea of becoming ill again, what does that do to you?'

'It's frightening, but to me I have accepted that, OK, I may be ill
again. Therefore I'll take the risk and be prepared to do it myself.
Of course they say, "You'll become ill and you'll cost the NHS a
lot of money." The nurses say that, not the doctors . . .'

'What do you feel if they say that?'

'It knocks your confidence back again. You have got to be really
sure of yourself and a strong person and be able to say, "I'll risk
it."'

Ben has travelled down the same road as Sarah but has now

reluctantly been brought to the conclusion that he puts himself at risk if he does without medication altogether:

'. . . I have medication, I take Depixol, a small amount, and I have a continual fight because I want to be off it . . . I don't like to think of myself as mentally ill, I like to think that I'll be free of it. But when I've been to hospital – there's a combination of factors, I hadn't taken medication for about a month or six weeks previous to going to hospital again – so there's absolutely conclusive evidence that you needed your medication! That was just a battle I lost! It is like a bit of a battle, I'll go in and I'll say, "I'm still taking medication, can we reduce it some more?" I would like to stop, I would much prefer to go into hospital once a week, say, than to actually take medication. But since the last time I went in I do feel that I probably do need it. So I've deferred to the doctor . . . But in some ways I do prefer – when it comes to the end of the medication, the end of the cycle, I'm a lot more active, and I do prefer to be in that state, my imagination is a great deal more acute.'

Back to the Hospital?

Though some of the people in this study continued to suffer from sometimes distressing experiences, none of them wanted to return to a mental hospital permanently. A harsh judgement on the benefits of hospital admission is given by Simon:

'I feel the hospital is pretty much a waste of time for everybody. The only time someone should be put into hospital is when they are definitely a danger to people and of course you are then talking of locking people away until they can be cured to some degree. But other than people like that, it's the wrong place for people and they should be treated outside. Perhaps GPs should be trained more in psychiatric work but most people get referred to, and end up in, hospitals.'

Simon feels that there is insufficient opportunity to talk through problems:

'I think it's not given enough importance and drugs are given too much importance. I think that's one of the things that's wrong. If we have hospitals in the future I think they have got to be changed in that sense. I think the whole emphasis has to be altered towards telling people about their problems rather than just turning them into vegetables and leaving them to sort their own problems out.'

'So you think there's an over-reliance on drugs?'

'Oh yes, I think generally they are understaffed and if they drug everybody they are easier to control. Give everybody their Mogadon, then they are going to sleep through the night. So whether you need Mogadon or not, you are given it. You may turn round and say, you don't need that and you are told, well, yes you do.'

A contrasting perspective on the mental hospital is provided by Roland, who now lives in a group home but returns to the hospital during the day to work in the gardens:

'Well, the hospital's got very good grounds, it's like living in the countryside, it's an old building and it's surrounded by trees and grass, it's got very good grounds and it's very peaceful. We get on with the foreman on the gardens, he doesn't make us work too hard, he has a laugh and a joke with us . . . I don't know, but it seems the only practical place for people like me, it's the only place where there's any peace and quiet and if you're not quite up to it people understand that you're maybe a bit slow or you've got your own rate of doing things and it's a bit easier than throwing you in at the deep end and saying, "You get on with it", because they might drown you, mightn't they? They might throw you into some difficult circumstances where you come across things that you can't cope with. I don't know, maybe there is another environment, maybe . . . But being in a hospital is definitely better than being stuck in a city, somewhere where everything's busy.'

We can appreciate why Roland likes to return to the hospital during the day when we learn that for Roland 'being stuck in the city' meant being homeless. If the choice were forced on him, he would again choose to live in the Church Army hostel in preference to the mental hospital but in his choice of words he makes palpable the experience of society of someone who is deprived of privacy and security:

'Well, the Church Army's OK because nobody says when you can come or go and there's nothing to do with the doctors. There's a lot of people there, there must be a hundred people there and you can, you're left up to your own resources, you get good food there but you've got to do your own washing, but you can get a bath and you've got your own cubicle. You can look after yourself, basically, but the only impression you get of society is that it's this big busy world, big hard world of cars zooming by all the time and you just don't – you know, you've got a desire for peace and quiet and the countryside and maybe just your own room somewhere, or maybe even sitting on your own with a few people watching television, not about fifty people all crammed in one room. You get a lot of fighting there, people fall out and get drunk – I got thrown out for fighting!'

'I Can See a Worth of Being Here'

Philip, who has been out of hospital for ten years, is less than sanguine about community care:

'. . . I don't know whether it's because the NHS is short of cash but the idea is to get people out of hospital into the community . . . I have managed to survive for ten whole years and it's a hell of a long time when you're suffering quite a bit . . . I wouldn't recommend it to anyone, that term of existence, it's been hell really over the ten years, but when you're at the bottom of the pile there's the old saying beggars can't be choosers and that could apply to my case.'

He feels betrayed by the health services:

'You are fearful of what might happen because at the present time the NHS seems to be overrun with patients who require not necessarily urgent treatment but cosmetic treatment and therefore the people like me who I think require continuous assessment have no recourse to the NHS, and instead of going into the emergency side of the service they are flitted away in other directions. The people who really need some money spending on them to lead some sort of satisfactory existence are not getting it . . . That's the principal problem. The illness itself is not fearful, it's the problem of how to get the proper treatment with the money available.'

Looking ahead:

'Quite honestly, just sometimes I feel very suicidal, I don't think
the future holds much at all . . . I'm now forty-five and when you
can go for – since this problem first started, virtually my whole life
I've been under some strain . . . and when you can go forty-odd
years and nothing much happens to improve your lot, I mean
you're virtually in the last third of your life and nothing has been
done . . . There might be a motive in ignoring people with illnesses.
I hope that the illness will go away but *they* hope that the person
having the illness will go away! . . . It's terrible really. It's really
negative all this stuff but really that's how it is . . . What you do
look forward to are the occasional times when you don't feel quite
as bad as you did . . . I do feel better on occasions and I don't
know why this is.'

While he does not want to be back in hospital permanently

'. . . I think I should occasionally have certain periods in hospital. I
am certain about that because I have to cope with everything to do
with this house as well as being in poor health. Paying bills, cooking
meals, washing – absolutely everything, and together with running
a house – you need to be more than fairly healthy to do it efficiently.
You can cope at some periods and not others . . .'

People like himself, he suggests, would feel more secure living in
the community if

'. . . you could be certain that you would get regular visits and
would have a physical or mental examination quite regularly, and
people could see the state that you were in at a particular time.
Not every six months – that's far too long. You might need to
be examined, say, every month to see how you are getting on. I
wouldn't mind that because you would know you could probably
last a month in feeling shocking . . . At the end of the month
you would know somebody would come and examine you and
possibly diagnose something and possibly have you in hospital
for a bit. Mainly it's your mind that needs a rest, because
physically I'm not too bad. I can get about, it's just mentally
you become exhausted, rather like an old person who needs a
frame to get about. Well, occasionally I need a similar sort of

frame to get about – it's not a physical frame, it's a mental frame.'

Sometimes he feels that living alone is not the best option for him:

'I think the ideal solution would be to go into a more supportive arrangement than living alone and trying to muddle through as I have done for years. But if I went out of this system . . . I don't know how much strain it's putting me under, I mean I don't really know. It's only if I went into hospital and came back after six weeks, I'd know the sort of strain I was living under. Looking at things from a distance rather than being in the middle . . .'

But the interesting thing about Philip is that though he complains that he has had to manage on his own with little or no external support for almost ten years, throughout this time he has to a large extent kept himself to himself and made little or no effort to make his needs known to official agencies. During this period he has been prescribed minor tranquillizers by his GP, but he has received no anti-psychotic medication: 'The fewer drugs I take, the better I feel . . . You're able to function as a normal human being as far as possible.'

He recognizes the contradiction himself:

'I said I hadn't seen anyone for ten years . . . I was saying earlier that I should be seen every month but I haven't been anywhere to see anyone for ten years! It seems crazy, doesn't it! You see, I'd rather keep myself quiet. It's the pride business – if I can manage I will do even if I feel terrible. I often think when I get my mental powers back that it's not a bad thing to be in here . . . I have a certain pride, I have a certain pride in trying to cope with whatever is wrong with me.'

Moreover, his experience of psychiatric functionaries has not been encouraging:

'I have little regard for psychiatrists. I've had bad experiences with psychiatrists and nurses, so I don't get in touch with people. They really do give you a punch in the guts. For instance, I said I was suicidal to a nurse and she said, "Why don't you do it then?"'

He particularly prides himself on maintaining his house in impeccable order:

'It's part of survival. I can actually see a worth of being here. I can make a difference to something, affect something . . . I feel as though I've accomplished something.'

Back to Square One?

A significant worry for many people is that if they experience a relapse they will find themselves pitched back to square one, as Simon put it. Not infrequently, 'square one' means a return to homelessness. In Vaughan's case, for example, the house in which he had been living remained empty for the four months he was in hospital and as a result it had been broken into, his possessions stolen and his flat set fire to. He had nowhere to go and found himself in effect abruptly discharged to the street. It distressed him that the doctor did not seem much concerned about the personal and material disruption that his admission to hospital had brought in its train:

'I saw the doctor on the Monday and he said, "You're going home on Wednesday." I said I had nowhere to go and he said, "Well, there's nothing I can do, you're better now and you can go home." So I was a bit bitter then, I thought I was just getting kicked out and nowhere to go.'

In his account of his own relapse, Ben describes how a person with a previous history of mental illness tends to be judged as incapable of playing an active part in managing his own crisis. He recognized that he had been under some stress and was having a problem sleeping which had made him a 'bit edgy', as he put it:

'The sleep problem comes from the worry and the work that I'm doing and the things that I'm involved in, the exhaustion if you like, and the ideas that I have and not getting things done – all these worries come together. In other words it's not just in my chemistry, it's to do with the life that I lead.'

While Ben recognized his own stress he felt, nevertheless, that he could be helped to manage it himself. However, friends who were acquainted with his history judged otherwise:

'I feel they overreacted because I had sleeping tablets in my pocket and I needed sleep as much as anything. The thing is, when I take those tablets I might sleep late, but it does give me a good night's rest and stops me from getting into really bad problems. It's becoming a common occurrence now, the sleep problem and the subsequent going into hospital – for the last three times it has been that cause.'

Ben would have preferred an alternative course of action:

'I think, to accept my solution of taking some tablets and having a sleep would be a lot better, and they would realize that if it didn't work after a good night's sleep, and I was still poorly, *then* they could take me in.'

He describes how the person with a history of mental illness easily becomes vulnerable to redefinition as a mental patient:

'You see, the problem is you can just look at me now, you can go next door, ring up, and you could have me in hospital on your word, not on my word. That is the problem and I could say, "I protest, I protest, I'm alright!" And I *would* protest, because I am alright. And you could say, "No, he isn't!", and you might have your own reasons for doing that. That's the problem of hospitalization and you would be doing it in the best of hearts – I'm not suggesting it's not concern . . . But I don't always like being in hospital . . . and if there is some credence to helping people in the community, it's no good when there's a problem just sending people into hospital. There has to be a solution other than that, I think.'[11]

Ben's relapse had considerable effects on the relationships he had established:

'It was upsetting with the friends I had made in the town independent of the hospital. Some of them knew that I had been in hospital, a lot of them didn't. For me to go into hospital and have them visit me, that was upsetting. I felt, if you like, I'd grown in self-confidence in certain things and it was a reduction, it was a step backwards . . . I like people to feel "Oh, he's alright" but I now have to convince them that I'm alright because of that. For me to have this relapse or whatever it was, I then had to re-establish that I'm kind of alright.'

For example:

'With friends, when I went in again, it has taken quite a long time to build up trust. Just little things, like baby-sitting, and it was five or six months before they would ask me again. Because they were worried – there was just this bit of "We had better not."'

The most important aspect of the repair work that he had to do in his relationships was 'building up that trust, that feeling again'. It all comes back, as he puts it, to the problem of stigma, of getting over the barrier of people 'thinking that you're mad because you've been in a mental hospital':

'Trying to get over that – that I'm alright, I'm a functioning being ... It's building up that kind of *trust*. It's a trust that you have to build up with any kind of human being anyway, but I feel that I've got that extra obstacle.'

But to a large extent his efforts have been successful:

'As people get to know me, they make contact and come to expect things from me and I expect things from them. They know the kinds of things I can do. Usually, and certainly in the kindest possible way, people know I have had an illness and say, "Don't let yourself get too pressured!" and although they are reacting to me in my illness, I certainly don't think they are doing it in any kind of malevolent way, they are doing it in a "We know if you do too much, or get too pressured, then you are going to have a problem" kind of way, and they are very kind about that, people who know.'

'Right Down at the Bottom'

Sarah described how the consequences of her mental illness led her to feel that she was 'right down at the bottom'. For many people being 'right down at the bottom' is as much as anything a desperate material condition. Harold describes how:

'I get by for food, just about. I don't eat expensive meals. I sometimes eat out in the café, the odd beer ... When I've finished there's very little left ... I buy tobacco, that's all. On average I don't spend more than £6 per week ... I can't go out at all.'

'What about things like, say in this weather you need a new pair of boots or something. What would you do about that?'

'Well, at a push – I've managed the last two years – if I could, I'd go to a cheap place and get them out of my weekly amount. I'd really scrimp and scrape that week, though.'

'I was just thinking – it's snowing outside – if you needed to get a thick coat, for example?'

'I've only got an anorak, but luckily, I mean, I got that anorak about two years ago now when I was in hospital. When I was in hospital I was able to get a little bit saved because I didn't have very much going out then . . . I couldn't manage to buy something like that now, I don't know what I'd do.'

As Jim's story illustrates, the stress of poverty may sometimes precipitate a relapse. Jim had been living in a Salvation Army hostel but decided to leave because he was tired, as he put it, of 'living with losers'. For a time he lived rough but hunger and lack of sleep affected his mental state and he was again pestered by voices, the 'fucking agitators' as he calls them. Eventually he was referred by his GP to the psychiatric out-patient department in the local general hospital. Jim recalled how for the past two days he had not been able to afford the price even of a cup of tea. The psychiatrist, he said, sat with a large mug of tea in front of him but declined to offer Jim one and terminated the interview when Jim tried to put his housing crisis on the agenda for discussion. For want of any alternative, Jim pushed himself to go to a reception centre from where some days later he was found a room in a lodging-house, mainly occupied by other homeless people. He does not have a room to himself and has no control over whom he shares with, the other occupant often staying only for a week or so. He has nothing to occupy him during the day, in the mornings he walks the streets and in the evenings mainly watches TV. His shoes pinch and he cannot afford another pair.

Not Integral Members of the Community

Particularly for people who already possess a low sense of self-esteem, the consequences of a mental illness can have a devastating effect. As Roland put it, 'Already I felt I was an inferior person and then being made a mental patient on top of this . . .' This is the outlook on life to which Henry has been brought:

'With schizophrenia you are not living, you are just existing. There is not a lot of future for you, but you come to terms with the illness. I don't like telling anybody but I do accept it. I am labelled for the rest of my life . . . I think schizophrenia will always make me a second-class citizen. I go for an interview for a job and the anxiety builds up . . . I haven't got a future. It's just a matter of waiting for old age and death.'

We can see why the anxiety builds up when he goes for a job:

'There is something I regret. I went not long since from the hospital to the Job Centre and I had to tell *them* I was schizophrenic. I was sat in front of the lady. I didn't want to tell them, but the hospital made me tell them. They had got a report from the doctor saying I was schizophrenic. But people are nervy . . . There was this lady sat in front of me as if she didn't know what to expect. They're nervy because they know you're schizophrenic, as though they feel "what's he going to do next?" It's all out of perspective.'

Ben aptly describes how many former mental patients find themselves negatively defined by their exclusion from any form of meaningful role:

'If you get classified as schizophrenic it becomes a kind of role in a sense – rather than being an artist, say, or somebody in society. If you are unemployed you are poor and you haven't actually got a clear identifiable role and then you do get this kind of problem. I know I wasn't really sure what I was in that sense and that seems to come as much from the social problems as anything . . . A lot of my difficulties come from that rolelessness. When somebody asks me what I do or what are you there is no definite answer – "I'm just unemployed", or I could say "I'm an ex-mental-patient."'

As a result the person is often made to feel useless. Sarah, for example, thinks that people see her as 'a pretty useless person':

'It's that feeling of being *useless* that bugs me more than anything . . . I think people brand me as useless . . . The only skill I've got is like talking to people and making them feel they're not the only one, or cheering them up, or making them feel a bit better. That's the only skill I've got, that's the only way that I can say, "Well, I'm helping someone", doing something that's a bit important . . .'

'Get Back to Your Ward!'

Naturally enough, the stances which people with a history of mental illness adopt are as varied as those of any other population group and the people illustrated here are by no means alike; there are wide variations in perception and belief, just as there are marked differences in condition and need. Perhaps most striking, in the face of professional accounts of schizophrenics as inarticulate, is their capacity to lend pointed and nuanced expression to their experiences. Across the variations we can identify a number of common themes and concerns, notably: the pauperization of lives; the cruel effects of stigma and the 'taint' of mental illness; the barriers to equality with other people, the experience of being made to feel less of a person or even an inferior person; experiences of powerlessness in their efforts to exert some control over their lives, not least in their dealings with the medical profession; and the demoralization produced by a health and welfare system that treats them as secondary sorts of people or as children. So, for example:

1. *Problems of Identity.* What becomes of the person who has had an illness like schizophrenia? Who does one say that one now is? In Ben's case, some people have learned to 'react to me in my illness', as he phrases it, and still treat him as an ordinary and capable human being. But this is evidently an achievement that is as exceptional as it is precarious, against the grain of established cultural sensibilities in which identities are judged to be irrevocably tainted or spoiled by a diagnosis of mental illness.

2. *Social Isolation and Exclusion.* The people illustrated here may not have to suffer the permanent exile of an older generation of mental patients but we may reasonably question whether they have been helped to belong in social life. Roland and Jim, for example, found themselves pitched into the anonymity of urban homelessness. Henry feels that schizophrenia has turned him into a second-

class citizen but it is not so much by the illness itself that he has been brought down as by the web of social and cultural forces that have turned him into a person seemingly devoid of worth and prospects.

3. *The Limitations of Services.* The majority of the people discussed here had a rather precarious and, by their own account, unsatisfactory relationship with psychiatric services in the community. Services seemed at best to provide regimes of benign containment in which the significant questions that concerned consumers about the value and direction of their lives were left unaddressed or obscured. So, for example, though medication was sometimes judged to be beneficial, it was also evident that delivered crudely as the primary (or exclusive) form of intervention it became a currency which devalued people's efforts to restore some dignity and purpose to their lives. Similarly, complain though he did about his neglect by psychiatric services, Philip had chosen to take himself out of the service system and, as we saw, the key to his decision lay in the importance he set on his own sense of worth.

It may help to set these remarks in a wider context. In a number of respects the accounts of these users of services underline what a number of studies have already shown, for example the blow to self-esteem that follows admission to hospital; the inadequacy of the information patients are given about the illness and about medication; failures to prepare patients for discharge and to provide guidance on such matters as housing and social security, and so on.[12] Drawing on Goffman's critique of institutional life, Kathleen Jones has described how we are 'no longer dealing with the unlettered patients of the early nineteenth century. The experience of hospital admission leads them to feel rejected. let down, betrayed by those they trusted; and once inside the hospital they feel that kindness from the nursing staff plus a few brief interviews with a doctor who prescribes for them is not enough to make up for their sense of loss of identity, loss of status, loss of the opportunity to communicate.'[13] Yet, as we have seen here, these various forms of loss may just as easily occur outside the asylum as inside it. As Philips's vivid account brings out, community care has among other things provided new opportunities for betrayal in the relationship between service providers and people with mental illness.

In the case of day care, studies have shown that a substantial level of unmet need for individual elements of care can coincide with quite high levels of overprovision. So, for example, there is evidence that substantial numbers of clients are placed in too dependent a setting. In one study only 40 per cent of current attenders at day hospitals had a profile of needs that warranted this form of intervention, and 25 per cent of them would have been more appropriately placed in some form of out-patient care receiving professional support.[14] Similarly there are indications that the 'chosen style of operation of some day and residential units is not directed towards exploiting the potential for autonomy that their clients possess'.[15] In a study of the views and experiences of patients discharged from Claybury Hospital, Nigel Goldie reports that in 'a few instances there were examples of people having well organized contacts with services. However, these were rather exceptional people who appeared to have organized these things for themselves.' The majority, by contrast, 'were prone to represent themselves as being at the mercy of services over which they had no control'.[16] Several of Goldie's subjects had come to view day centres 'as part of a system that is still seeking to control people and further to place them in a dependent relationship to the service providers'.[17] One person said of such places: 'They're just like being back in hospital, you are not left alone, always being told to do something.' In most cases the only action users feel able to take to register dissatisfaction with the regimes that are provided for them is to leave or, in the psychiatric jargon, engage in 'non-compliance'.

But the understanding of the social fate of people with mental illness, and the limitations on the choices open to them, plainly involves much more than the service system. As Steen Mangen has written, there is

... a range of problems about promoting autonomy among a socially deprived group which cannot be resolved within the confines of a service system. Directly at issue is the marginalized position of the long-term mentally ill in society ... Their common social handicap stems from their denial of access to the full rights of citizenship, which extend beyond conventional civil and political rights to economic and social welfare. Viewed from this perspective, many long-term users of psychiatric services are profoundly disadvantaged: their relative poverty imposes massive restrictions on choices available to them in daily life and thus can be the major determinant of the level of autonomy they attain.[18]

Yet, as Mangen points out, 'most British mental health workers have relied on traditional professional spheres of action, providing broadly drawn occupational rehabilitation programmes', and they have in consequence tended 'to underplay any political implications of their interventions with clients'.[19] So, for example, in a study in which patients with long histories of psychiatric disorder were questioned about their own skills and problems, the researchers were led to judge certain categories of responses as seemingly obscure or irrelevant. Thus patients listed 'a number of problems which, from the point of view of staff, would be regarded as "facts of life" or stresses for which a day hospital could offer no direct intervention, such as lack of paid employment, shortage of money and chronic illness in the family'.[20] The irony of this judgement is that it is cast within a theoretical framework in which social disadvantage is recognized to be a crucial component of social disablement among people with severe mental illness. Yet from the perspective that is offered, it would appear that the task of the day hospital in relation to the demoralized mental patient is to foster, if not an attitude of resignation to the decrees of fate, at least a compliance with the division of labour in which pressing social and material questions are always someone else's business. This form of verdict on how the line of relevance is to be drawn nicely illustrates Nigel Goldie's remark that 'being a professionally trained person means assessing what can be done for a client in terms of the skills of that profession; it does not mean seeking to understand what the client wants from his/her point of view'.[21]

Yet it may, perhaps, be argued that if we are not to fuel the demoralization of people with mental illness, and stigmatize them still further, we do indeed stand badly in need of psychiatric theories that try to grapple with what users of mental health services themselves want. In opposition to the more facile assumptions about deinstitutionalization that were current in the 1960s, in particular the belief that discharged mental patients could quickly get over their illness and rejoin the market, critics have rightly identified the persisting vulnerabilities of certain groups of people and their need for long-term support. Yet in attacking the prevailing psychiatric assumption of the period, these critics have left intact the social and moral assumption that goes with it, namely the belief that individual worth is determined by the market-place and only those who show themselves to be economically capable are to be valued as integral to society.

Indeed, far from becoming an object of professional concern, the marginalized position of the long-term mentally ill in society has been taken very much for granted. Social psychiatrists have declared an interest in helping to maintain vulnerable patients 'in an appropriate setting in their own community, free to come and go and to participate in an urban environment'.[22] But unless accompanied by a willingness to address the constraints on participation in their urban environments which most users of services have to contend with, to look critically at what 'participation' amounts to in practice, assertions of this kind are inevitably rather empty and fail to offer people with a history of mental illness any grounds for social hope.

As we shall see later, at the present time the significant debate is not between those who dispute the reality of long-term mental illness and those who recognize it, rather it is between those who are prepared to challenge the assumptions about the terms of membership afforded to people with a history of mental illness and those who settle for a highly impoverished view of the place of the former mental patient in the community. Fundamentally, this debate is about power relationships. The terrain in which users of mental health services and the various groups concerned with their well-being now find themselves is being remade by wider social and political changes, not least in the reorganization of the health and social services. The erosion of the paternalistic structures of the post-war welfare state has been accompanied by new forms of demand for citizenship rights from disenfranchised groups, and clashes have inevitably arisen between the interests of sections of the professional service establishment and other concerned parties on the one side and the interests of groups of users and their advocates in their struggles for citizenship on the other. 'Continuity of care' is doubtless an appropriate nostrum but, for want of a sufficiently critical application, it can become a euphemism for the containment and pacification of the insane poor.

The 'rediscovery' of chronic mental disability in recent years is better told as the rediscovery of the association between pauperization and the demoralization of people suffering from mental disorders. By contrast with the 'lost' and submissive mental patients of the asylum era, many of the new generation of service users do not use services 'in the tractable fashion of their predecessors but rather as wary, often angry, consumers demanding response to their broad needs for social and economic support'.[23] One of the most detrimental features of the asylum system, Denis Martin declared, was 'the love of power which such a system tends to foster'.[24] As we saw earlier, there are still those who hanker after the benevolent authoritarianism of the asylum era and are intent upon promoting a politics of retrenchment, a regrouping of forces around the asylum, in order to distance themselves from the changing and sometimes turbulent relationships in the community and the threat to established power structures these pose.

Looking back over the history of the transition from hospital to community-based services in this country, Ann Davis concludes that the revaluation of the person with a history of mental illness has not so far been taken very seriously:

Most medical, nursing and social-services staff retained in their hearts and minds the notion of consumers as damaged individuals who needed advice and management. Professional preoccupations with the difficulties, problems and 'weaknesses' of consumers rendered them passive recipients of services controlled by professionals who decided what was 'best'. The consequence for consumers has been that most community-based provision has replicated the all-too-familiar relationships of institutional life. Such relationships serve to confirm the worst fears that consumers have about themselves. They focus on helplessness and inability and so sap confidence and a sense of self . . . It is a fundamental change in the hearts and minds of those working in our mental health services that has been missing over the past three decades.[25]

An indication of just what has been retained in the hearts and minds of service personnel is conveyed by a recent experience of Ben's. In preparation for a visit from one of my colleagues to discuss the next stage of a project in which he and a number of other users had been engaged for some time, Ben had kindly undertaken to reserve a room in the psychiatric department of the local district general hospital. On presenting his request to a member of the staff, he was at once reprimanded for his audacity in seeking to secure a space normally reserved for doctors and nurses, and told, 'Don't be so silly, get back to your ward!' Now Ben as it happens is an old hand in the business – he was not to be put off by this rebuff and eventually secured his aim by another route. That he had in fact no ward to get back to is only part of the point, for 'ward' in this piece of professional invective is effectively a figure for the mental patient's place in society.

We need, I believe, to try to understand this admonition not so much as a reflection of shortcomings in the training of this or that member of a hospital staff (though doubtless it is also that), but rather as an expression of an attitude towards people with mental illness, and their place in the human and social scheme of things, that is rooted in the history of the social organization of responses to insanity over the past one hundred and fifty years. To uncover some of these roots may help us understand both what is implicated in the project of closing the asylum and why attitudes such as this continue to possess contemporary force.

3 The Asylum and the Dehumanization of the Insane

From the House to the Barracks

If any period merits the title of what Michel Foucault termed the Great Confinement, one historian has argued, it is the nineteenth century. In Foucault's provocative account, the insane were increasingly confined to institutions during the classical period, the 'long eighteenth century', from about 1660 through to 1800.[1] But in the English case at least, the heyday of the institutionalization of the insane had not yet arrived. To be sure, from the late seventeenth century onwards it did become increasingly common for lunatics to be confined in madhouses but, as studies have shown, these institutions were not promoted by the state but were instead private entrepreneurial initiatives, comprising what has been termed the 'trade in lunacy'.[2]

During the nineteenth century, however, the state became increasingly involved in the institutionalization of the insane. The County Asylums Act of 1808 permitted local authorities to build county asylums for those unable to afford private treatment, and from 1845 it became obligatory for counties to provide adequate public accommodation for pauper lunatics. The motives of early Victorian lunacy reformers were in important measure therapeutic and humanitarian rather than custodial. As Andrew Scull has said, one of the distinguishing features of the lunacy reform movement was its conviction about the redemptive power of the institution. The era of moral treatment produced a new sensibility towards insanity, in which the madman was no longer seen as someone in whom all rational faculties had been suspended but instead as a wayward individual who, if placed in the appropriate moral regime, could eventually be restored to the world of sober, rational, self-determining citizens.[3]

But as the century wore on, all this was to be discarded and a very different sensibility would emerge. To a considerable extent, the history of the Victorian asylum reveals the victory of custodial realities over rehabilitative good intentions. Contrary to the intentions of early Victorian reformers, the Victorian asylums became gigantic warehouses for the chronically insane. The celebrated Retreat in York, the small Quaker asylum which did more than any other institution to promote the cause of moral treatment, had been designed to accommodate as few as thirty patients. According to Anne Digby, it must 'have given the impression of a well-run country house', with a prevailing atmosphere of 'controlled openness' in which both the gates and the front door 'stood open to the world'. Quaker visitors from the area regularly took tea or dinner at the asylum and patients who were near recovery were encouraged to reciprocate these visits. All in all, the 'interpenetration of the asylum by the outside world meant that the patient's isolation was minimized and his social identity – usually that of a Quaker – was retained as much as possible.'[4]

The Retreat was a 'small house just outside the city walls',[5] but by the middle of the century a radically different moral topography had come to supervene and asylums increasingly became closed institutions, built in many cases at a considerable distance from the city. In debates about the appropriate design for pauper asylums earlier in the century, it was recognized that the intimate scale of institutions like the Retreat was no longer sustainable. None the less it was claimed that 'from 100 to 120 are as many as ought to be in one house; where they are beyond that the individual cases cease to excite the attention they ought; and if once that is the case, not one half the good can be expected to result'.[6]

This was indeed a prescient warning, for as the century unfolded the metaphor of the 'house' became increasingly inappropriate as a description of asylum reality. The ten asylums which were built in the twenty years following the County Asylums Act of 1808 numbered on average 115 inmates each, but by the mid-1840s the average size was around 300 inmates, though the Lancashire asylum housed over 600 inmates and the Middlesex Asylum at Hanwell around 1,000. By 1870 the average size had gone up to 542 and by 1900 to 961.[7] London had a higher rate of lunacy than the rest of England and Wales, and after the newly created London County Council took control of the management of lunatics in the region in 1888 it set about expanding the system of mass segregation; in addition to existing asylums such as Colney Hatch, and those already planned such as Claybury, which opened in 1893, the LCC commissioned a range of new asylums to include Banstead, Hanwell, Cane Hill, Bexley, Horton, Leavesden and Caterham, some of them housing as many as 2,000 patients, 'standard design barracks on a regimented layout'.[8]

The population of England doubled in the last half of the nineteenth century, but the number of certified lunatics increased more than fivefold, from 20,809 in 1844 to 117,200 in 1904. The most significant increases in the asylum population occurred among pauper lunatics. So, for example, between 1844 and 1870 the numbers of private lunatics rose from 4,072 to 6,280 and of pauper lunatics from 16,821 to 48,433. In the London region some 15,000 pauper lunatics were confined in asylums in 1891 and by 1909 the population had risen to just under 26,000. Furthermore, in this same period the proportion of pauper lunatics in asylums in England and Wales judged to be curable by asylum superintendents fell sharply. In 1844 it was estimated that 15.4 per cent of pauper lunatics in county asylums were curable; by 1860 the number had fallen to 11.2 per cent and by 1870 to 7.7 per cent.

Within the space of a remarkably compressed period, then, the 'loose and scattered madness of the country' had been brought under observation in vast warehouses of seemingly intractable lunatics. From being 'the instrument of regeneration', the asylum had become 'the dustbin of the incurable'.[9] In attempting to understand the nature of the asylum problem which contemporary policies purport to tackle, therefore, it is above all this late Victorian legacy which we need to consider. For, as Roy Porter has remarked, 'it is nineteenth-century gates which are being opened to disgorge their patients, and nineteenth-century orthodoxies about the decent and efficacious thing to do with the mad which have been discarded'.[10]

The Poor Law and the Pauper Lunatic

How is the transformation of nineteenth-century asylums into vast custodial institutions to be explained? On the evidence that has emerged it is apparent that the asylums were not simply dumping grounds for the aged and broken but came to accommodate an extraordinarily diverse collection of people, many of them still in their prime. In the asylums at Lancaster and Wakefield, for example, the median age of admission in the 1850s and 1860s was in the late thirties.[11] But who exactly were these people who came to swell the ranks of the chronically insane? Were they genuine cases of chronic insanity or troublesome people who in various ways posed a threat to social order?

One view of this question has recently been given by a psychiatrist, Edward Hare.[12] In Hare's opinion, questions about social regulation are secondary to the primary determinants of nature. The increase in the admission rates to asylums in England and Wales in the last half of the nineteenth century, he argues, reflects a real increase in the rate of incidence of insanity. Moreover, such an increase took the form, he postulates, not of a surge of milder cases but of an epidemic of severe cases of insanity, in particular of that virulent form of mental illness which is today classified as schizophrenia. A number of European countries, and perhaps also the United States, were subjected to a slow epidemic of schizophrenia from the early decades of the nineteenth century onwards, to be 'attributed to the changing effect of some specific causal factor of a physical nature'. Such a hypothesis, Hare suggests, can help us account for why it was judged necessary to construct the Victorian asylums in the first place, and also for the subsequent pressures on them – the sharp rise in the admission rates as the epidemic of schizophrenia gathered pace and hard cases started to accumulate. Ratepayers were often reluctant to accede to the demand for new asylums but that they did so suggests that the reasons for 'that demand must have been urgent, compelling and inescapable'.

As to why nature should specially have chosen paupers for this fate, Hare does not tell us, and his argument has prompted a lively riposte from the sociologist and historian of psychiatry, Andrew Scull.[13] Contrary to Hare's naturalistic account, Scull argues that the boundaries of what constituted madness expanded considerably in the nineteenth century. Thus 'a wide range of nineteenth-century observers commented on how much laxer the standards were for judging a poor person to be insane, and how much readier both local Poor Law authorities and lower-class families were to commit decrepit and troublesome people to the asylum, individuals who, had they come from the middle and upper classes, would never have been diagnosed as insane'. So, for example, William Ley, superintendent of the Littlemore Asylum, described how 'Orders for the admission of paupers into the county asylum are given more freely than would be thought right as regards the imputation of lunacy towards persons equally debilitated in body and mind who have the means of providing for their own care.'[14] Where Scull proposes that the surge in pauper recruits to the asylum drew largely from the reservoir of 'mild cases' of insanity, Hare claims that such cases would not have been deemed sufficiently urgent to warrant the construction of so many beds. But as Scull astutely remarks, the definition of 'urgent' in this context is 'a matter of complex social definition'.

Not the least interesting aspect of this process of definition is the fact that Victorian alienists had only limited control over the selection of candidates for the asylum, or the means by which they got there. To understand the expansion in the asylum population properly, it has been suggested, we must look to the location of the public asylums within the Poor Law system. Public asylums were 'first and foremost Poor Law institutions and it was the character of the Poor Law that largely determined their nature'. The Poor Law 'affected the numbers, flow and characteristics of the inmates to be found within them; it affected the size and scale of the institutions; it affected the resources available to them, including the numbers, qualifications and attitudes of the medical men and the attendants who worked with them; and it affected the responses to policy initiatives to improve and reform them'.[15]

Through its abhorrence of outdoor relief in particular, the Poor Law system inevitably came to structure social responses to those who were economically dependent and incapable of work. On the basis of his investigations of the Lancaster Asylum in the middle decades of the nineteenth century, John Walton suggests that most of those admitted were not so much the 'inconvenient people' characterized by Scull, as 'impossible people in the eyes of families, neighbours and authorities'.[16] So they may well have seemed, but the likelihood is that the assessment of 'impossibility', and the subsequent ejection of people from their homes on to the road to the asylum, was occasioned less by a reduction in the threshold of familial tolerance than by sheer economic and practical necessity.

This is not to say that the Poor Law authorities embarked on the process of casting out, as it has been described, at all lightly. Indeed the contrary appears very often to have been the case. In the first place, the certification procedures were drawn extremely tightly to protect the sane against unwarranted detention and, more especially, from the standpoint of the Poor Law authorities the asylum was the last resort, after other measures had been tried and failed, not least because it was a good deal more expensive than the workhouse. On Busfield's reading of the situation, because the asylum was the institution of last resort people only got there rather late, by which time their problems were of a long-standing and chronic nature. Thus the Report of the Metropolitan Commissioners in Lunacy for 1844 commented that it 'has been the practice in numerous instances to detain the insane pauper at the workhouse or elsewhere, until he becomes dangerous or unmanageable; and then, when his disease is beyond all medical relief, to send him to a lunatic asylum where he may remain during the rest of his life, a pensioner on the public'.[17]

Forgotten Pauper Lunatics

But if, in general, authorities were more reluctant to embark on the process of 'casting out' than has sometimes been suggested, they were equally reluctant to provide for the 'bringing back' of those who had been so cast out. In the last decades of the century the proportion of inmates in asylums in England and Wales who were held to be 'probably curable' by asylum superintendents fell to below 10 per cent. To assign someone to the asylum meant in effect that the authorities had given up on the person. Determined as it was by the requirements of the Poor Law to maintain a system of custodial control and to obviate demands for 'outdoor relief', the 'administrative inertia of the asylum system developed a built-in bias against cures and discharges, especially when patients' families and friends were less than eager to have them back'.[18] Of the small numbers who were discharged, many were readmitted, but, as Walton relates, the exigencies of Victorian society in general, and of the Poor Law system in particular, hardly promoted a propitious environment for the reassimilation of the pauper lunatic. Once past the asylum doors, for example, the pauper lunatic ceased to be entitled to relief.

If the asylum was a last resort, it was then an extremely final one. What the combination of pressures in the system for regulating the poor conspired to produce, Joan Busfield has suggested, was not so much an expansion in the boundaries of insanity as such, as an expansion in the boundaries of the types of insanity that were deemed to warrant detention in an asylum. Various categories of people who might previously have been perceived as 'partly mad', or as curable, were more readily seen as 'wholly mad' and as hopeless cases. Furthermore, delays in receiving treatment, together with the indignities they suffered at the hands of the Poor Law system, meant that the curable were more readily transformed into hopeless cases, the partly mad into the wholly mad. If the evidence suggests that these were not simply troublesome and inconvenient people wrongly consigned to the regimens of psychiatry, no more does it suggest that these were in the main victims of a naturally deteriorating form of chronic insanity. The interesting questions are therefore, perhaps, about the social and economic conditions under which what were previously manageable forms of incapacity came to be judged as unmanageable, the 'partly mad' as 'wholly mad', attracting official certification as career lunatics. It is just here, perhaps, within this mix of administrative and economic contingency, that the notion of the 'urgent case' came to assume a new and more complex definition.

As we have seen, the asylums were not intended as repositories for the excommunicated. Far from it; in their original purpose and design they were seen as reformatories through which the wayward and unproductive could be brought into more promising and acceptable lines of communication. Assessed in the light of these motivations, the project was a dismal failure. 'Casting out' may have been a reluctant procedure but in the vast majority of cases it was a final one. Within the competing pressures of Victorian society, the asylums provided a refuge for people for whom there was apparently no viable social place. Considered as refuges, they may have served their function well enough, but they did so in the context of a social order which had decided that it did not want these people in its midst and at best could only care for them in their classification as hopeless cases. The preponderance of asylum inmates 'resigned themselves to the routines of asylum life, and the downward spiral of crumbling personal identity, mental decrepitude, and the inevitability of burial as a forgotten pauper lunatic'.[19] A psychiatrist reported to the House of Commons in 1877 that within these gigantic asylums

... the classification generally made is for the purpose of shelving cases; that is to say, practically it has that effect ... in consequence of the treatment not being personal, but simply a treatment in classes, there is a tendency to make whole classes sink down into a sort of chronic state ... I think they come under a sort of routine discipline which ends in their passing into a state of dementia.[20]

The consequences of what was taking place were not lost on prominent observers such as Henry Maudsley, who in his presidential address to the Royal Medico-psychological Association in 1871 attacked the asylum system:

The confinement, the monotony, the lack of interest and occupation, the absence of family relations, which are inevitable in any asylum ... do, after a certain time in most cases, more than counterbalance the benefit of seclusion. The patient has no proper outlet for his energies, and outlet is made for them in maniacal excitement and perverse conduct; he goes through recurrent attacks of that kind and finally sinks into a state of chronic insanity – becomes an asylum-made lunatic.[21]

Those who 'advocate and defend the present asylum system,' Maudsley argued later in the same year, 'should not forget that there is one point of view from which they who organize, superintend and act, regard the system, and that there is another point of view from which those who are organized, superintended and suffer, view it'. Thus to 'the medical officer these are not so many *individuals*, having particular characteristics and bodily dispositions, with which he is thoroughly acquainted, but they are apt to become so many lunatics, whom he has to inspect as he goes on his round of the establishment, as he inspects the baths and the beds'. While there may well be 'some chronic lunatics who have been in asylums for so many years that it would be no kindness to remove them – who have, indeed, so grown to the habit of their lives that it would be cruel to make any change', this is hardly to be taken as 'argument for subjecting anyone else to the same treatment in order to bring about the same result'.[22]

Maudsley was only one of a number of contemporary critics of the Victorian asylum who in a number of respects prefigure, and may well be said to equal, the invective of the asylum critics of our own period. Yet trenchant though they may have been, they were to no avail. The spirit of the times, and the available scope for alternative courses of action, worked against them. To have discharged harmless lunatics from the asylums, and permitted them some form of outdoor relief, would only have aggravated the scourge which the Poor Law Amendment Act of 1834 had been designed to eliminate. As Andrew Scull puts it, discharged mental patients would have become 'beneficiaries of something approximating a modern welfare system while their sane brethren were being subjected to the rigours of a Poor Law based on the principle of less eligibility'.[23] In the words of a contemporary Poor Law guardian, 'outdoor relief cannot be given to a single immoral or improvident individual without tempting that individual's neighbour to follow in the same steps'.[24]

Certainly, as the century wore on, in an effort to make more space in the workhouses for troublesome elements in the community who were claiming outdoor relief, incentives were offered to local authorities to search out 'urgent cases' among their workhouse populations. In 1877, for example, Henry Maudsley argued that the sharp increase in the rate of admission of pauper lunatics to asylums could be attributed to the so-called 'Four Shilling' Act of 1874 whereby the government granted four shillings towards the local-authority cost of maintaining each asylum patient – or, as Maudsley put it, 'an Act whereby the government said, in effect, to parish officials, "We will pay you a premium of four shillings a head on every pauper whom you can by hook or crook make out to be a lunatic and send into an asylum."' As Maudsley went on to remark, this was 'a direct premium on the manufacture of lunacy'.[25]

From the point of view of public policy, the enormous expansion of the asylum population was an undesirable development, an unanticipated consequence of earlier efforts at lunacy reform. Yet there was no viable place for these distressed people within the Victorian order of things. The inflexibilities of labour requirements, and of the Poor Law system of regulation, provided little or no scope for the category of the 'sheltered worker', for those who were only partly well and could manage only at their own pace. Furthermore, it was just the ambiguity of the 'partly mad' and 'partly able' that the authorities most disliked about them. If they were 'partly mad', then they could also be 'partly bad'. The labile character of madness, which was often remarked on, far from making the lunatic seem more appealing, actually rendered him all the more dangerous.

Psychiatry and the Dehumanization of the Insane

From the point of view of the psychiatric profession, there was the awkward question of how to legitimate itself, to justify its existence, in these new and unforeseen circumstances. It had not chosen this chronic population and these were hardly the kinds of patients desired by a fledgling profession anxious to establish its prowess as a curative agency. However, by dint of a process of social selection over which the psychiatric profession had limited control, socially unwanted people were thrust upon the asylums and arrived there fettered by a final and unshakeable judgement as to their social worth.

Confronted by this 'motley crowd of persons of weak minds or low spirits', psychiatry delivered the final sentence upon them.[26] The inflexibilities in the Victorian regulation of the poor and incapacitated came to be mirrored in the increasing inflexibility of psychiatric perceptions and judgements. In the last decades of the century, the idea that insanity was largely incurable was divested of its controversial or contestable aspect and taken very much for granted. The locus of psychiatric exclusion was reproduced in the scientific frameworks in which insane people were classified and analysed; they were abandoned both to an asylum and to an intellectual framework which declared them incomprehensible. It is just here, perhaps, that psychiatry came to make its most notable and enduring contribution, in helping to complete the process of sealing and closure in which insane people were enveloped, and to establish the hegemony of psychiatric 'difference'. Asylums became custodial rather than curative institutions and psychiatric ideologies provided a convenient shield to distract from searching moral questions about the social fate of vulnerable groups of people. As John Walton argues, 'a widening range of problematic behaviours and circumstances could be blamed on the medical problems of individuals rather than on the deficiencies of society at large: a mode of explanation which was conveniently compatible with *laissez-faire* principles, and posed no challenge to the existing economic order'.[27]

Even if Edward Hare is mistaken in his epidemiological surmise, he is surely correct in bringing the whole question of schizophrenia on to the historical agenda. For there is no doubt that in the minds of late nineteenth and early twentieth century psychiatrists a large majority of the new recruits to the asylum population were suffering from dementia praecox, the precursor of what we now know as schizophrenia. The 'discovery' of dementia praecox by Emil Kraepelin, and the formulations that came to be given of the condition, must be seen against the wider background of responses to the 'social question', the problem of how to account for the unregenerate poor, those who had either spurned progress or been rejected by it. Influenced by theories of urban degeneration, psychiatry came to see in the embodiments of this burgeoning, collective problem that were brought before it the signs and expressions of a constitutional unfitness and of a relentless slide into degenerative insanity.

At a debate held by the Royal Medico-psychological Association in 1909 to discuss Emil Kraepelin's theory of dementia praecox, a Dr Robert Jones of Claybury Lunatic Asylum objected to the term on the grounds that it was unduly pessimistic and appeared to exclude by definition any possibility of recovery.[28] In the view of most of his colleagues, however, Jones had misperceived the true nature of the course of the disease. Thus a Dr Stoddart invoked the standard of the 'useful worker' to justify Kraepelin's usage and asserted that among dementia praecox patients 'mentation is so enfeebled' that they are 'totally incapacitated from ever doing any useful work'. Dr Devine urged similarly that in 90 per cent of the cases where the symptoms of dementia praecox are observed, 'such mental deterioration will follow as will lead to a permanent incapacity to lead a useful life', and thus 'one knows one is dealing with a disorder which is the commencement of a downward career leading to mental deterioration'. And Dr Hayes-Newington said that he took the term dementia praecox to 'admirably denote the quiet collapse of jerry-built brains under the strain of their own weight or on the first contact with the social responsibilities of adult life'. In 1914 one authority described how 'patients in asylums may be roughly divided into two distinct groups, namely those who have a prospect of recovery, forming about 10 per cent, and the hopeless chronic cases who make up the remaining 90 per cent'.[29]

Manfred Bleuler, the psychiatrist who has perhaps done more than anyone else to further our understanding of the history of schizophrenia, has described the dogma of 'incurability in principle' which held sway in this period:

The clinician who discovered after years of observation that there was an improvement, and who found an abundance of inner life, of emotional perception, of human rationale in his chronic schizophrenic patient – rather than the expected inexorable progression of the disease – almost had to be ashamed of his discoveries. On the other hand he felt secure and in concert with the accepted hypotheses if he was able to record an increasingly severe state of idiocy and dehumanization of the patient.[30]

Bleuler describes how the chronic mental patient came to be sealed in his otherness and conceived as suffering from a 'final and irrevocable loss of his mental existence':

So it happened that the clinician became increasingly accustomed to seeing in his schizophrenic dementia cases an autistic attitude on the part of the patient. The patient and those who were healthy had ceased to understand one another. The patient gives up, in abject resignation or total embitterment, any effort to make himself understood. He either no longer says anything or says nothing intelligible. In so doing the naïve observer declares, out of hand, that the patient has lost his reasoning powers.[31]

By the end of the century, then, we have travelled a long way from the ideals of the Retreat in their dedication to maintaining channels of communication between the asylum and society. The relationship between mental patient and society had been all but severed and the mental patient isolated from ordinary understanding; in place of painstaking efforts at dialogue we find elaborate structures of excommunication. We cannot account for this simply by the shortcomings of total institutions, for it involved also positive psychiatric structures, sins of commission, a historian has suggested, as much as sins of omission.[32] As Manfred Bleuler has shown, influential concepts in psychiatric theory, and in the management of madness, served to legitimate a process of sealing off in which the humanity of asylum inmates was systematically denied.

The Severance of Rationality and Ethics

In order to appreciate the significance of this history of segregation and excommunication, it may be useful to look at some of the unforeseen developments that stemmed from it and to locate these in the context of peculiarly modern attempts to devise rational solutions to social problems. In a recent study, the sociologist Zygmunt Bauman has highlighted the destructive potential inherent in the modern civilizing process. One of the major accomplishments of the rationalizing tendency, as codified most forcibly in the institutions of modern bureaucracy, has been to create the means whereby the requirements of rationality have been emancipated from the interference of ethical norms and moral inhibitions. The rationalizing tendency reveals as one of its primary concerns, Bauman argues, the silencing of morality, as indeed 'the fundamental condition of its success as an instrument of rational coordination of action'.[33] From this point of view, modern society may make immoral conduct more rather than less plausible and in fact entail a significant loss in moral capacity. Modern social achievements in the management of morality include distancing – whereby the sense of responsibility of one social group for another is eroded – and the technology of segregation and separation.

Responsibility, Bauman argues, arises out of the proximity of the other person. If proximity is eroded, responsibility is silenced and 'may eventually be replaced with resentment once the fellow human subject is transformed into an Other. The process of transformation is one of social separation.' Bauman describes some of the stages in this process of transformation:

Definition sets the victimized group apart (all definitions mean splitting the totality into two parts – the marked and the unmarked), as a *different* category, so that whatever applies to it does *not apply to all the rest. By the very act of being defined, the group has been targeted for special treatment*; what is proper in relation to 'ordinary' people must not necessarily be proper in relation to it. Individual members of the group become now in addition exemplars of a type; something of the nature of the type cannot but seep into their individualized images . . .[34]

Members of the victimized group are then removed from their ordinary stations in life. The group is now

. . . effectively removed from sight; it is a category one at best hears of, so that what one hears about it has no chance to be translated into the knowledge of individual destinies, and thus to be checked against personal experience . . . Concentration completes this process of distantiation. The victimized group and the rest do not meet any more, their life processes do not cross, communication grinds to a halt, whatever happens to one of the now segregated groups does not concern the other, has no meaning easy to translate into the vocabulary of human intercourse.[35]

This becomes a somewhat chilling description when we understand the part that it plays in Bauman's argument, for Bauman's purpose is to show that the passage from the transformation of the fellow human subject into an Other to the annihilation of the victimized group is a direct and logical one. The programmes of extermination carried out by the Third Reich were, he argues, not so much a distortion or aberration of the modern civilizing process as one of the most accomplished products of the modern world. This history may be seen to hold some relevance for our concerns when we consider that the extermination of unwanted groups implicated not merely European Jewry but in addition various categories of the 'socially unfit', most notably the mentally ill. If we are to try to understand the nature and roots of the problem we are trying to tackle in closing the asylum, we will need to explore these events in a little more detail.

The justifying concept in the murder of the mentally ill was the concept of 'life unworthy of life', first promoted by the psychiatrist Alfred Hoche in 1920. According to Hoche, mental patients were nothing but 'human ballast' and 'empty shells of human beings'. Putting such people to death, he wrote, 'is not to be equated with other types of killing . . . but is an *allowable, useful act*'. As Professor Robert Lifton has remarked, Hoche was in effect saying that the mentally ill are *already* dead.[36] A number of 'educational' films demonstrated the economic drain on German society caused by the 'mentally dead', such as *Opfer der Vergangenheit*, 'The Victim of the Past' (1937), which contrasted 'healthy German citizens', for example girls performing gymnastics, with the regressed occupants of back wards.

It is not known exactly how many mental patients were murdered. For Germany itself, estimates have been given of between

80,000 and 100,000, but Robert Lifton suggests that the actual figure was twice this amount. One difficulty in establishing the precise figure is that it is known that many doctors and institutions were permitted to continue murdering their patients even after the programme had been officially proscribed in 1941 following protests by a few prominent Church leaders.[37] Furthermore, the murder of the mentally ill was not confined to Germany alone. So, for example, Poland, scene and symbol of so much else in these hideous years, was also the site of some of the most brutal killings of mental patients, numbering some 15,000, in asylums across the country.[38] Indeed, it was only after the murder of the inmates of a mental hospital in Poznan in October 1939 that gas installations were fitted in seven mental hospitals in Germany.[39] And research has also shown that in Vichy France in the same period, psychiatrists cooperated in the name of science in the death by starvation of some 40,000 mental patients.[40] In addition, the expertise gained in the German mental hospitals was to prove useful elsewhere. When it was decided to convert the concentration camp at Auschwitz-Birkenau into an extermination camp, a group of prisoners was dispatched to the mental hospital at Sonnenschein to be gassed in order to refine the technical knowledge required for the extermination programme. Subsequently, technical personnel from the German mental hospitals were also to lend their expertise to other extermination camps in Poland.[41]

A complex administrative system was established to carry through the extermination programme, including the creation of a bogus company called the Community Patients' Transport Service:

Using grey postal vans so as not to attract too much notice in rural areas, the Transport Service would then collect the patients concerned, and transfer them to asylums like Grafeneck or Hadamar where they were gassed. Although at first some patients were glad to be going on an outing, the regular arrival of the vans which brought no one back soon led to harrowing scenes and the use of sedatives and handcuffs.[42]

How was all this possible? This is Primo Levi's description of his encounter with Doktor Pannwitz in Auschwitz-Monowitz:

Pannwitz is tall, thin, blond; he has eyes, hair and nose as all Germans ought to have them, and sits formidably behind a complicated writing-table. I, Haftling 174517, stand in his office, which is a real office, shining, clean, and ordered, and I feel that I would leave a dirty stain on whatever I touched.

When he finished writing he raised his eyes and looked at me.

From that day I have thought about Doktor Pannwitz many times and in many ways. I have asked myself how he really functioned as a man ... above all when I was once more a free man, I wanted to meet him again, not from a spirit of revenge, but merely from a personal curiosity about the human soul.

Because that look was not one between two men; and if I had known how completely to explain the nature of that look, which came as if across the glass window of an aquarium between two beings who live in different worlds, I would also have explained the essence of the great insanity of the third Germany.

One felt in that moment, in an immediate manner, what we all thought and said of the Germans. The brain which governed those blue eyes and those manicured hands said, 'This something in front of me belongs to a species which it is obviously opportune to suppress. In this particular case, one has first to make sure that it does not contain some utilizable element.'[43]

The German psychiatrist and historian of psychiatry, Klaus Dörner, has recently attempted to uncover the secret of what he terms the Pannwitz look. Like Bauman, Dörner believes that the solutions propounded by the Third Reich were rational and logical solutions to modern problems. The modern problem to which he directs particular attention is once again the 'social question', the tendency of a modern, progressive society to generate a 'social ballast' or 'social waste' which it does not know how to dispose of. Modern citizens have become preoccupied with the question: *'Was machen wir Bürger mit denen, die nicht so sind wie wir, deren Leistungswert sie industriell unbrauchbar macht; wofür sind sie da und wie gehen wir mit ihnen um?'* ('What should we citizens do with those who are not like us, the people whose ability to perform renders them unproductive; what are they here for, and how are we going to deal with them?').[44] So far as a group of people ceases to figure within the human picture that we have of a society, it then becomes difficult to recognize them as people. We may then be brought to ask 'whether they are not superfluous, not just from an economic point of view but also morally, and come to feel pity for them in the way that we do for children or animals'.[45]

There was nothing especially novel about the concerns of National Socialism over the 'social question'. The closing decades of the nineteenth century and the early decades of the present one are littered with ideologies of 'social waste', efforts to comprehend, and propound solutions to, the problem of the 'socially unfit' (*die Gemeinschaftsunfähigen*), prominent among them the psychiatric ideologies of dementia praecox and schizophrenia. The question of how to rid a society of its social ballast so as to free it to develop its industrial, scientific and cultural potential was a widely shared one. The problem to which the extermination of the mentally ill proposed a solution, the very language in which the problem was cast, the fears and preoccupations on which it went to work, none of these were invented: they were ready and waiting. Where National Socialism differed from previous attempts to solve the 'social question' is that it was willing to risk a painful but final solution of this burdensome problem.

The secret of the Pannwitz look, Dörner argues, is this: *'alle Menschen mit der Frage anzublicken, ob sie Menschen oder Dinge sind'* ('to scrutinize everybody with the question, are you a person or an object?').[46] In the case of the mental patient, the answer to that question had already been delivered. The ideological and social conditions in which mental patients ceased to be recognized as fellow human subjects, and had become objects, were already well established, and the process of definition, separation, segregation and concentration described by Bauman had long taken place. Psychiatrists had already come to look upon their patients in the way that Doktor Pannwitz looked upon Primo Levi, not out of hatred but because the human bond or connection between them had been broken.

The name which Dörner gives to the attitude which made the killing of mental patients possible is *'tödliches Mitleid'* (deadly compassion). Many psychiatrists and their staff, he says, were against the transportation and murder of their patients. But their resistance had crucially been weakened. The medicalization of 'inferior people' had had good effect, and psychiatrists and others had come to see it as their social and professional duty to help restore the social body to good health. The value and worth of mental patients had already been reduced in their eyes, so that when it came to the critical moment they were unable to identify with their patients or to defend them. To say this is not to doubt that most of these psychiatric functionaries were exemplary doctors, motivated by compassion and concern for their patients. However, to appreciate the sense in which this particular expression of compassion is appropriately described as 'deadly compassion' we may look at the following account by Robert Lifton:

Just one psychiatrist, Professor Gottfried Ewald of Gottingen, openly opposed the medical killing project . . . At a planning meeting called by Werner Heyde on 15 August 1940 to enlist prominent psychiatrists, Ewald refused to participate in the project and was asked to leave . . . When given an opportunity to speak, Ewald stated, 'On principle I would not lend my hand to exterminate in this way patients entrusted to me.' He pointed out that schizophrenics, the largest patient group concerned, were not as 'empty and hopeless' as claimed, and could well benefit from new forms of therapy just then being developed. After giving additional arguments and making clear his refusal to become an expert, he was joined by two other psychiatrists. But those two reversed themselves, Ewald testified, when Professor Paul Nitsche, Heyde's next in command and a man with considerable professional standing, spoke passionately of having personally lived through the tragedy of coping with a mentally ill brother-in-law and urged the group not to oppose the extermination of the mentally ill. As Ewald said nothing more and clearly had not changed his point of view, Heyde 'dismissed' him . . .[47]

Echoing Manfred Bleuler's description, Lifton tells us that most German psychiatrists, in common with the majority of their counterparts working elsewhere, were 'committed to the idea of schizophrenia as an organic, incurable disease, whose natural course was deterioration. Indeed, for many, professional pride depended on that view. Any effort to penetrate the psyche of a schizophrenic patient as a means of understanding and a form of treatment was viewed by these psychiatrists as "unscientific" and therefore a professional and personal threat.'[48] As if to demonstrate the potency of the prevailing ideology of schizophrenia, it has been suggested that in some cases doctors and nurses tried to save their charges by diagnosing not schizophrenia but some other disorder.[49]

The extermination programme was officially halted in 1941 not, so Lifton tells us, in response to protests from psychiatrists and other physicians, many of whom were directly involved in carrying out the programme, but in response to pressure from a few Church leaders 'who gave voice to the grief and rage of victimized families with ethical passions stemming from their own religious traditions'.[50] The arguments of Bauman, Dörner and Lifton converge to suggest the same conclusion: psychiatrists, by contrast with those families who voiced their protests through the agencies of the Church, were unable to show themselves ethically passionate. Compassionately passionate they may well have been, but not ethically passionate.

In the encounter with their patients, psychiatrists saw themselves only as taking part in a suffering which was not their own. The communal meaning of suffering had been erased and the psychiatrist had ceased to be a partner with the suffering patient.[51] Powered by a characteristically modern but ethically moribund understanding of rationality and scientific inquiry, psychiatry had assisted in lending authority to the depersonalization and debasement of the figure of the mental patient. In distinguished representatives like Professor Paul Nitsche (later to be hanged for his contributions to psychiatric betterment) we are witness to a professionally legitimated breakdown of moral capacity in which rationality and ethics had become severed, and the humanity of the mentally ill subject obliterated.

4 Broken and Flawed Individuals

The Dehumanization of the Mentally Ill

What, then, do these historical considerations imply for our contemporary agenda? In a striking image Manfred Bleuler contrasts his own perspective with that of the type of psychiatrist who 'is inclined to compare the impoverished personality after a schizophrenic psychosis with the condition after psychosurgery or localized cerebral diseases'. Instead, Bleuler prefers 'to compare it with the impoverished personality after long-standing frustration in a concentration camp or after an uneventful, unsatisfactory life during which the person's talents and abilities had no occasion to develop'.[1] In pointing the contrast in this way, Bleuler brings the problem of the dehumanization and debasement of the person with a schizophrenic illness to the forefront of discussion.

To understand why he is right to do so, we may turn to Richard Warner's masterly study of the fate of people with schizophrenia in Western societies over the course of the present century. A psychiatrist who has also trained as an anthropologist, Warner has attempted to relate the problem of schizophrenia to political economy and to demonstrate that the lives of people with schizophrenic disorders are to a large extent shaped and determined by the organization of the material conditions of life in a given society. Bequeathed to us by the Victorian asylum, Warner suggests, we have the legacy of a public psychiatry which had become the science of regulating paupers, a legacy with which we are still living today, not least in the official operating perceptions of the mentally ill.

Warner marshals a sizeable body of evidence to show that changes in the outcome of schizophrenic illness reflect changes in the perceived usefulness of the schizophrenic in the productive process. The recovery rates for schizophrenia in industrialized societies, he argues, are closely linked to economic cycles and the requirements of the labour market, with periods of high unemployment generating an increased population of socially disposable people and a more pessimistic view of schizophrenia. There have, of course, been numerous examples of therapeutic enthusiasm but these have always had to fight against the current and have failed to remedy the structurally precarious position of the mentally ill. The underlying preoccupation of mental health policy over the past hundred and fifty years, Warner suggests, has been with the management and control of disposable people. He is led to the position that we must view people with schizophrenia as forming part of what Marx termed the 'relative surplus population' of the unemployed, known as the 'industrial reserve army'. Thus they are to be found among the 'stagnant' category of this population, fated to 'extremely irregular employment' and to conditions of life which 'sink below the average normal level of the working class', and also among the 'lowest sediment', who dwell 'in the sphere of pauperism'.[2] The historical evidence suggests that the treatment

. . . of the great majority of the mentally ill will always reflect the condition of the poorest classes of society. In the absence of some powerful political counter-force, the outlook in schizophrenia is unlikely to get better. Despite the fact that an improvement in conditions of living and employment for psychotics may yield higher rates of recovery, this consideration will remain secondary . . . Efforts to rehabilitate and reintegrate the chronically mentally ill will only be seen at times of extreme shortage of labour – after the other battalions of the industrial reserve army have been mobilized. At other times, the primary emphasis will be one of social control.[3]

In Warner's portrayal of the estrangement and degradation of the mentally ill there is a disturbing echo of Primo Levi's moving account of the 'drowned' in the concentration camp:[4]

The status afforded the mentally ill is the very lowest – lower than that of ex-convicts or the retarded. Even after five years of normal living and good work, according to one survey, an ex-mental-patient is rated as less acceptable than an ex-convict . . . Western society maintains schizophrenics in poverty and creates for them social disintegration with pariah status and a disabled role . . . In the stigma of mental illness, the most debased status in our society, we see the utmost in painful estrangement of one human from another. And in the schizophrenic's own acceptance of this same dehumanized stereotype we witness the loss of his or her sense of fully belonging to humankind.[5]

The Politics of Deinstitutionalization

And here we are brought to the ambiguous politics of deinstitutionalization, for it is evident that, ministerial pronouncements to the contrary, a number of factors have weighed in the decision to transfer mental patients to the community. Andrew Scull has put forward the argument that the exodus from the mental hospitals in Britain and the United States has been powered by the rediscovery of outdoor relief, namely the development in the post-war era of welfare programmes which enabled the indigent and disabled to be maintained more cheaply outside institutions.[6] The trouble with this argument, however, is that it fails to account for national differences in the timing and style of deinstitutionalization policies, and to explain these variations we must look, Warner suggests, at 'differences in the perceived social value of the inmates of the institutions, and especially at the importance of their contribution to the labour force'.[7] In the post-war period the demand for labour, rather than the need for cost-cutting, may have provided the immediate driving force to deinstitutionalization. So, for example, the countries which played the lead role in the development of social psychiatry in the years following the Second World War – Britain, the Netherlands, Norway and Switzerland – were among those with low unemployment rates and, in the case of Britain, a labour shortage. Deinstitutionalization is therefore 'in some circumstances a sign of progressive efforts towards community care and rehabilitation of the mentally ill', but equally 'may elsewhere indicate the opposite – the abrogation of responsibility for the welfare of a segment of the poor'.[8]

It is against this background of governmental parsimony that the debate about the role of psychotropic drugs in making deinstitutionalization possible assumes a special importance. Warner adduces evidence to suggest that the influence of psychotropic drugs in emptying the mental hospitals has been exaggerated and in crucial respects misrepresented. So, for example, in the USA the rate of mental hospital occupancy as a proportion of the general population was declining before the introduction of anti-psychotic drugs.

Furthermore, significant changes in hospital and community psychiatry in northern Europe preceded the introduction of anti-psychotic medication. As we saw earlier for the British case, in a number of countries the discharge rates from mental hospitals increased in the period 1945–54 before the introduction of anti-psychotic medication, and the advent of such drugs in 1954 often had little impact on hospital discharge rates. The revolutionary changes which preceded the introduction of anti-psychotic drugs in certain countries, Warner suggests, may also explain why the discharge rates of a number of hospitals were only marginally affected by the arrival of the drugs. So, for example, data from Norway suggests that the drugs had little effect on those hospitals which already had high discharge rates and were using the new social therapies; on the other hand on those hospitals with low discharge rates and poor rehabilitative regimes they had a marked effect.

To be sure, the advent of drugs had a major impact on the back wards of asylums in the USA, but Warner questions the assumption that the reduction in the hospitalized population of schizophrenic patients is convincing proof of the efficacy of these agents. The argument that drugs have been a major factor in producing modern recovery rates is a misleading one. Viewed in a historical perspective, it is clear that the outcome of untreated schizophrenia in the early part of the century was not as bad as was supposed. Furthermore, the introduction of anti-psychotic drugs has done nothing to compensate for the marginalization of schizophrenic patients in social life. Drugs have certainly been a crucial instrument in the disposal of mental patients but the preoccupation with the 'technical fix' has obscured recognition of the web of moral and social relations in which the identities of ex-mental-patients are either made or broken. In the USA in particular, the celebration of drug treatment has resulted in the neglect of other forms of service provision. And most significantly, perhaps, the very need for drugs has been fuelled by the failure to tackle the social problems of former mental patients. Not infrequently, schizophrenic patients have been 'thrust into environments in which they can only survive with the aid of drugs' and 'too often the psychiatrist is called upon to wedge the schizophrenic into an ill-fitting slot because an appropriately therapeutic setting is not available, affordable or even considered feasible. In these circumstances the prescription becomes a document in a political process'.[9]

The Professional Dialogue with the Pauper Lunatic

Implicit, and at points explicit, in Warner's account is a critique not merely of the external forces that constrain the destiny of the person with schizophrenia but also of the understanding of the schizophrenic patient that has been developed in the most influential traditions of psychiatry. A recent discussion of the history of the disease categories of dementia praecox and schizophrenia helps us to identify the extent to which the politics Warner discusses has been reproduced in the framework of schizophrenia itself. The psychiatric perception of the dementia praecox patient, it has been suggested, was informed by a stigmatizing political discourse about the urban poor and drew on a number of representative preoccupations of the period with 'psychological weakness', 'psychic degeneracy', 'deterioration' and above all the constitutional basis of the 'socially unfit'. The Victorian asylum thus became '. . . a site in which stigmatizing symbols were concentrated, refined and applied to those who could not or did not engage in productive social relations and thus any disease category coined by psychiatric experts within these institutions would emerge from and remain saturated by this stigmatizing discourse'.[10]

The pauper lunatic came to be conceptualized as the converse of Darwinian man and we should view the category of dementia praecox as:

. . . the product of a clinically accurate but politically saturated discourse generated by an emerging European professional class in dialogue with the insane of a pauper class, a discourse which was inclined to characterize the latter in terms of an endogenous, biological flaw which leads to a failure of the capacity to be productive, to compete and adapt, and ultimately to an evolutionary decline.[11]

Once 'a label of dementia praecox had been affixed to a person', historians of psychiatry have informed us, 'he became a case number awaiting the ultimate fate of deterioration'.[12] Perceived through the ideological lens of individualism, the insane were interpreted and categorized as 'broken individuals', as demonstrating a 'quintessential failure to achieve the qualities of successful individuality in capitalist society, a failure to achieve psychic unity, autonomy, self-containment, full possession of thoughts, and willed, rational, purposive action directed to useful production'.[13] Arguably, notions of broken and biologically flawed individuality have been carried over into the psychiatric framework of schizophrenia in which the illness is seen as residing within the core of the patient's identity as an individual person, as a feature of his or her basic nature. The substitution of the term schizophrenia for that of dementia praecox

. . . enabled a subtle but powerful transformation wherein a noun denominating a disease could be rendered into an adjective predicating a person. This is the transformation from a patient being diagnosed or suffering from *schizophrenia* to a patient being a *schizophrenic*. Hence, qualities of the disease came to pervade the total identity of the patient . . . Patients who in the first instance are described as experiencing the onset of an episode of schizophrenia become redefined through this subtle but powerful transformation into patients who have had the seeds of schizophrenia in their biological and biographic origins, who come to express their schizophrenic identity in all aspects of their person, and who remain schizophrenic even after recovering from that initial episode.[14]

So, for example, in the United States, 'The term "chronically mentally ill" has come to be practically synonymous with a person with schizophrenia . . . Variations on the theme of "once a schizophrenic, always a schizophrenic" still persist in plenary addresses at national meetings, in conferences with families, in case supervision, in academic classrooms, and in the DSM-III manual itself.'[15]

The argument here is not that these sorts of people have somehow mistakenly been judged as suffering from mental illness but that what we are dealing with here is a culturally specific way of thinking about the problem. The relevant contrast is with the way in which similar conditions are interpreted and dealt with in other societies. For example, as Leo Eisenberg points out, '. . . if a disorder is "explained" by spirit possession, then it is not intrinsic to the patient; once appropriate ritual exorcizes the demons, the patient is restored to his or her former self. This is in contrast to the Western view of schizophrenia as a chronic biological disorder and of the recovered patient as being "in remission" rather than "cured".'[16]

He then goes on to set this observation in the context of the finding that people with schizophrenia from Third World countries are less likely to have a chronic outcome than patients with similar conditions from industrialized countries: 'The way we formulate the diagnosis and the way society responds to patients with the disorder *do* have consequences for course and outcome. That is the message in the data ... What the course of disease reveals is its social history.'[17]

Implicit in what Eisenberg says is the idea that there may be a destructive component in Western conceptions of the schizophrenic patient and that notions of flawed individuality may reinforce a view of people with mental illness as Other. But to what extent does the perception of the person with schizophrenia as a flawed individual still prevail? Warner certainly suggests that it does and part of his endeavour is to try to rescue our understanding of the lives of people with mental illness from such notions. Mental health professionals, he argues, are not only 'likely to hold attitudes towards mental patients which are similar to those of the general public; they may be even *more* rejecting'. Furthermore, 'professional conceptions of mental illness may reinforce the popular tendency to dehumanize mental patients'. In 1981, for example, the *American Journal of Psychiatry* published an article in which it was demonstrated that people with schizophrenia are capable of experiencing human emotions such as depression. It is 'an important clinical issue', the authors concluded, that 'chronic schizophrenics do become depressed when they are aware of their marginal lifestyle in the community'. As Warner asks, 'How could the editors of the *Journal* possibly imagine that such findings were worth publishing? Only by assuming that a number of their readers would have doubts about the human qualities of their schizophrenic patients.'[18] Similarly, studies of the language of schizophrenic patients have been published which report the startling discovery that, contrary to established professional assumptions, the 'abnormalities of behaviour' which emerge, for example, in the patient's interview with the doctor are not always in evidence and that 'it may well be that schizophrenic patients, like the general population, respond quite differently to different situations'.[19]

To take another instance of moral estrangement in professional dealings with the long-term mentally ill. Warner recounts how in the United States

... homeless, male schizophrenic patients are frequently admitted to hospital, hungry, dirty, sleepless and floridly psychotic. When, after some meals and a good night's sleep, their mental state dramatically improves, hospital staff claim that the patient has 'manipulated' his way into free board and accommodation. More benign observers argue that the patient's improvement is evidence of the efficacy of the dose of the anti-psychotic medication which he received on admission. In fact, such patients often improve as readily without medication. The florid features of their psychosis on admission are an acute response to the stress of their abject poverty and deprivation.[20]

People with schizophrenia are 'scroungers' and 'manipulators', constituents of an undeserving underclass. So far as they wish to gain acceptance in the mental health system, they must adopt a suitably compliant attitude and behave as patients are supposed to behave when put under the doctor. In a recent discussion of young, adult chronic patients, Sue Estroff provides us with some additional insight into the vocabulary of 'manipulation':

The term 'young adult chronic patient' deserves to be eliminated from professional discourse. Increasingly it serves as a misleading and ill-tempered designation for persons aged eighteen to thirty-five who have severe and persistent psychiatric disorders. The literature associated with this label reveals a substantially negative, accusatory attitude. Members of this group are called 'hateful patients', 'demanding manipulators', 'unwelcome patients', and even worse. These descriptions refer to younger persons who are defiant, who often prefer to take their own drugs rather than ours, who deeply value freedom, who often have not yet been broken in spirit by institutions or phenothiazines, and who refuse the role of 'good patient'. Many of them are not declining help. They may be seeking to avoid the stigma of the mental health system and the submission required by the role of mental patient.[21]

Chronicity in Schizophrenia

One way of defining the project of closing the asylum is to say that it is about releasing people with disorders like schizophrenia from the despair into which historically they have been pitched. But to put it in these terms is at once to see that it involves much more than a change of locus and engages also the controversy about the nature and causes of chronicity in schizophrenia, or what has become known as the 'negative symptoms' debate. Chronicity in schizophrenia, the question has been asked, is it a fact, a partial fact or an artefact?[22] The answer is that we are not entirely certain, but that the controversy around the question continues to rage.

In important respects the custodial history of the asylum in which the mental patient was shut away from society is recapitulated in the traditional psychiatric account of schizophrenia as a narrative of loss in which the pre-illness person is engulfed and even destroyed by the force of the disorder. In the traditional framework, schizophrenia is not so much an 'I have' illness, as an 'I am' illness, a condition which the person can be said to 'become'. If we ask 'who and what existed *before* the illness' and who and what persist *during* and *after*, one answer is that there is no 'after' with schizophrenia, only a 'before'.[23]

So how are we to conceive the person with a history of schizophrenic illness now that he is no longer shut away in the asylum? The most important issue here is around the interpretation of social disablement. In the view of the British social psychiatrist J. K. Wing, the level of social disablement is 'usually determined by multiple biological, psychological and social factors, each of which can vary in influence over time, independently of or in potentation with the others'. Wing distinguishes between 'intrinsic' impairments, social disadvantage and adverse self-attitudes. The term 'intrinsic' is used to describe 'disabilities that persist over long periods of time whatever the changing circumstances. It is neutral as far as theories of causation are concerned, though the possibility that biological impairments (whether environmental or genetic) are involved is implicit until disproved.'[24] The interaction between these various aspects is a crucial dimension of Wing's theory. As he describes it, in most cases of schizophrenia the degree of social disablement is 'determined by a mixture of intrinsic impairment, social disadvantage and personal reaction'.[25] However, the question then arises, how do we distinguish between these components? When are we looking at an example of a negative symptom that is an expression of an intrinsic impairment and when at one that is best accounted for by social disadvantage or adverse self-attitudes? The crucial issue is one of interpretation and it is here that Wing's account conflicts with the models proposed by a number of other theorists, in particular the vulnerability model espoused by Joseph Zubin and his colleagues.

The major point of difference between J. K. Wing and vulnerability theorists is over the interpretation of negative symptoms, or what is sometimes termed the clinical poverty syndrome. Where the model proposed by Wing suggests that negative symptoms are an 'intrinsic' or 'primary' disability, the argument from vulnerability theory is that only florid symptoms should be classified as primary handicaps. The vulnerability hypothesis assumes that 'the concept of schizophrenia does not imply a chronic disorder so much as a permanent vulnerability to develop the disorder'.[26] On this view, negative symptoms belong within Wing's category of secondary or external disabilities. Vulnerability theory takes the position that negative symptoms are neither an inevitable consequence of schizophrenic disorders (as argued by Kraepelin, for example) nor an intrinsic feature of such disorders. It argues instead that negative symptoms are 'essentially an artefact or a social consequence of having been identified, labelled, and treated as schizophrenic by medical specialists, relatives, close friends, and other members of the patient's social network'.[27] Factors such as social isolation, labelling and loss of social skills may result in a deterioration of the patient's coping ability and generate what has been termed a 'social breakdown syndrome' which may frequently be mistaken for permanent psychopathology. In a large proportion of cases, Zubin provocatively suggests, the negative symptoms of schizophrenia may be just a side-effect of the 'noxious niche which post-episode schizophrenics occupy in life'.[28]

Person–Disorder Interactions

Implicit in the vulnerability model is the idea that we need to provide more space for the person in our conceptual frameworks. We can understand what is involved here a bit more clearly if we turn briefly to some recent studies of person–disorder interactions among people with a history of schizophrenic illness, in which the conceptual distinction between the person and the disorder is made explicit. The focus of these studies is on the developing relationship between the person and the illness over time and the results to date suggest that the self is not necessarily engulfed by the disease, nor is there an inevitable rupture between the pre- and post-breakdown self. John Strauss, professor of psychiatry at Yale University, describes how the interest in person–disorder interactions arises from 'one major lesson that people with severe mental illness appear to be trying to teach us'. This lesson

. . . is reflected in a question once posed by one of our subjects. During an interview early in our research, she said, 'Why don't you ever ask what I do to help myself?' What she and others suggest is that the person as an active agent interacts with mental disorder in a crucial way that influences the course of that disorder. Thus, in contrast to some models of mental illness . . . my hypothesis is that the role of the person in mental disorder is not peripheral, merely as a passive victim of a disease to be fixed by medicine.[29]

Strauss and his colleagues identified a change of attitude in many of their subjects that in retrospect was a key turning-point in their illness careers:

Somehow, after an extended period, they found themselves wanting not just to live with their illness but to have a life along with it or in spite of it. Some stated that they came to accept their disorders. But this was not the kind of giving-up acceptance or resignation that often seems generated by the attempts some professionals make at helpful teaching (e.g. 'You have an illness like diabetes and will have it all your life. You'll need to stay on medication and there are certain things you'll never be able to do.'). The acceptance described by these subjects was one that involved hope for a better life and the resolve to work for it.[30]

Of special importance here are the strategies by which some people attempt to resist engulfment in a concept of self as mentally ill and to surmount their identity as a mental patient. Stephen Lally has recently described a series of stages from patient denial that they are mentally ill to a condition in which 'patients come to view themselves as mentally ill and see this as an all-encompassing, permanent view of self'.[31] Traditionally this process has been seen as a realistic process of adaptation to the effects of a chronic illness in which patients learn to accept a definitive change in themselves and to alter their expectations of life. However, Lally proposes that it may be more accurate to read it as a process of adaptation in a social and cultural context in which mental illness is given a very negative meaning and in which the role options open to the mentally ill are severely restricted. If this perspective is correct, then it clearly becomes important to learn how to 'stop a periodically psychotic person from becoming a full-time mentally ill person in self-concept'.[32]

One of the issues that concerns someone like Ben, whom we discussed in Chapter 2, is how to live a worthwhile life despite vulnerability to mental illness. Similarly, Sue Estroff found that most of her subjects were willing to acknowledge signs of illness, yet at the same time what '. . . they resist and reject are notions that those signs mean that they are incompetent, failed or somehow revised individuals because of these problems. Many make what we call "normalizing statements" in order, we hypothesize, to stress and reassert their similarities with others and to retain claim to their persisting, unrecognized, not-disordered selves.'[33]

The position of many of her subjects, Estroff suggests, is captured by the remark of an ex-mental-patient: 'You are not your illness! Find another role besides mental patient!' She is brought to the ironic conclusion that 'The loss and disorder of person so character-istic of our conceptions of schizophrenia may be at least partly our own invention, and one of the many ways in which we desert the person who has schizophrenia . . . *Becoming a schizophrenic* is essen-tially a social and interpersonal process, not an inevitable conse-quence of primary symptoms and neurochemical abnormality.'[34]

The negative-symptoms debate clearly has important impli-cations for the kinds of attitudes which psychiatrists encourage patients to hold and for how they assess such attitudes. In the contrasting stances of J. K. Wing and John Strauss we have a controversy between two leading psychiatrists over how people with schizophrenia should envisage themselves, and over the contri-butions of such self-concepts to the outcomes of the very illnesses they are attempting to treat. Wing claims that the majority of people afflicted by schizophrenia 'have to learn to live with schizo-phrenia much as one might have to live with diabetes or cancer or an amputated limb'.[35] On the other hand, John Strauss and his colleagues argue thus:

The contributions of treatment interventions to apathy and withdrawal may . . . be particularly powerful in schizophrenia. Some of the most common treatment efforts may inadvertently create the opposite effect from the one intended. Patients with schizophrenia are often told that they have a disease like diabetes. They are told that they will have the disease all their lives, that it involves major and permanent functional impairment, and that they will have a life-long need for medication ... Stigma, discouraging 'therapeutic' messages, social dysfunction, and the problems schizophrenia often generates in functioning cognitively may all interact over time to make remaining engaged, involved, and hopeful particularly difficult.[36]

Achieving Desegregation

In similar terms, Richard Warner suggests that the sorts of features that have generally been seen as characteristic of chronic schizophrenia, such as depression, apathy, irritability, negativity, emotional over-dependence, social withdrawal, isolation and loneliness, loss of self-respect and of a sense of time, are in fact not so very different from the typical responses of unemployed men to their situations. These features are often seen by psychiatrists as inherent aspects of the illness but they may, in fact, to a considerable extent be socially induced. Much of the so-called 'defect state', Warner argues, 'may be attributed to the purposeless lifestyle and second-class citizenship of the schizophrenic ... Depression and withdrawal may be merely the characteristic response of the unemployed person. Diminished spontaneity and enthusiasm can be the outgrowths of an aimless existence. Negativism may be little more than the recognition of the unequal power and status of patient and therapist – a reaction to the social control function of psychiatry.'[37] To label such problems 'as biological deficits helps the professional cope with his or her frustrations, but it also increases the pessimism regarding treatment and the stigma which attaches to the patient'.[38] For example, a number of studies have shown that people with a history of schizophrenia have a highly restricted network of social contacts and that the collapse of the patient's social network appears to be a consequence of the illness, occurring after first admission. But it was evident from some of the examples we gave earlier that the capacity to make and sustain social contacts may be as much affected by material constraints and the shame of poverty as by an inherent vulnerability in relationships.

An implication of what Warner is saying is that if patients are to recover, they will need to reject a lot of what psychiatrists and other mental health professionals have come to believe in. We should not assume that good outcome is necessarily associated with patient compliance or acceptance of a mentally ill identity. Patients with 'insight', Warner suggests, may tend to function less well than expected and become excessively dependent, and the patient who functions well, by contrast, may be inclined to reject treatment. He proposes counter-intuitively that 'patients who accept that they are mentally ill will have the worst course to their illness, that those who reject the label from the outset might do better, and that the patients who show the most improvement will be those who accept the label of mental illness but subsequently are able to shake it off'.[39] The patient should therefore be helped to see 'his or her low self-concept as a product of the larger society ... To achieve desegregation, the mentally ill must first confront their debased status. As in any process of consciousness-raising they should expose, through sharing of experiences, the hidden social indicators of power and status – to discuss openly the subtle influences of stigma.'[40]

Warner sets out a provocative agenda for deinstitutionalization that puts some moral spine into the discussion. He delivers an assault not only on cheese-paring governments but also on liberal psychiatric traditions for their tendency to domesticate patients and reproduce the Otherness of people with mental illness. He asks that we understand deinstitutionalization not simply as the transfer of mental patients from one location to another, and the creation of an alternative network of services, but as embracing a much more systematic revaluation of the kind of people we take people with mental illness to be and of the disadvantage to which they have been subject. The management of the mentally ill should aspire to something more than the regulation of paupers. And all this is highly germane to the present moment, as we shall see.

5 Citizens and Paupers

From the Mental Patient (Person) to the Person (Mental Patient)

Today, mental patients are being told that they are to be discharged as patients and to rejoin the community as ordinary persons. Indeed, in a number of countries, to acquire permanent tenure as a mental patient is more difficult than to acquire tenure in, say, a university department; the norm these days is of temporary, short-term contracts. On one reading, these developments promise the deliverance of people with severe mental illness from the constraints of the regimes in which they had previously been maintained, regimes in which they had been sentenced to a life-long servitude as mental patients, excluded from society and exiled in the space of their illness. Seen in this light, the closure of the asylum heralds the return from exile of a large group of people who had previously been rejected by society and their reassimilation into social life.

A rather less sanguine account of what policies of deinstitutionalization actually amount to suggests, as we have seen, that they have by and large been powered by more expedient motives. On this reading, far from returning home after a long period of exile, many people with mental illness are being ejected from the refuges which over a long period had protected them from the brunt of market forces and told to go away and shift for themselves as best they can. On this view, all the talk about providing new opportunities for individuals to flourish and to determine their own lives is just a rhetorical disguise worn by those governmental agencies who are intent upon dumping a group of people whom it has become too costly to maintain in the old welfare style.

One way in which to summarize the consequences of custodial policies is to say that what they produced was an individual whose identity as a person was secondary to their identity as a mental patient. On some accounts, of course, the person was in any case altogether lost to the illness, quite apart from the effects of the institutional regime itself. But whichever way we look at it, and even in more progressive regimes where people may have conferred on them the rights and recognitions of what has been termed the 'abstract individual', the category of the person is secondary to a primary identity as a mental patient, to a form of confinement not merely in a place but in a whole way of seeing and understanding.[1] What the asylum produced, we may suggest, was a mental patient (person).

Nominally at least, the thrust of current policy is to overturn this legacy and to inaugurate a shift in perspective from the mental patient to the person. It proceeds from the recognition that to conscript people with mental illness as full-time mental patients, and force them to renounce their social identities on account of their psychiatric histories, is for the most part both unnecessary and undesirable. The maladies from which people suffer may to varying degrees persist, but none the less the framework in which they should be helped to conduct their lives is that of personhood rather than mental patienthood. From this point of view, the onset of a severe mental illness need no longer be a barrier to ordinary human recognition and the entitlements of citizenship. We might therefore now say that we live in a society in which by and large the intention of policy is to produce not so much a mental patient (person) as a person (mental patient). To put it slightly differently, we might say that the person with mental illness is now primarily thought of as 'partly mad' rather than 'wholly mad'. This recognition is in effect embodied in recent legislation. Thus in England and Wales the 1983 Mental Health Act granted more autonomy to patients, not least rights to refuse treatments, than had previous legislation, in which the decisions of the physician held sway.

Needless to say, the notion of the person (mental patient) is clearly open to a number of sometimes conflicting ideological interpretations. For example, we may choose to cast it in terms of the reappropriation by the former mental patient of his own identity and the struggle he has to undergo to tackle, among other things, the legacy of stigma. Or we may frame it in terms of the way in which a person must learn to live with mental illness. What, perhaps, we can be said to be living with today are the complications and ambiguities of the 'partly mad' perspective, the varying uses to which it can be put, some of them cynical, some enlightened. Thus it may equally be used as a means to empower people with mental illness or as an administrative device to divest people of specialized support. It marks a new direction, certainly, but we cannot assume that it testifies to a change of governmental and psychiatric heart, to a revaluation of the worth and social competence of the person with mental illness. Some American observers have recently given an appropriately ironic account of the consequences of the contemporary shift in perspective. Contemporary mental health policies, they remark, are 'inclusionary' policies: 'By inclusionary, we mean a change from the mentally ill being forcibly excluded from society to their being forcibly injected back into society . . . That is, they are now mostly included in society rather than mostly excluded from it.'

Most alarmingly, perhaps, we do not quite know what to make of these people who have come back to live amongst us:

Ironically, mental patients may be more of a mystery today, living among us, than they were when hidden away in the asylum. We do not know them, because they are neither outside society in the world of exclusion, nor are they full citizens – individuals who are like the rest of us. Being neither other nor self, they are a new kind of social construction.'

Neither other nor self. This captures very well the ambiguity in the social construction of the person (mental patient). By contrast with its counter-image, it suggests a positive direction but it hints equally at uncertainties and unresolved questions both over the terms of membership or belonging that are to be offered to these returned exiles and over the concepts and vocabularies in which we might appropriately describe them and relate to them.

In an intriguing study of a small French town which since the turn of the century has played host to a colony for the mentally ill and where former patients from the local asylum are transformed into lodgers who reside with foster-parents in the community, Denise Jodelet has described some of the uncertainties and ambiguities around this new kind of social construction that underlie the placid surface of integration. For the townspeople of Ainay-le-Château, the experience of living in close proximity with former mental patients has brought with it the disquieting discovery that many of these people are not generally as peculiar or different as the prevailing stereotypes of the mentally ill had led the inhabitants to suppose. Though reassuring in certain respects, the discovery of ordinariness has created a new uncertainty and the inhabitants of Ainay-le-Château worry, for example, that people from another region visiting the town may experience difficulty in distinguishing between the inhabitants and the former mental hospital inmates. In consequence it has become necessary to erect various barriers to maintain a distance from the former patients, both directly in the organization of the household and in the language that is used to describe the relationship with the lodgers to outsiders. The former mental patient, we learn, is 'never truly treated as "a" (worker, child, friend, etc.) but rather "like a" (worker, child, friend, etc.)'. The lodgers come to inhabit a 'universe of the "as if"', in which though they are in the house, they are never truly of the house, and are indeed neither quite other nor self. They are treated '"as if" they were "children", "part of the family", "employees", "work-mates", or "not at all like animals", even if no one goes so far as to say that they are "like part of the furniture"'. As one foster-parent put it: 'They have their room, they are . . . we are . . . it's a family, so to speak.'[3]

'Partly Mad' and 'Partly Bad'

Much has been written about the 'criminalization' of the mentally ill, the process by which people suffering from mental illness have been deflected from the mental health system to the criminal justice system. Shortcomings in social provision for former mental patients, not least in housing, have undoubtedly augmented the prison population and in some cases the prison has come 'to replace the asylum as the place of sanctuary for the mentally ill'.[4] A recent study suggests that as many as 37 per cent of prisoners in English prisons suffer from a psychiatric disorder, including 2 per cent from a psychosis. As the authors point out, though the prevalence of psychosis in prisons is comparable to that in the general population, it still amounts to quite a large group – roughly 730 prisoners at any one time. Overall just over a thousand prisoners were judged to require treatment in a psychiatric unit, a large proportion of them in a facility offering conditions of medium security.[5] Other studies have shown that while the courts are empowered to make hospital orders they have become disinclined to do so, not least because there are currently only 600 medium security beds, a considerable shortfall on the 2,000 recommended by the Butler report.[6] As is well known, ordinary psychiatric hospitals are reluctant to give houseroom to convicted criminals with chronic conditions; moreover the recent NHS reforms provide them with ample financial disincentives to do so and 'fail to address the question who will pay for the treatment of such patients in the future'.[7]

It may, however, be misleading to attribute the criminalization of the mentally ill solely to pressures exerted on the prisons by the mental health system. Interestingly, the shift in perspective on the mentally ill is mirrored by similar changes within the criminal justice system, both in England and Wales and in the United States. The person (mental patient) may be as much a product of the criminal justice system, and of a seemingly enlightened policy in which mentally disordered offenders are viewed as only partly mad and held responsible for their acts, as of mental health policy. What has happened in England and Wales, Simon Verdun-Jones tells us, 'is that a defendant's mental disorder is no longer relevant to the issue of criminal responsibility. Instead the issue has now become relevant exclusively to the process of sentencing. In short, all mentally disordered offenders are considered to be partly mad and partly bad.' The attempt to separate the 'bad' from the 'mad' in terms of their criminal responsibility has largely been abandoned and the 'insanity defence is virtually dead and buried'. 'Badness' rather than 'madness' is the focal consideration and mental illness only enters the lists late in the day, as rather a secondary matter. In some twelve states in the United States the verdict of 'guilty but mentally ill' has been introduced as an alternative to acquittal by reason of insanity, and results in the accused being convicted and sent to prison but 'assuages the conscience of the jury by requiring that the accused receive treatment in the prison system'.[8]

From a 'therapeutic' standpoint such measures may seem unduly punitive, but criticisms have also been made of regimes of coercive benevolence whereby mentally ill offenders are forcibly diverted to the mental health system. So, for example, Saleem Shah proposes that 'In view of the consequences that are typically associated with such diversion (e.g. indeterminate confinement, the social stigma of being considered mentally ill or "insane", and the possible loss of such civil rights as obtaining a driver's licence, etc.), if given a choice it is likely that many defendants may opt to forgo the promised benevolence and accept the determinate criminal sanctions.'[9]

Person (Mental Patient) or Pauper (Mental Patient)?

It must be admitted that the realities of life experienced by many ex-mental-patients have made the exchange of a mental patient identity for that of a person (mental patient) look decidedly ambiguous. To be sure, the emphasis on the 'person' rather than the 'mental patient' has set a direction for contemporary striving, in particular perhaps for the striving of ex-mental-patients themselves and the less stigmatizing self-definitions many of them have come to entertain for themselves. In important respects, the homogenized identities of mental patients warehoused in asylums have yielded to a much more diversified culture that has permitted the emergence of a more varied set of career trajectories and of richer and more nuanced identity prospects for people with mental illness.

Yet the life chances of some people with mental illness have if anything been degraded still further. Community care in Britain at the present time, it has recently been said, is 'an unknown quantity with an unknown distribution round the country'. Depending on the good or bad fortune of his location, 'a young man with severely disabling chronic schizophrenia might block an acute psychiatric bed for a year, enter a slow-stream rehabilitation ward, move to a hostel in the centre of town, return to his parents' home, stay in bed and breakfast accommodation, or sleep in a cardboard box'.[10] As has been widely remarked, the hopes that have been entertained of resettling the disadvantaged into integrated communities in which they will benefit from a 'network of reciprocal social relationships' have paid scant regard to the realities of late-twentieth-century British society.[11] As the Social Services Committee acidly commented, 'The concept of community may be more resilient than the reality. One submission put it bluntly: "In the majority of cases, the community does not exist." '[12]

On the available evidence, the transformation of mental patient (person) into person (mental patient) can also plausibly be read as a profoundly retrogressive move in which people with mental illness are returned to the undifferentiated predicaments (joining the ranks of the homeless or the criminal) in which they found themselves in the era before the Lunacy Reform movement and the construction of the asylums in the nineteenth century. Release from the stigmatizing discourse of psychiatry may not entail much more than the freedom to be picked up in the stigmatizing discourse of poverty. It has properly been pointed out recently that the association between mental hospital closures and the increase in the population of the homeless in Britain has been considerably exaggerated. 'This assumption conjures images of elderly long-stay patients being turfed out of the hospitals that have been their homes for twenty or thirty years into the cold, dirty streets.'[13] Some such people can certainly be found among the homeless but to a much greater extent the population of the homeless mentally ill is made up of younger people who have never been long-term hospital inmates and throughout their illness careers have always been beneficiaries of community-based care. What this evidence demonstrates in the British case, then, is not so much the consequences of hospital closures as the failure of policies that proceed under the banner of the person (mental patient) to provide reliable alternatives to mental patienthood for a sizeable group of vulnerable people.

If assignment to an asylum as a mental patient was not infrequently a certification of hopelessness, it did at least provide a structure of protection. Indeed, it is part of the awkward legacy of caring for the mentally ill that the stigma and the protection have been closely intertwined. In dismantling the structures of mental patienthood, however, and holding out the promise of a life beyond the asylum, we may in some instances be removing the limited but crucial vestiges of protection which the welfare state had to offer the mentally ill. In urging ex-mental-patients towards the community we may under some circumstances be doing no such thing, but rather removing them from a familiar and known community and pitching them into dismal isolation.[14] We can focus the ambiguity around the direction of contemporary policy in the following way: is it to be about dismantling protective structures of psychiatric provision and returning the mentally ill to the ranks of the poor? Or are we to see it as an effort to overcome the conditions of disadvantage to which the mentally ill have been subject and in which they have to a considerable extent been treated as an alien caste? If the intention of policy is to transform the mental patient into a person (mental patient), the reality of what is delivered may be a pauper (mental patient).

Certainly, judging from psychiatry's equivocal relationship to the chronic mentally ill over the past century it can plausibly be argued that the mentally ill are being turfed out of the mental hospitals, not because they have succeeded as patients, taken their medicines and got better, but precisely because they have failed as such. As Geoff Shepherd tellingly remarks, people with chronic mental illness sit very uneasily within a conception of service that is built round notions of 'patients' and 'treatments' and aspires to a curative rather than a custodial function:

Being a 'patient' should be a temporary condition. You get ill, you receive treatment (take your medicine) and you get better. While you are 'ill' you are excused the normal duties and responsibilities of life; when you get better you have to take them up again. Thus, the idea of a *chronic* patient is a contradiction in terms. You cannot be a proper patient and be untreatable at the same time; it just does not make sense. It also becomes difficult to justify the expenditure of scarce, therapeutic resources on people who are not going to get better ... Thus, chronic patients represent a problem. They are an embarrassment to a scientific and technological culture which is used to being able to sort out its problems.[15]

Far from providing access to the entitlements of citizenship, the transformation of the mental patient (person) into the person (mental patient) may mean that the person's health care needs are now bracketed and all but ignored. Critics have for long lamented the medicalization of madness and the incorporation of the insane within medical institutions, but today, under some circumstances, discharged mental patients may find themselves excluded from adequate medical care altogether. This, indeed, is what is suggested by evidence about the inability of hard-pressed acute psychiatric services in inner-city areas to cater for the needs of the homeless mentally ill.[16]

The Asylum Reopens as a Public Shelter

If we want to identify a significant contemporary icon for what is happening in this respect, we cannot do better than turn to the situation in the United States, where the closure of wards in state mental hospitals has been pushed much further than elsewhere in the industrial West. From a maximum in-patient population of 558,900 in 1955, numbers had fallen to 132,164 by 1980. Resources intended for the support of people with severe mental illness have frequently been diverted to more tractable and socially acceptable groups. As a number of observers have noted, the Community Mental Health Centre system, which was established in the USA to take over the function of the state mental hospitals in providing care for the seriously mentally ill, has increasingly tended to concentrate its energies on the 'worried well', and the proportion of individuals with diagnoses such as schizophrenia admitted to the centres has sharply decreased.

So where are ex-mental-hospital inmates to be found in the USA? In November 1986 the National Institute of Mental Health admitted that the whereabouts of 58 per cent of people with a history of schizophrenia was unknown. As many as 937,000 of these people had been lost to aftercare, and only 17 per cent were in receipt of out-patient care.[17] To those who walk the streets of New York and other North American cities, however, their whereabouts is all too evident, and it is estimated that approximately one third of homeless people in the USA are seriously mentally ill. In his recent study of the homeless mentally ill Fuller Torrey vividly describes some of the most egregious instances of the conversion of mental patient (person) into person (mental patient). He recounts how early in 1989:

New York City officials announced a new policy of discharging some patients from psychiatric wards of city hospitals and *placing them directly in shelters for the homeless.* Two of the shelters, they said, would be staffed with psychiatrists, nurses, social workers and a recreation aide, thus being essentially like a hospital ward in the middle of a homeless shelter. Mentally ill individuals can now therefore make a full circuit, from a state mental hospital to public shelters for the homeless to psychiatric wards of city hospitals to public shelters for the homeless that are set up like psychiatric hospital wards. This is the *planned system* . . .[18]

Furthermore, New York City has recently been sued by advocates of the homeless and forced to reopen a decommissioned building at Manhattan State Hospital as a shelter for the homeless to rehouse many of the same people who had previously been inmates of the hospital. Testimony from the inmates suggests that conditions are now appreciably worse than they were when the institution functioned as a mental hospital.[19] Some years ago that fearsome scourge of the psychiatric establishment, Thomas Szasz, berated psychiatrists for providing shelter for the homeless under the title of a supposedly scientific and therapeutic regime.[20] Are these now, we may wonder, the kinds of facilities, stripped of all therapeutic pretensions, that Szasz seemed to be advocating in place of the mental hospital?

Studies have also documented the extreme distress precipitated in homeless people by the shock of entry to municipal shelters or the enforced migration from one condition of homelessness to another.[21] The endless migration of the homeless mentally ill, Fuller Torrey writes, 'is like a medieval pilgrimage, which goes on year after year, with hardships endured in order to attain grace. Unfortunately for the mentally ill, the best they can hope for from their involuntary pilgrimage is survival.'[22]

Mad or Undeserving

'So, here is the heart of the matter,' Catherine Grimshaw writes, 'care in the community implies a process of revaluing citizens called mentally ill. Of necessity this means narrowing the gap between those who have and those who have not, by actively promoting an anti-poverty strategy. Therefore, no government which is serious about closing hospitals can simply sit back, cut spending on state benefits and let market forces determine the shape of tomorrow's society.' She goes on to describe how former mental patients find themselves transformed into ordinary 'citizens' within the structural constraints imposed by a government which 'saw in the overhaul of social security the opportunity to save money regardless of the social and economic consequences of keeping large numbers of people on the poverty line'.[23] The persisting vulnerabilities of many of these ex-patients, and the lack of work opportunities provided for them, mean that these 'citizens' quickly find themselves drawn into the politics of invalidity and become welfare claimants. This is the experience of one such person in attempting to negotiate a furniture grant:

I got an appointment to see a member of staff at the DHSS who told me that I wasn't entitled to it. I knew my rights and told him them! He made such comments as, 'You don't look mentally ill to me', 'What is wrong with you?' and 'When will you stop being ill?'. He was unhelpful and wouldn't say whether or not I was likely to get the money. In the end my social worker and my key worker at the hostel helped me to sort it out. I got the money but it was made so difficult for me to claim that many people would have been put off.[24]

As Grimshaw comments, 'No matter how diligent the welfare rights practitioner, he or she is as powerless as the claimant to manufacture the fundamental changes needed to improve the benefit structure and to overcome the stigma and prejudice that clings to those who engage with it.'[25] The government remains seemingly 'wedded to the old stereotypes of the "undeserving poor" and the necessity to control them'.[26] Furthermore, because by comparison with physical disability mental health problems tend to be less 'visible', it is more difficult for ex-mental-patients to escape the ascription 'undeserving'.

Here then is another aspect of the ambiguous status of the person (mental patient). In Chapter 2 we saw that disclosure of a psychiatric past, particularly in an employment interview, often results in redefinition as a mental patient. Yet here we see that the effort at disclosure by someone who plays the part of an ordinary citizen is seen to lack legitimacy. In the one case the person finds himself absorbed by the power of his psychiatric past, in the second he finds himself unable to make a legitimate claim upon it as a feature of the kind of person he is now. Pinioned between the images and assumptions of the asylum and the Poor Law, the ex-mental-patient discovers that his psychiatric affiliation is either a menace or a bogus credential. The choices open to him appear to be those of 'Get back to your ward!' or 'On your bike!'

Where the House Becomes a Hospital Annexe

One variation, as we have seen, is simply to convert mental patients into paupers (mental patients) as a more expedient means of dealing with them. Another is to ensure that the promised delivery from mental patienthood never happens, as in the phenomenon of 'transinstitutionalization', whereby after the mental hospital closes inmates are moved to other institutions, often in the private sector. This is an industry that has been most keenly promoted in the United States but there are signs that it may grow in the United Kingdom also and that there may well be incentives for health and social services to transfer people in need of long-term care to the private sector.[27]

It is just as important, however, to look at what happens when genuine attempts are made to provide the structural conditions for personhood as an alternative to mental patienthood. In England, for instance, a number of cases have emerged of the use of property legislation as a device to discriminate against people with a history of mental illness and prevent them taking up residence in local communities. An example is the experience of eight former mental patients in Bath – as fitting a place as any from which to explore the machinations of what one historian has termed a 'hegemonic rational culture of the propertied and the polite' in its attitude to mental illness.[28] Previously long-stay patients at a hospital which was due for closure, the eight residents had moved into two four-bedroomed detached houses on a new estate which had been purchased by the local health authority. As in countless other resettlement schemes of this kind across the country, we may reasonably assume that these former mental patients had been carefully prepared for the move and were looking forward to it as an opportunity to re-establish themselves at last in ordinary life. Indeed, we might be forgiven for thinking that this, among other things, was what community-care policy was supposed to be all about.

However, a rude shock was awaiting them, for unbeknown to them the property company which developed the estate had already commenced proceedings against them by the time they moved. No complaints had been received from the neighbours, indeed one neighbour described how 'the nature of these people's illness makes them rather reclusive . . . we see so little of them – they are very quiet and shy people'.[29] None the less judgement was passed in the High Court that the health authority had infringed the property laws and the ruling was supported by the Appeal Court. One of the Appeal judges recognized that

In many respects the way in which these two houses were being used was indistinguishable from the way in which other houses on the estate were used. It was central to the Care in the Community policy that that should be the case. The intention was that occupants were weaned from their reliance on institutionalized care and progressively assisted to take their place in the community.

However:

Private houses were normally used as accommodation for the owner or a tenant and his family. None of the occupants of these two houses were owners or tenants, nor were they members of the Health Secretary's family. They remained patients in NHS care at least in that they were ineligible for social-security benefits and relied on the NHS for their food and household requirements. That underlined the special nature of their occupation and the special use which was being made of the house. They had a resident house leader who was a registered nurse and two daily support workers, all employed by the NHS ... No emphasis of the residents' ability to treat the houses as their permanent homes nor of the advanced degree of autonomy which was given to them in the running of them could obscure the Health Secretary's continuing responsibility for their care or the incidental powers vested in him.[30]

In virtue of the Health Secretary's responsibility to 'provide supervision and support for the residents', the houses were therefore being used 'for public and not for private purposes. It was neither the Health Secretary's private dwelling-house nor the residents'.' Lord Donaldson, Master of the Rolls, averred that: 'If a label can be attached to such a use, it seems to me that of "hospital annexe" or "mental health hostel" ... This is not a use which would be regarded as a normal use of a private dwelling-house.'[31]

The crucial argument, then, is that these are not really ordinary people at all. What appears to be a group of ordinary people in search of an ordinary home in which to live is shown to be no such thing; the people are shown for what they are, as first and foremost mental patients; and what they took for a private house on an ordinary street is shown to be an annexe of the mental hospital. The mental hospital from which these people emerged may well have closed, been razed to the ground even and all its assets stripped, its Victorian fittings such as pine doors and brass handles sold to adorn the interiors of suburban villas, but none the less these residents are still marked by their attachment to an absent hospital. If they fondly imagine that they have left the mental hospital for a life elsewhere, as far as the law is concerned they are still in hospital. The effect of the rhetorical conversion of an ordinary house into a hospital annexe is to put these former patients back in their place and ensure that the terms of membership of the community available to most other citizens are denied them. If the opportunities for discrimination in property legislation are to prevail, for these unfortunate people and others like them the asylum will apparently never close. As one commentator sardonically remarked, 'At a stroke, then, this judgement has dealt a blow not just to these particular people who will have to move out but also to community-care policy. Ex-patients cannot live in the community like anyone else because the court has defined them as patients who are not like anyone else.'[32]

Welfare Paternalism

One way in which to describe the promise that is held out by the shift from the mental patient (person) to the person (mental patient) is of deliverance from a tradition of welfare paternalism in which the beneficiaries were the passive recipients of care and the voice of the mentally ill was all but silenced. As has been said, the experience of people with mental illness in society has generally been 'one of disempowerment, loss of control over their lives, a sense of being on the receiving end, and of being a passive recipient'.[33] Those who have criticized current policies have often enough invoked the vocabulary of 'caring' to mark the contrast with the unscrupulous and cynical practices they see before them. But what is overlooked here is the widespread desire for participation and empowerment among users of mental health services and the criticisms that have been made of the tradition of welfare paternalism. From what users of services say, it appears that the reproduction of client docility under new professional auspices, no matter how well resourced, is not what they seek. In a recent article, Michael Ignatieff has described the welfare mould from which many users want to break free and has nicely castigated those who have tried to defend the welfare state by contrasting the 'uncaring' policies of the Conservative government with their own 'caring' attitudes. The 'citizenship ideal of post-war liberals and social democrats', he writes, 'stressed the passive quality of entitlements at the expense of the active equality of participation. The entitled were never empowered, because empowerment would have infringed the prerogatives of the managers of the welfare state.'

As a political question, Ignatieff argues, welfare is about rights, not caring. To 'describe the welfare state in the language of caring is to misdescribe it, and to misdescribe is to deceive'. To do so is to reinstate Poor Law principles and to understand the welfare state as a civic pact between haves and have-nots, care givers and care receivers, in which entitlements are a matter of moral generosity rather than of right. As Ignatieff aptly remarks, 'only someone who has not actually been on the receiving end of the welfare state would dare call it an instance of civic altruism at work'. Notions of the 'caring society' evoke for Ignatieff 'the image of a nanny state in which the care we get depends on what the "caring professions" think it fit for us to receive'. He would, he goes on, much 'prefer to live in a society which struggles to be just, which respects and enhances people's rights and entitlements'. Simon spoke for a number of the ex-patients we discussed earlier when he described how demoralizing it felt to be part of the community mental-patient system, 'you're sort of tied to the strings of the hospital, the apron strings of the hospital, you're being treated like a child ...' The critical issue, Ignatieff suggests, is not to 'tie us all in the leading strings of therapeutic good intentions', but 'the struggle to make freedom real' through the shared foundation of a 'citizenship of entitlement'.[34]

It is in the light of criticisms like these that we can be helped to identify the shortcomings in the liberal psychiatric traditions of the 1960s and 1970s. Consider, for example, the writings of Douglas Bennett, for many years one of the leading figures in the British tradition of social psychiatry. Rehabilitation for psychiatric patients, Bennett tells us, is 'principally directed to the recovery or initiation of appropriate social roles'. Socialization will play an important part in this, since it seeks 'to help a disabled person to acquire or regain the habits, beliefs, attitudes and motivation which will enable him to perform satisfactorily in the roles expected of him in society'. In contrast to earlier perspectives in which it was assumed that either there was little or nothing to be done about the handicap or that at most psychiatric care could 'provide shelter, concede the weakness, and make allowances', Bennett describes a progressive ideology of psychiatric rehabilitation in which the focal task is to attempt to modify the disability, and compensate for it, by developing other abilities.[35]

Bennett provides a benign and dedicated approach to failings in socialization for role performance, but the problem with it is that the failures of mental patients are entirely individualized. Cursory reference is made to secondary handicaps and the impact of stigma, but what is missing is an understanding of the dialectics of disability and of the constraints and perplexities of the field of social and cultural forces in which people with a history of mental illness have to try and make something of their lives. Here, for example, is what Sidney, a young man with a history of several hospitalizations for schizophrenia, has to say about his difficulties in striking up relationships with women. In an encounter with a woman in a pub, for example:

I might have got talking to her but I would have had to cut off at a certain point because I knew that once she found out about the background she'd lose interest ... It would have been more difficult to carry on with the relationship ... I have actually avoided getting into relationships because of the difficulty I would have in explaining what I'd been through, and what it all means, to someone ... If I met someone in a pub or a club or whatever, and I liked her, if I felt that she'd never known anything about mental illness, never experienced anything to do with it, I'd avoid talking to her ... because it would seem pointless to me. I'd just stop it dead.

In Bennett's normative scheme of things, the ability to form relationships with members of the opposite sex is surely to be reckoned an important accomplishment, but we entirely misapprehend what Sidney is telling us if we cast his difficulty in this sphere as an individualized failing or weakness. If we want to understand what it is like to be in Sidney's position in his encounter with a woman in a pub, we can only do so on the basis of a reading of the history through which people like Sidney have been brought to see themselves, and have come to be seen by others, in a singularly dismal light. The displacement and estrangement that Sidney experiences is in important measure not so much a property of the individual case as a social construction to which authoritative traditions in psychiatry, whether by intention or by default, have amply contributed.

For want of a moral critique of the norms by which people with mental illness have been judged and the barriers on their participation in social life justified, we are inevitably trapped in a view of the mental patient as a failed, if not broken, individual. Bennett, for example, clearly does not consider it a legitimate part of his business to assist his patients to confront their debased status as second-class citizens. In this regard, perhaps the most notable thing about the writings of Bennett and others in this tradition is that we never hear from the patients themselves. Indeed, the schizophrenic is for the most part represented as a reluctant, incapacitated and largely inarticulate actor who only by the most patient ministrations of psychiatric expertise can be encouraged to do anything at all. What Bennett and others deliver are psychiatric monologues, ventilated only by reference to other psychiatric monologues. These accounts are a notable advance on what has gone before but they lack the depth that can come only from an ethically and historically informed understanding of the predicament of the former mental patient in social life and from a willingness to confront the complications that result from an entry into dialogue. Notwithstanding the sympathy and concern of these psychiatric protagonists, mental patients continue to be numbered among the 'non-men who march and labour in silence'.[36]

Empowerment

However, some users of mental health services have made it their business to develop a critical consciousness of themselves as second-class citizens. In important respects psychiatry has been forced to relinquish some of its control over people with mental illness and where some have been lost to welfare services and become homeless, others have begun to think of themselves in new ways, to press not for the reinstatement of welfare paternalism but for more participative solutions, and to join with the new form of class struggle characterized by Ralf Dahrendorf as the struggle for citizenship. In common with other disadvantaged groups, ex-mental-patients are in possession of certain civil rights, but 'until traditional entitlement structures are broken and elements of a civil society created' we cannot legitimately say that they have arrived as citizens, 'they have merely gained a new vantage point in the struggle for more life chances'. As Dahrendorf says, 'The crucial fact about the underclass and the persistently unemployed is that they have no stake in society. In a very serious sense, society does not need them. Many in the majority class wish that they would simply go away; and if they did their absence would barely be noticed.'[37]

Here is an account by Vivien Lindow, a woman who has managed to establish herself in a more critical and distanced relation to the categories of 'mental illness' and 'mental patient', of the forces that conspire to make it very difficult for people with mental illness to see themselves as anything other than mental patients:

It was the casting out, the stigma, that felt most damaging ... Having been given, and accepted for lack of an alternative, a label of 'mentally ill', I did not feel that my opinions were valid. Many aspects of the treatment itself confirmed this view. Society's discrimination against people who have received psychiatric treatment, in not accepting us for proper jobs and proper housing, adds to this. Unlike criminals, society does not forgive our former diagnoses after a period of time ... It is difficult for a person who has been treated for years as a 'mental patient' to realize that her (or his) thoughts and actions are valid and could make a difference. At this stage I had a vague awareness that I needed to join with others towards political action. The thought that I could play a part in bringing about change was alien to all that I had learned about my worthlessness during my upbringing and in the psychiatric system ... One of the things that we service users have in common is this shared experience of total powerlessness. We learn to define ourselves by the roles and diagnoses given to us by psychiatrists, take them into ourselves and feel helpless to influence our own lives ... With our powerlessness goes poverty of an enduring and humiliating nature.[38]

Vivien Lindow describes her experience in terms of a shift from a definition as a mental patient to a self-definition as a survivor. 'I learned,' she writes, 'of the term "survivor" and it really fitted as a self-definition. It was much less pejorative than "mental patient".' We can see this as one way in which the former mental patient may learn to reappropriate his or her identity. As Peter Campbell, himself a user or, as he prefers to describe himself, a recipient of mental health services, has recently argued, it is perhaps inevitable

that in breaking from traditional conceptions people with a history
of mental illness should now come to describe themselves in a
number of different terms. The question of the appropriate language has itself to be seen against the background of powerlessness:

One of the difficulties is that much of the language used has not been
chosen by those it describes. It should not be expected that when people
do assert their power and choose terms of self-description they will necessarily arrive at an agreed term. Although it may be untidy to have numerous
descriptions – consumer, user, recipient, system survivor – this may well
be a truer reflection of the complicated realities which other (externally
sanctioned) labels such as 'mentally ill' have previously concealed.[39]

As we have seen, numerous questions arise for ex-mental-patients
in the community: how to locate themselves in relation to medical
definitions; to medication; to psychiatric services; to organized
groupings of ex-patients; and to their own psychiatric histories.
There has, of course, been a long history of resistance to organized
psychiatry, and the protestations of the 'anti-psychiatry' movement
of the 1960s, together with the emergence in the same period of
groups such as the Mental Patients Union, share in important
respects a common lineage with the declamations of John Perceval
and the Alleged Lunatics' Friends Society of the 1860s.[40] While
there are certainly affinities between a number of contemporary
pressure groups and this critical tradition, it would none the less be
quite misleading to attempt to assimilate either the diverse struggles
of ex-mental-patients in the community or the more formal groupings which have emerged in the 1980s into a single oppositional
stance. As Campbell aptly remarks, since the late 1960s 'there has
been a tendency to define any coherent opposition to the psychiatric
system as being part of the "anti-psychiatry" movement'.[41] In a
review of the various groups, some of them directly connected with
service provision and some of them operating outside the system as
pressure groups, which broadly comprise the contemporary self-
advocacy movement, Campbell stresses their ideological diversity:

Those involved in self-advocacy, for example, hold a range of views on
whether 'mental illness' exists as such, and whether or not collaboration
with the psychiatric system is desirable. In addition, the ways that self-

advocacy groups are working are often far more pragmatic than in the anti-psychiatry movement. In a sense, mental health self-advocacy could be characterized as reformist, seeking ways of changing and improving the existing systems, rather than taking up dogmatic ideological positions.[42]

The thrust of contemporary debate is less to commend one version of how people with mental illness should view their predicaments at the expense of others than to highlight a number of shared themes and issues, notably the need to transform the professional–patient relationship and permit more power for the patient. Writing in the early 1980s, Peter Sedgwick characterized the debate about psychiatry in terms of a conflict between those who were eager to press for better services and more resources and those who were mainly aggrieved by the social-control functions of psychiatry and the ambitions of psychiatric expansionism.[43] Some ten years later, it can perhaps be said that the 'better services' lobby has won the argument, though surely not the cause, and the significant debate is now about the *nature* of services and the power structure of such services. A recent discussion of consumer participation in mental health services from the World Health Organization provides a representative emphasis in proposing that 'In planning and evaluation, professionals and consumers should respect each other's expertise and experience, with a more balanced weight being given to the views of each. This implies a move away from the assumption that consumers have little insight into their own capabilities and limitations and a move towards recognition of the contribution that consumers can make.'

One of the words which usefully encapsulates the concerns of contemporary protagonists, it is suggested, is 'empowerment':

Users of the mental health service systems are often viewed as deviant and the labels 'illness' or 'madness' are stigmatizing. Services may be paternalistic and a medical model of care can put great weight on the views of the doctor ... The paternalism of current services taken together with the stigmatizing effects of a diagnosis of mental illness can produce a climate which reduces considerably the ability of individuals to control their own lives. Fundamentally this issue is about power. Many consumer organizations will argue that they are working towards empowering the primary consumers of services to be able to control their own lives once again and that such empowerment also requires control over service delivery and the planning, development and management of care.[44]

Old Services in New Places?

There are, of course, numerous examples of innovation in community provision in Britain, some of them well documented, but concerns have been expressed about the nature of some of the changes that are taking place:

Much of the current impetus for change derives from the NHS bureaucracy and its preoccupation with more efficient use of resources tied up in the mental hospitals. The vision of alternative provision is poorly defined, however, and there is considerable danger that, rather than developing new services, the relocation of resources will merely reproduce old services in new places. In our view the scale of this challenge has been underestimated. Real change in psychiatric provision will only be attained where it is possible to achieve new status for people with psychiatric disabilities, new roles for staff and new public attitudes all within a single movement for reform.[45]

In some residential facilities, certainly, the mental hospital, together with the roles and attitudes that derive from it, has been painstakingly reproduced. So, for example, a strict demarcation may exist between the territories available to residents and those for the exclusive use of staff, such as separate toilets. More especially, in many residential establishments

users are even segregated amongst themselves, particularly on sex lines. Like children, they are regarded as being unable to cope/deal adequately with emotions, especially those involving sexual relationships. The solution is usually to separate the sexes in terms of:

– their bedrooms (and, in some establishments, even sitting-rooms) being separated into separate 'wings';

– monitors (for example, electronic switches tripping off lights on a control panel) are used in other buildings where there are not separate wings but staff still wish to see who is entering whose room;

– toilet facilities even in buildings professing to be 'like home' are separate for the sexes, unlike a really normal home.[46]

Even where they possess more opportunities to exercise choice than in the asylum, ex-mental-patients are still seriously constrained. The following account of the fortunes of discharged mental patients in social life in the United States presages a development which we may come to see in the United Kingdom in the 'contract culture' of the reformed National Health Service. Though the ex-mental-patient is now commonly described as a consumer, 'it may be more accurate to suggest that such patients have been included in the new mental health system as both commodities and consumers'. These people

have become valuable to service providers in both the public and private sectors by virtue of the money that can be obtained from third parties for their care. After all, the essence of a commodity in the market-place is that it can be used to generate money as it is processed, improved or simply stored. Patients are used by service providers for this purpose. The movements of patients, therefore, have become the stuff of which markets are made.

The patient may have been delivered from the asylum but he has not become a player:

Patients have some flexibility and power, but it is an odd, negative kind of power – if patients disappear, the ability of the service provider to earn income is in jeopardy. So the patient must stay 'in play', without being a player, caught between the world of income and self-sufficiency and the world of institutions and labels.[47]

The demand for well-resourced services may not seem to require justification but it is sometimes forgotten that the critical issue of power is also involved. To understand how this is so we may look briefly at the Programme for Assertive Community Treatment (PACT) and the Mobile Community Team (MCT) based at the Dane County Mental Health Centre in Wisconsin, which specialize in a form of aggressive community outreach and have been lauded even by their critics as among the best community mental health programmes that the United States has to offer. According to the American sociologist Leonie Bachrach, deinstitutionalization is about attending to the service needs of the chronic mentally ill in the community rather than in the hospital. The problem for younger patients in the contemporary cultural milieu of the person (mental patient), she claims, is that they are given mixed messages

– sometimes they appear to be patients and sometimes not – and the prescriptions and proscriptions of mental patienthood are no longer available to them.[48]

For this cultural malady psychiatric community outreach has now devised a remedy by staying in contact with patients wherever they may be and actively involving them in the service system. The Mobile Community Team describes its intentions thus:

MCT is designed to provide a support system for severely disabled psychiatric patients in the community . . . The main goals of MCT are to reduce the frequency and duration of psychiatric hospitalization and to increase self-esteem and independence . . . The MCT team is reluctant to allow clients to drop out of the programme or for services to clients to lapse . . . Costly and, perhaps, dysfunctional hospitalization can be averted if staff can be 'gate-keepers' and it is MCT's policy to work assertively to keep clients in the programme. If clients do not keep appointments, do not appear for groups customarily attended, or do not follow medications regimens, MCT staff will seek out the client and make serious efforts to keep the client involved. Letting services lapse because of oversight or letting clients be lost because they are tired of being involved is quite unacceptable to the programme.[49]

So what does this intensive exercise in psychiatric incorporation really amount to? Clearly enough, it assists in keeping people out of hospital and in meeting some of their basic needs but what else does it achieve? To throw some light on these questions we may turn to Sue Estroff's searing critique of the PACT programme in her book *Making it Crazy*, perhaps the most detailed ethnographic study of the lives of people with chronic mental illness in the community yet undertaken. According to Estroff, the clients she studied had no alternative but to view themselves as mental patients or 'crazies'. Even at the subsistence level, in securing housing, food and other basic requirements, they found themselves 'enmeshed in a complicated system oriented to psychiatric disability – a system in which their identities or roles as crazy people are the means by which they "make it" or survive'.[50] The roles, expectations, stereotypes and responses fashioned around these clients in the community programme were not markedly different from those that accompany the backward patient in the mental hospital. If primary symptoms had been their only difficulties many of them could have worked or had relationships with normal people:

But this was not the case. For clients developed fears and avoidance of others, feelings of inadequacy and incompetence; and both appreciation for and repugnance towards themselves and their psychotic processes. They did this within an interpersonal, social and cultural context that conveyed to them that they were different from normals because they experienced these thoughts and feelings. More importantly, their difference was evaluated as a negative condition, a disease that required medical treatment to eliminate or diminish it.[51]

In Estroff's view, the effect of this and similar programmes is not to help deliver people from mental patienthood but to perpetuate it, and the end result is 'stabilization within the realm of negative differentness':

Not only do we describe these persons as pathologically dependent but we contribute to their dependencies. Not only do we view them as unintegrated within the community but we isolate them by constantly reminding them of their incompetencies and by introducing them to peers (in treatment programmes like PACT) with whom they may be more comfortable.[52]

Estroff's account is borne out by more recent observations of the Dane County programmes. Two independent psychiatric observers who studied the MCT programme found it to be comprehensive: it could 'provide directly or arrange everything any client might need'. But this was not all that they found, for they went on to characterize it as 'proactive, intrusive, and controlling'. As a discharged mental patient in Madison, Wisconsin, it is, we learn, 'almost impossible not to be treated and followed' and 'very hard to escape the mind police'.[53] Programme staff were shown to hold a paternalistic view of their chronic clientele:

for example, the we–them distinction is clearly made by programme staff with regard to the chronic psychotic client. This was pretty clearly stated when we were told that the Mental Health Center staff didn't like to be in the kitchen when the Mobile Community Team's clients were there, as they were just too unpleasant. This attitude . . . may make it difficult for clients to preserve or gain any power. We did not, in our meetings with people at the Mental Health Center, find anyone, with the exception of the director of the Support Network, who showed much investment in client-run programmes or was seriously concerned with ways to preserve and enhance client power.[54]

Heirs to a much older tradition, these programmes are evidently a means of gathering up the loose and scattered madness of the city and bringing it under daily observation. Contemporary ex-mental-patients may well worry about mixed messages: the whisper has gone round that in bringing them back from the places in which they had been put, society may after all want to give them something to hope for; but some experiments in social psychiatry appear to indicate that the most that they can hope for is some stability within their social misery.

Compulsory Medication?

An example of the complications introduced by the shift from the mental patient (person) to the person (mental patient) is nicely brought out in the recent debate in England about Community Treatment Orders, under which patients in the community could be compelled to take medication. The government has shown a healthy scepticism for these proposals, as indeed have many mental health professionals, and it appears unlikely that they will be implemented. They are, however, interesting for what they reveal of the reluctance on the part of some psychiatrists in particular to recognize that the patient in the community is not the same as the patient whom they knew in the mental hospital. We may, perhaps, see them as an instructive example of institutionalized thinking in which an attempt is made to reproduce in the community the concepts and styles of patient domestication and management that derive from the hospital setting.

Under the envisaged legislation, a Community Treatment Order would be made either when the patient refused to continue with his medication or when his relatives detected signs of relapse. The patient, it is assumed, would in all likelihood comply with the requirements of the order and the characteristic cycle of the deterioration and relapse would at last have been broken. Matters are not so straightforward, however, for as Lucy Scott-Moncrieff, a mental health lawyer who has produced a spirited critique of the Royal College of Psychiatrists' proposals for such legislation, rightly points out, the order is designed 'not only to persuade the persuadable but also to compel the unpersuadable'. And the ex-mental-patient in the community is likely to be rather less persuadable than his hospitalized counterpart:

It may be argued that patients who have been admitted to hospital seldom continue to resist physically the administration of injections. However, the situation for people in hospital and people out of hospital is very different. It does not take very long for most patients to realize that the best way of getting out of hospital is to cooperate with the medical and nursing staff. Equally, it will not take very long for such patients to realize that if they cooperate with a Community Treatment Order there is no reason for it ever to end. In these circumstances, I think we can expect to see numbers of patients totally refusing to cooperate with a Community Treatment Order.[55]

But, in any case, on what basis would an order be made? Consider, for example, a situation in which the doctor and approved social worker are summoned to the house by anxious relatives because the patient has discontinued his medication:

If the patient is symptom-free (when the doctor and approved social worker are there) and off medication (even though the residue is still in his body) I think that there might be some difficulty in claiming that someone is suffering from mental illness. One can say that they have suffered and maybe that they are likely to suffer but to say that because they have suffered they must now be suffering seems insupportable.[56]

A powerful argument against the introduction of Community Treatment Orders is the evidence about the side-effects of antipsychotic medication. Furthermore, studies have shown that maintenance medication does not benefit all who take it. In view of these uncertainties, it can plausibly be argued that 'it will always be difficult to be sure that refusal of medication by someone who is not currently psychotic or hospitalized is irrational or incorrect'.[57] But underlying these considerations, and the judgements that any particular ex-mental-patient may make in the light of them, are awkward questions about the rational status of someone who has suffered in the past and may suffer again in the future, but is not obviously suffering in the present, from a severe mental illness. In some traditions of psychiatry, as we have seen, the person with a history of schizophrenia even when in remission is none the less taken to be a flawed individual. On this view he is always a questionable, even suspect, person and unlikely to be able to judge for himself what is in his best interest. Speaking from a rather different standpoint, Professor Julian Leff has recently declared in favour of the rationality of non-compliance; he invites us to entertain a concept of the recovered schizophrenic as a 'completely sane' agent whose judgement should not be put in question simply in virtue of his psychiatric history or suspicions about what that history might portend for the future. Leff envisages a situation in which a relapsing patient who has responded to medication in the past is made subject to a CTO: '. . . they then recover, and say, "I don't want to take this medication any more, I'm perfectly well now." You then say, "But you've got to because you are on a CTO."' In such a situation, remarks Leff, 'you would be compelling someone, who is completely sane, to do something against their will. That seems to me a very dangerous ethical situation . . .'[58]

Similarly, a user of psychiatric services questions the 'underlying assumption that the reason most people cease taking prescribed medications is because they lack "insight" – in other words they are, in some fundamental way, just not capable of knowing what is good for them'. Compelling people with a history of mental illness to take medication, the writer continues, 'may be a simple way of sorting out the relationship between care systems and their recipients to the satisfaction of society', but it masks a deeper malaise. 'Could it be that people stop taking their drugs, indeed opt out of contact with services altogether, because they see a completely new psychiatrist every third out-patient appointment, are told "talking therapies" are no use to them because they are "psychotic", are given medications which do not do the positive things for them which have been promised but have harmful negative physical effects?'[59]

This type of explanation will not satisfy all those who worry about the failure of ex-mental-patients to take their medication, nor indeed should it. It is not difficult to think of instances where other factors are pre-eminent. But we should not for this reason neglect it, for it points to complexities in the relationship between care systems and users which proposals for Community Treatment Orders fail to take into account. Indeed, Community Treatment Orders provide a handy tool for those who may be tempted to reduce the complexities of community provision for people with mental illness to the mechanics of drug delivery. Once such legislation appeared, cost-conscious health managers and accountants may be drawn to the view that a Community Treatment Order 'provides much better value for money than the provision of staff and facilities to build up trust so that people can take medication voluntarily'. It will then 'come about that even those mentally ill people who wish to take advantage of community facilities will have those facilities withdrawn from them'.[60]

The trouble with these proposals, Scott-Moncrieff concludes, is that they attempt to 'equate the position of a mentally ill person in the controlled environment of a hospital with the position of the same person in the uncontrolled environment of the outside world. What are appropriate powers in one situation are either dangerously inadequate (in terms of suitable treatment) or too restrictive (in terms of civil liberties) in the other situation.'[61] The liberties which people with mental illness enjoy in the community inevitably introduce risks, and sometimes the effort to draw users into the contract for their treatment will break down, but the tensions and uncertainties which these produce for mental health professionals and for relatives are not to be resolved by the reinvention of the domesticated mental patient.

It may be useful to enlarge briefly here on the question of side-effects. On some American evidence the real dangers may be in the other direction: not so much that some patients may decide to discontinue their medication but that many may continue taking it without having sufficient understanding of the damage that they may be inflicting upon themselves. In a recent discussion in the *American Journal of Psychiatry* the authors point out that the high risk and potential irreversibility of tardive dyskinesia which includes symptoms such as facial grimacing and distortion, protrusion of the tongue and difficulties with speech and swallowing, means that the obtaining of informed consent must hold special importance in relation to patients receiving long-term neuroleptic drug therapy. 'To be adequately informed, a patient must understand the nature, benefits and risks of the proposed treatment as well as the benefits and risks of the alternative choices, including no treatment.' One study showed that only 32 per cent of psychiatrists routinely informed their patients about the risk of tardive dyskinesia. Furthermore, for informed consent to be meaningful it must be 'viewed as an educational process and not as a single isolated event marked by the signing of a consent form'. The question of informed consent for neuroleptic treatment imposes a special responsibility upon the physician, in as much that a 'number of patients requiring this medication have cognitive deficits that may impair their ability to learn about side-effects' and for lack of such learning they may persist in taking medication that results in 'a potentially irreversible side-effect in a large percentage of patients'. The challenge, the authors write, 'is to effectively treat these patients while respecting their individuality and their autonomy. Informing patients about their illness and the positive and negative aspects of treatment is the first step in an educational process that may span years.'[62]

British psychiatrists are aware of the dangers of the routinization of drug administration but point to the financial constraints which hinder the promotion of more sensitive practices. Thus one psychiatrist acknowledges that 'the present stereotyped drug regime administered to all patients cannot be the best clinical practice' and that he is in no doubt that many patients 'do very well on smaller amounts than what are usually regarded as "standard" doses'.[63] The advantage of maintenance therapy, however, is that it is relatively inexpensive. To adopt an alternative approach, for example one that dispenses with continuous medication and prescribes oral neuroleptic medication for brief periods only at the first signs of relapse, would require greatly increased resources for the careful monitoring of patients over long periods of time, together with the education of patients and informal carers, and these are presently available only in a few centres. The danger here is that the pressure on psychiatrists to come up with cost-effective solutions may lead them to understate the adverse effects of continuous medication. For some patients, however, the 'greasy, masked facies, stooped posture, "dancing feet" and slow, shuffling gait' which mark them out in a crowd may indeed lead them to judge that the effects of the cure are worse than the disease itself.[64]

The Legitimation of Ambiguity

Critics have countered traditional assumptions about the dissolution of the person in schizophrenia by arguing that in significant measure the disadvantage which he experiences derives from our tendency to subsume the person under concepts of disorder. None the less, to attempt to bring him back into his own and envisage him as someone who can stand apart from his illness raises some awkward questions. Someone like Ben clearly does not want to be defined by his history of illness or by his psychiatric attachments but he is willing to recognize the category 'disorder' as a tendency in himself that sometimes comes to the fore and which he has to reckon with. He may not identify it in conventional psychiatric terms but recognize it he certainly does, and in his case we can usefully invoke the framework of a person–disorder interaction.

But things may not always be so clear. Some years ago Elizabeth Bott provided an illuminating discussion of some of the interpersonal processes between schizophrenic patients and their relatives that may culminate in the redefinition of the person as a chronic mental patient. In Bott's view, while 'illness' is clearly a factor in chronic hospitalization, it is 'less important than the use the patient and his others make of it in relation to each other'. She describes some of the consequences of the redefinition of the person as a mental patient when his behaviour in the family proves intolerable:

Such redefinition, distressing though it is, takes some of the pain out of the patient's behaviour, for it makes it unintended; he does not mean it; he is not responsible for himself. But this very redefinition is what makes it such a terrible thing to do. It annihilates the person's identity as a responsible adult and is fraught, for the relatives, with anxiety and fear of revenge, often unacknowledged. It is done because the relative thinks it has to be done for his own psychic survival. His identity is being destroyed and the destroyer must be removed. But the fault is defined as residing in the illness, not the person. The person the relative used to care about has ceased to exist. He is not himself.[65]

From the standpoint of the patient:

... having an 'illness' absolves him of responsibility and entitles him to care. But the stigma is enormous, and admission to hospital, especially for the first time, is a catastrophe. It alters one's sense of oneself irrevocably, a fact that people who work constantly in hospitals tend to become almost unaware of.[66]

Read in one way, Bott's account helps us understand what may be involved in converting a person into a mental patient, the process of 'closure' that may ensue when 'what used to be a relationship is dismembered into illness in the patient and health in the relative'.[67]

As a result the pre-illness person appears to have been abolished, and we are now confronted with someone who is 'wholly mad', his identity permanently spoiled by his illness. Is not this just the kind of process, we may wonder, which the revolution in mental health policy we are concerned with is trying to get away from? But this is only part of the story for, as Bott aptly remarks, the process of closure is one to which the 'patient may obligingly and even cunningly contribute'. To conceive the patient as an innocent victim in this scenario, she continues, is to ignore 'the extent to which he controls and manipulates both his associates and himself to destroy the basis of thinking and gratification both for himself and for them'.[68]

In one aspect Bott demonstrates very starkly how casily and irrevocably the process of closure may develop, but what she also demonstrates are the instabilities that the experience of madness inevitably introduces into the interpersonal scheme of things. By introducing a conceptual distinction between the 'person' and the 'disorder' we implicitly acknowledge that for much of the time at least we are dealing with someone who is only 'partly mad'. In doing so we accord the person a significant degree of respect as someone who is responsible for himself, but as we have seen we have also to concede that as well as being 'partly mad' the person may also be 'partly bad'. Studies of mental hospital environments have shown that patients were rarely as incapacitated as they were taken to be, but actually talented and resourceful agents trying to salvage some dignity for themselves. Critics of total institutions have tended to use the identification of this talent to offset the medical account of the patient as 'wholly mad'.[69] And in important respects rightly so. But, as Bott suggests, patients can show themselves to be resourceful in quite varied ways. In hospital, for example, patients who want to stay 'know how to bchave as if they were more ill, and patients who want to leave know how to behave so as to seem less ill'.[70]

One of the effects of current policies has been to make it much more difficult to bring about the kind of closure which Bott describes. The option of chronic hospitalization is not so readily available to relatives as it used to be. The thrust of policy has been to vindicate the partiality of madness and this as we have seen is laudable and necessary, for the stigma of mental illness and mental patienthood has inflicted untold damage on countless lives. In many cases this may work well enough, but the irony of the matter is that in seeking to detract from the irrevocability of madness, and in some measure to leave it behind as a phenomenon that belongs in a past era, we are brought face to face with the cruel nature of the problem. For the painful truth about mental illness resides as often as not precisely in its ambiguity and resourcefulness. Indeed, it is just this which may sometimes be a special source of suffering for those who have to live with a mentally ill person. Life would be much more tolerable if the individual were identifiably 'wholly mad'.

To live with the 'partly mad' individual may then be to have to live with the ambiguous and unresolved; a combination, perhaps, of the 'mad' and the 'bad', with no official confirmation of either. Not untypical of our own time, it would appear, is less the legitimation of mental patienthood than the tacit legitimation of ambiguity. From the point of view of the relative the plausibility of the putative patient in some contexts is part of the problem. From the point of view of official agencies it may indicate that there is an insufficient basis for compulsory intervention. Those who have most intimately to do with the person have to live with him in his several aspects; those who meet him occasionally are confronted only by his external presentation of self. This problem was well understood by Cervantes in the sixteenth century: 'All the physicians and all the authors in the world could not give a clear account of his madness. He is mad in patches, full of lucid intervals.'[71] And it was recognized by George Brown and his colleagues in their studies of the families of people with schizophrenia in the early 1960s:

Patients can often show some control over the expression of their disorder, and this may be influenced by environmental factors. It was fairly common to be told by the relatives of a disturbed patient that when strangers called or he visited the doctor, 'he is like you or me'. The most startling examples of this came from a few employers who reported quite acceptable conduct in patients who at home had behaved in a very disturbed manner.[72]

Before 1983 the rationality of the person with mental illness received little or no support in legislation. For example, nothing was said about consent in the 1959 Mental Health Act. As Philip Bean has indicated, the Percy Commission – the Royal Commission which preceded the 1959 Act – was able to justify compulsory detention from the nature of mental disorders themselves. That is to say: '... patients may not know they are ill, and if they are unwilling to receive the form of care considered necessary there was a strong likelihood that unwillingness was due to a lack of appreciation of their condition, deriving from the mental disorder itself'.[73]

In other words, as Bean neatly summarizes the argument, by definition mental patients were considered to be unable to give consent. The 1983 Act, by contrast, introduced a perspective in which consent was given a due place as a legitimate principle, though it has hardly succeeded in eliminating conflicting definitions of consent, and some would argue that the new consent procedures 'have not shifted the relative power of medical practitioners in terms of their patients where the one is seen as knowledgeable, responsible and rational and the other is not. The onus is still on the patient to show he is rational or aware unless proven otherwise.'[74] From the standpoint of relatives' associations, however, it is precisely the enlargement of patients' rights that has sometimes proved detrimental to patient well-being. In his discussion of patients' rights Bean acknowledges that 'as a method of promoting social change, rights are of limited value. On the one hand they can improve the patient's perception of himself, prevent intrusion and, perhaps, set standards. On the other they rarely promote new, more humane, and perhaps even more efficient methods of handling patients.' The problem here is that patients' rights and patient care derive from different sources:

There is one view that a man should be protected from those who could care for him, for all are prone to abuse him. The other view suggests that patient care deals with the whole person and requires direct intervention in aspects of his life. The former can be traced to a Kantian view that paternalism is the greater evil, or to Mill where the sovereignty of the individual is paramount, the latter from a view that mental illness is debilitating and to cure the patient becomes an ethically justified task.[75]

Arguably, it is, however, a narrow interpretation of rights that enforces this division. On a broader understanding of rights that is concerned not merely with civil but also with *social* rights, and that displays a concern with the person in the various facets of his existence – for example, with the provision of opportunities for him to engage in productive work – and, just as importantly, with the rights of relatives to be accorded proper recognition in their tasks as carers and to receive adequate support, the severity of the antinomy between rights and care may at the very least be softened. Indeed it is precisely because some relatives have been isolated in their tasks, and the social rights of patients and relatives neglected, that relatives' associations have sometimes been forced into reactive positions. In such beleaguered and lonely conditions of existence it is scarcely surprising that the National Schizophrenia Fellowship should report that anxious relatives not infrequently resort to the police as the agency seemingly most willing to intervene and the most promising route to the official legitimation of the tribulations that beset them.[76]

The 'Contract Culture'

The framework in which the British government proposes to provide renewed impetus to the transformation of the mental patient (person) into the person (mental patient), and establish the structures and procedures through which it can be securely accomplished, with benefits to consumers and carers alike, is set out in the policy discussions and legislation that have followed in the wake of the Griffiths Report. The broad thrust of the new policies is familiar enough. The day of the 'bureaucratic, encompassing state' is now deemed to be over and public-service provision will henceforth be consumer- rather than producer-led. As has been pointed out, quite the most radical thing about Sir Roy Griffiths's report is that he took as his starting-point not so much the organization and delivery of *services*, as the needs of the individual. His assumption was that 'members of the priority groups are disadvantaged, therefore they need someone to look after their interests; an agent to ensure that services are provided but not necessarily to provide them directly'.[77] Instead of providing authorities we will therefore now have enabling authorities, placing more weight on case management and social-care planning, and stimulating a competitive market in social welfare in place of the more traditional producer-led system of provision. In the development of a 'mixed economy' of care, and of a 'contract culture', it is envisaged that the competitive stimulus of the market will provide more efficient mechanisms for reducing costs and for improving the quality of care. The demise of the monopolistic system of provision will offer consumers wider choice and make it more likely that they will find a service which meets their needs.

The White Paper *Caring for People* set out the government's response to the Griffiths Report, and the changes proposed in this and other White Papers have now been enshrined in the NHS and Community Care Act 1990. Under the new legislation, local authorities will now largely act as brokers in the planning and coordination of community care and are charged with responsibility for developing a mixed economy of care, to include voluntary and private services. At the core of the new arrangements, which are being phased in over a three-year period, is a system of case management in which case managers (most likely social workers, home-care organizers and community psychiatric nurses) will identify people in need of formal care; assess individual needs; act as brokers in the planning of care; monitor the quality of care; and regularly review the need for care. Since April 1991 local authorities have been in receipt of a specific grant for mental health services from central government, made available to them on the basis of social-care plans agreed with the appropriate district health authorities.

A number of concerns have been expressed about the future of the much-vaunted consumer in the 'contract culture'. For example, though the case-management function is certainly a promising one, it may also prove conflictual. Pressure on resources and on budgetary management may generate tensions between a client advocacy role and a management and allocation role, with the result that the scope for advocating the preferences of individual service users may be much reduced.[78] An additional source of concern is that the pluralism envisaged by the new proposals is not guaranteed. Though the 'contract culture' will provide more scope for voluntary organizations, in the competitive market-place the smaller agencies may find themselves squeezed out. Moreover:

Contracts between social service departments and the voluntary sector will probably concentrate on the most concrete schemes (accommodation and day care) at the expense of less visible, more innovative ideas such as 'user participation' and advocacy. While the new policy may reasonably divert public money towards services that have proven track records, it may unreasonably narrow consumer choice and impoverish community care.[79]

Furthermore, in the competition for scarce resources voluntary organizations may be driven to accept contracts for services 'on the cheap', with detrimental effects on the quality of care for the consumer. So, for example, the regional director for a national mental health charity has recently argued that we are witnessing a gradual 'voluntarization' of the welfare state, a process in which voluntary organizations are being used as an insidious tool by the government in the privatization of public services.[80]

There is, it has been remarked, 'something of an irony in the fact that in the terminology of contracting, the "client" is no longer the user, but has become the local authority department managing the contract'. Indeed much of the debate in the wake of the Griffiths Report 'has been dominated by discussions about modes of provision rather than the importance of ensuring choice and influence for the consumer'.[81] Though the preoccupation with consumerism is a product of disenchantment with the bureaucratic forms of the welfare state, consumerism as envisaged by Griffiths does not necessarily promise participation. Consumerism implies 'choice in deciding whether we wish to "buy" or not but true participation . . . as partnership and sharing in common, does not necessarily follow'.[82] Traditionally mental health service development has been based on the authority of professional knowledge but the rationale for a more democratic approach has been clearly stated: 'The mental health field is not one where experts know best. There is no single body of knowledge that informs the service and many different theoretical and practical perspectives are employed to help an individual.' In addition, given that the experience of mental illness involves a considerable degree of loss of control, 'if contact with mental health workers further limits or prevents people gaining control over their lives, then the legitimacy of the service is challenged'.[83]

In reality, it has been claimed, the government is operating with a highly stunted notion of the consumer. Though there have been some encouraging reports of mental health user groups working with purchasing authorities in a consultative capacity and playing a significant role in the planning and monitoring of services, for the most part the internal market in health services has so far turned out to be not a market driven by consumers at all but 'a highly managed market, driven by negotiations between managers of purchasing health authorities and managers of provider units', in effect a managerial paternalism in place of the old medical paternalism.[84] Similar uncertainties surround the debate about quality assurance in welfare services and the flurry of efforts to provide scientific backing for the assessment of quality. It hardly needs saying that quality is a notoriously slippery concept and some experiments in the evaluation and promotion of consumer satisfaction emit a strong odour of public relations, appropriate enough perhaps to the world of commerce, but hardly to the sphere of welfare in which a genuine concern with consumer well-being must endeavour to promote equality and empowerment.[85] Only by placing the empowerment of service users squarely on the agenda for reform, it has been argued, can we ensure that the consumer 'turns out to be a lively, talkative, participating individual, not just a passive recipient of improved *marketing*'.[86]

The new reforms call out for effective inter-agency collaboration and, as has rightly been said, failure to provide it 'will lead to such potential chaos that service users' needs will be less well served in future than they are now'.[87] However, *Caring for People* was decidedly vague about the mechanisms of collaboration between health and social-care agencies. In the light of the long history of administrative fragmentation and of professional and ideological rivalry in the organization of mental health care, this is a matter of some moment. Responsibility for mental health care is, for example, still very unclear. Though local authorities have been nominated as the 'lead agency' for community care, health-authority control over the specific grant for mental health implies that 'the money could be withheld if a proposed community project does not suit a medical model'.[88] For these reasons, also, there is potential scope for conflict between consultant-led services and services organized on a case-management model. At present medical staff largely make their own decisions in the designation of key workers. 'Will it be enough, as one consultant quipped, to ignore the new proposals for community care and simply rename key workers as case managers? Or will social services want more say?'[89]

But the central problem is the allocation of resources. For some time there have been widespread allegations of asset-stripping, whereby funds acquired from the sale of mental hospitals are siphoned into other areas of the health service to the detriment of community mental health care, and these concerns have not been allayed by the refusal of the government to endorse proposals to 'ring-fence' funds for the care of people with chronic mental illness. Thus one director of social services envisages 'some departments spending the specific grant for mental illness on child care and justifying this action by calling it preventative psychiatry'.[90] The sum allotted to the specific grant is in any case paltry and the National Schizophrenia Fellowship calculated in 1991 that even if the national grant for that year of £30m had been paid in full (which it was not), it would have provided for the care of only three thousand people with schizophrenia. Mental health, particularly that section of it which provides for the care of people with long-term mental illness in the community, bids fair to perpetuate its historical role as the Cinderella service. For community mental health care to transcend its pauperized existence, the government would need dramatically to increase

... the proportion of the £1.4bn NHS mental health budget that is spent on local mental health services. At present over half is spent on the 40,000 psychiatric patients remaining in hospital. If we conservatively estimate that about 180,000 (0.5 per cent) of the 36 million adult population of England suffer from severe forms of mental illness then less than half the total expenditure reaches the 78 per cent of severely disabled patients who live in the community.[91]

Against this background, it is hard to disagree with the conclusion that recent developments in mental health policy 'represent something of a "double-edged sword" at this stage. They can be used either dramatically to improve the autonomy and dignity of service users or further deny them choice and status in our crowded society.'[92] A recent discussion from the King's Fund College has set out some of the shifts in orientation, and possible futures, which the development of the 'contract culture' might permit (Figure 3). Clearly, the delivery of such futures is dependent upon the appropriate allocation of resources and Figure 4 sketches the interaction between value orientations and resources.

	Now	Possible future
User views	see selves as disabled/ desire for conventional service	see selves as citizens/ demand for social change and individual support
Social perspectives	caring, altruistic, Victorian	modern, individualistic, holistic
Professional views	part of the system	struggling to develop autonomy for users
Political options	incorporated provision	tolerance, diversity, 'green' solutions

Figure 3

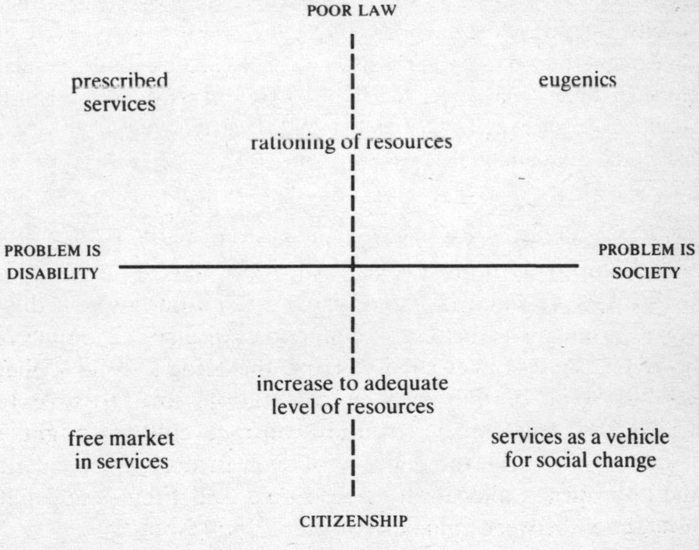

POOR LAW

prescribed
services

rationing of resources

PROBLEM IS
DISABILITY

eugenics

PROBLEM IS
SOCIETY

increase to adequate
level of resources

free market
in services

services as a vehicle
for social change

CITIZENSHIP

Figure 4

Reproduced from Hawker and Ritchie, 1990

The promise that is held out is of a framework for social care which parts historical company with narrow patient-bound conceptions of the subjects of care and locates health-care needs within a richer and more nuanced understanding of the social needs of the person. In breaking from professional and institutional monopolies, the 'contract culture' offers potential scope for a far more pluralistic and accountable array of service forms. But we may be justly sceptical as to whether it will promote a real step forward in the revaluation of people with mental illness and their struggle for citizenship, or simply deliver the renewal of outdoor relief under more diverse auspices.

6 'Give Us Some Hope!'

The Conflicts of Deinstitutionalization

The problem of an asylum is the problem of a society. In recent years politicians have berated the mental hospitals for their inertia and resistance to change but polemics like this are misleading for what they imply of the independence and autonomy of the mental hospital. The Victorian asylum was not some lurid construction of psychiatric ambitions but pre-eminently a social product, and it became what it did because powerful social forces willed it to do so. The real questions, then, are not about dismantling the mental hospitals as such but about the prospects for manufacturing the social and political will adequate to the task of bringing back and reassimilating into society what had been thrust into the mental hospital. The paradox of the mental hospital, Elizabeth Bott told us, is that it has always been 'in a situation of trying to help an individual on behalf of a society which does not recognize its wish to get rid of the individual as well as to help him'.[1]

Yet, of course, it has not quite always been so. Today it is perhaps easy to be forgetful of the optimism that was invested in the asylum in the first half of the nineteenth century in which the asylum took on for a time

. . . a status as panacea equivalent to the steam engine, the rights of man, or the spread of universal knowledge. Madness could after all be cured, reason could be restored. The asylum was the magic engine in which this could be achieved. The asylum superintendent or doctor was the new exorcist for a scientific society. Those visiting institutions such as the York Retreat might have been pardoned for exclaiming that they had seen the future and it worked.[2]

But by the closing decades of the century if the asylum was still a panacea it was a panacea of a drastically different kind, and the 'noble dream' of restoring reason to the victims of derangement had been largely shattered. By this time the existing asylums were bursting at the seams, wings and annexes had been added, and a new round of asylum construction put under way. Whatever benefits the asylum may have delivered to this expanding population, the notion that 'all but a small proportion might actually be cured had essentially been abandoned' and the asylum 'came to be thought of not as an engine for cures but more as a territory over which the alienist held suzerainty, an imperial colony or fiefdom to be managed with justice, economy and administrative flair'.[3]

Very properly, the new history of psychiatry, inspired to a considerable extent by the writings of Michel Foucault, is now being written not simply as a history of disease or affliction but as a history of power relationships; not surprisingly, within this unfolding saga the question of psychiatric power, and in particular the hold of the psychiatric profession over the empire of the asylum, looms large.[4] Yet among other things the lessons of deinstitutionalization show very clearly that there are other forms of power to reckon with apart from psychiatric power. Displays of psychiatric conceit and self-congratulation have, perhaps, masked the extent to which psychiatrists have not so much been overlords of independent fiefdoms as lieutenants in a politically sanctioned operation in the disposal of the socially unwanted and unproductive. As Bott's paradox implies, while the psychiatric profession may have lent its authority to the mutation of potentially remediable lunatics into hopeless cases, it was powerfully assisted in doing so by other social forces. Though they may not always have worn them lightly, psychiatrists have generally tended to wear the prejudices of their age.

To appreciate just how embedded is the asylum in a wider field of power relations, and the enormous resistances that are thrown up to the creation of a more promising set of career prospects for people with mental illness, we have only to look at the effects of the Italian psychiatric reform act of 1978, the notorious Law 180, which sought to legislate away the asylum. On the best available evidence it appears that:

1. Contrary to expectations, the reform has not brought about profound changes in the general picture of psychiatric care in Italy.

2. It has lacked coordinated control, and no effort has been made by administrators and politicians to implement it consistently.

3. The planned closure of mental hospitals has only been very partially carried out and in the 'opinion of many practitioners the "quality" of care provided by the psychiatric hospitals today is, except in a few praiseworthy exceptional cases, even worse than that, by no means exemplary, which existed before the reform'.

4. In some places the psychiatric wards in general hospitals have reproduced some of the worst features of the old mental hospitals, such as physical restraint of patients and the indiscriminate use of drugs.

5. The proposed network of alternative services for the care and support of people with long-term mental illness has been poorly developed and widespread recourse has been had to old people's homes and other institutions.[5]

The Italian reformers had rightly seen that the asylum was an instrument of 'emargination' (*emarginazione*), the social process by which socially redundant and unworthy people such as mental patients are isolated and segregated from society, and they aimed to bring about an 'effective dismantling of the hospital structure and an effective abolition of the asylum as a discrete place for canonizing disease and institutionalizing emargination'.[6] By dint of such an exclusive focus on the asylum, however, it largely escaped the reformers' attention that emargination showed rather less discretion over where to make itself felt. As a consequence they found themselves drawn into some rather peculiar alliances. As Richard Mollica explains, 'left-wing ideologues and fiscal conservatives on the right found themselves aligned on the issue of dismantling the asylum' but what the reformers 'did not anticipate was that, once the asylum was dismantled, politicians would refuse to finance a community care system because it would be much more expensive than the former custodial care'.[7]

The Italian reforms have undoubtedly brought about some genuine innovations which have justly received a high international profile. But these are evidently scattered oases in a fragmented system of directionless hospitals, dispossessed of any motivation to change, and porous community psychiatric services. In the effort to achieve comprehensive reform by legislative fiat the reform movement came up against entrenched and widely distributed resistance to providing more hopeful and dignified career prospects for people with mental illness. In the absence of a concerted political and social will to carry such changes through, some things have improved but others, notably and poignantly in the hospitals themselves, have got rather worse. The quick legislative fix has turned out to be anything but that.

Though it would certainly be premature to pronounce on the demise of the asylum, it would appear to have fallen out of favour in many parts of the world. For example, a survey conducted by the European Region of the World Health Organization in 1982 reported that among member countries there was now a clear policy commitment to reducing mental hospitals in size and importance and to shifting the focus of service development from the segregated mental hospital to the community.[8] It would, however, be a mistake to think that in Britain and elsewhere mental hospitals are being scaled-down or closed in answer to some widespread, shared understanding of the failure of the asylum project, a change of governmental heart by which an unreasonable reason has recovered its senses and determined to make amends for the way in which a previous era had invalidated and marginalized the poor and the mad. Critiques of the asylum which have declared an interest in the moral relations of its inmates have as often as not provided a convenient fig-leaf under which to enlist support for changes in policy. Mental health policy has for long been embedded in a complex field of social and political forces and even where we may be tempted to furnish a progressive reading of a given line of innovation, this will never suffice as a complete account. At each point new developments quickly find themselves locked in a conflictual struggle such that what seems to presage a new chapter in the struggle for citizenship and social rights by a disenfranchised group may from an opposing position dangle the prospect of more efficient means of managing the socially marginal and more cost-effective rationalities of disposal. What *can* be said with some certainty is that the conflictual struggles around deinstitutionalization, not least the arguments over how policies of deinstitutionalization are to be understood and defined, are as much a typical product of modern societies as the creation of the asylum itself.[9]

Defending Mr Dick

The awkward and conflictual experience of deinstitutionalization is unquestionably chastening, and it must surely encourage us to view with more sympathy the problems with which the asylum has traditionally had to deal. As a consequence we should look upon the asylum with less acrimony, be less inclined to regard it as a malevolent actor and accordingly be more modest in our expectations. But just because we witness the re-creation of what seem to be old problems in new places, we should not for that reason be tempted to retreat into traditional solutions and residual styles of thought. Above all, perhaps, we must avoid the tendency to tunnel vision, to resolving the numerous variations in the social fate of people with long-term mental illness in the community into a single image or slogan, and endeavour to maintain a more nuanced and differentiated perspective. So, for example, from some journalistic accounts it would appear that the figure of the homeless person under the arches is to be made to carry the burden of the consequences of community-care policies as a whole. Community care, such images encourage us to believe, was a well-intentioned policy that has gone awry and can now be judged a failure. The homeless mentally ill are certainly a neglected group and it is wholly necessary that concerned observers should persist in imaging their predicaments; but if we are to reach towards a more differentiated picture of the fortunes of the long-term mentally ill in the community it is equally necessary that we introduce countervailing images. So, for example, a recent follow-up study in the London area of more than five hundred patients with schizophrenia who had been discharged from hospital over a ten-year period revealed that at the point of follow-up the great majority had permanent homes and only one was in prison. Moreover, less than 1 per cent either of the patients themselves or their relatives requested the patient's return to in-patient care.[10]

By contrast with the political *réclame*, the social reality of the prospects genuinely available to people with long-term mental illness in the community is, of course, bathetic. For want, among other things, of worthwhile and secure employment opportunities the identities of former mental patients are, as we have seen, only precariously grounded in social life. Much remains to be done, not least in the provision of services that 'are local and accessible, comprehensive, flexible, culturally and ethnically appropriate, accountable, equitably distributed, and based on need and that offer continuity of treatment and care'.[11] The experience of the hundred or so community mental health centres, arguably the anchors of a local mental health service, which have been established in Britain in the past few years has not been altogether encouraging and some recent research suggests that clients with long-term mental illness may easily be neglected in favour of a more promising clientele.[12]

None the less there are innumerable examples of good practice and an abundance of projects, small and large, which provide indications of what, under a more hospitable political climate, could be helped to grow more widely. Perhaps the most striking feature of the changes in the mental health culture over the past decade or so is that we have been helped to recognize the strengths of people with mental health problems. As one distinguished lay observer commented recently, 'in a previous era no one would have believed that people diagnosed as schizophrenic or manic depressive could eventually be capable of providing advice on policy and planning. But this is just what is now happening.'[13]

We can mark some of these shifts in consciousness in an organization like the National Schizophrenia Fellowship which for a number of years maintained an intransigently patronizing attitude towards its constituents, tending to represent them as either pathetic or dangerous, and seeming to care rather little for promoting their independence and dignity. However, there are welcome signs that the Fellowship has now reassessed its orientation and a recent annual review no longer speaks of 'schizophrenics' or 'sufferers', but instead describes how the Fellowship seeks to support 'men and women with experience of severe mental illness, their carers and relatives', and to foster a 'positive response to mental illness'.[14] We might, perhaps, suggest that the influence of Betsey Trotwood has made itself felt within Fellowship circles, in the robust defence that she gives of Mr Dick. Readers of Dickens's *David Copperfield* will recall that when David first met Betsey Trotwood she had been a generous champion of Mr Dick for some ten years, not least in his endeavour to complete his Memorial, a labour which was constantly interrupted by the appearance in it of King Charles I, some of whose troubles after his head had been cut off had mysteriously been put into Mr Dick's head:

'Is he – is Mr Dick – I ask because I don't know, aunt – is he at all out of his mind, then?' I stammered; for I felt I was on dangerous ground.

'Not a morsel,' said my aunt.

'Oh, indeed!' I observed faintly.

'If there is anything in the world,' said my aunt, with great decision and force of manner, 'that Mr Dick is not, it's that.'

I had nothing better to offer than another timid, 'Oh, indeed!'

'He has been *called* mad,' said my aunt. 'I have a selfish pleasure in saying he has been called mad, or I should not have had the benefit of his society and advice for these last ten years and upwards . . .'

'So long as that?' I said.

'And nice people they were, who had the audacity to call him mad,' pursued my aunt. 'Mr Dick is a sort of distant connection of mine; it doesn't matter how; I needn't enter into that. If it hadn't been for me, his own brother would have shut him up for life . . . A proud fool! . . . Because his brother was a little eccentric – though he is not half so eccentric as a good many people he didn't like to have him visible about his house, and sent him away to some private asylum-place . . .'[15]

We should not, of course, expect a relatives' association like the National Schizophrenia Fellowship to be unreservedly sympathetic towards Betsey Trotwood's style of reflection and it is scarcely surprising (and from the standpoint of a pressure group doubtless necessary) that in some of its proclamations the voice of Betsey Trotwood should on occasions cede to that of Mr Dick's brother. To understand why this should be so we need among other things to take account of the singular disposition of Mr Dick, for not quite everyone with experience of severe mental illness has the charm and good humour of Mr Dick. Though it is wholly necessary to offer a robust defence of those like Mr Dick who can be helped to lead relatively independent lives in the community, it is equally important to recognize that the concerns of Mr Dick's brother possess a legitimate claim in respect of a minority of patients who stand in need of more specialized and protected conditions of long-term care, for example in medium secure units. If there has some-times been a tendency to project a minority of 'hard cases' as representing the whole, it needs to be understood that the promotion of a 'positive response to mental illness', and the defence of the interests of the more capable majority, can only be secured through a reciprocal acknowledgement and defence of the needs of the more vulnerable minority.

Comrades or Incurables?

Mirrored in some of the contemporary alarms about the fate of the mentally ill in the community is the unresolved problem in the history of the asylum presented by that burgeoning group of patients who failed to live up to the curative aspirations that were entertained for them. The history of the Victorian asylum disclosed two stark options, that the patient be deemed either curable or incurable. For those patients unable to conform with the standards of normality and social achievement laid before them, their psychiatric keepers had no alternative recourse in their moral frameworks but to identify them in their broken individuality as incurable cases. For these chronic mental patients there was no viable social place, no means of securing a dignified niche for themselves either in social life or in the moral concepts that society at large entertained of them.

In the era of deinstitutionalization, pharmacological enthusiasts and sociological critics of the asylum have joined forces in furbishing a modern version of curative aspirations, the latter in entertaining the hope that the whole problem of chronic mental illness could be put down to the legacy of the asylum and that if we could only get the moral relations right the problem would disappear. As we now know, this was a forlorn hope, not least because we have been unable to get the moral relations right and some people with mental illness are as demoralized in social life as ever they were in the asylum, but also because (whatever the arguments about the causes of disability in an illness like schizophrenia) many such people are indisputably intrinsically vulnerable and in need of long-term support.

In the face of these perplexities we may be tempted to reproduce the doctrine of the 'hopeless case' and the biologically flawed individual, and to hanker after the asylum as though it had once offered a solution to the placelessness of the poor and insane. So, for example, some of the campaigns that have highlighted the isolation of former mental patients in the community following the closure of hospitals have tended to assert the profile of rather inadequate and incompetent people, uncared for in their illness. Because the identities of former mental patients in the community are insecurely grounded, they are inevitably vulnerable, both in themselves and, just as importantly, to misrecognition by others. Confronted by these not infrequently uncertain and perplexed people, some observers have taken fright and decided that many former mental patients are unable to cope in social life. But the evidence we looked at earlier, and the users of services we encountered in Chapter 2, suggests that this is only a very partial and often highly misleading account of how things stand. What must compel our attention is not so much natural inadequacy as an understanding of structurally produced inadequacy, the social forces that conspire to render the person with a history of mental illness incompetent and demoralized. Consider, for example, the case of Ian, a man in his late thirties with a long history of schizophrenic illness. The management of his illness has now been brought under control and his main concern at present is to identify some form of socially valued project in which he could play a useful part. He has, however, been disheartened to discover that his psychiatrist continues to impress upon him a view of himself as only a community mental patient who must be 'content to be on the sick and cope and manage as best' he can. Ian now speaks of hating himself:

Well, I don't know about hating myself, it's just people's attitudes to mental illness. They won't give you a job, they won't give you any sort of responsibility. I applied to do voluntary work at a place where they look after kids and you go and help out generally, and I applied and told them I had been a student teacher and told them I had had nervous trouble and been in hospital, and they never wrote back and never offered me a position. So that was voluntary work!

Reporting on some of his recent research, Richard Warner has posed the question, 'Have we now traded the earlier institutional neurosis for a new existential neurosis which will similarly stand in the way of recovery?'

Most professionals would argue that a person diagnosed as mentally ill needs to understand that he or she is mentally ill in order to benefit from treatment. Our study, however, indicates that a sense of mastery over life is essential if someone is to get any benefit from the knowledge that he or she suffers from a 'mental illness'. But one of the consequences of accepting that one is 'mentally ill' is a loss of the sense of self-mastery and self-esteem. This is the Catch 22 of being 'mentally ill' in Western society – that one loses the very psychological strength which is necessary for recovery in the process of gaining knowledge and insight. Conventional treatment programmes, moreover, with their element of control, cannot help much in replacing that lost sense of mastery.[16]

An astute discussion from the USA of poverty and disability nicely lambasts the tendency of the prevailing health-care model to obscure understanding of structurally produced incapacity: 'Fix the illness first and then free the person to triumph over adversity! Unhappily, for far too many, the model does not work. For many disabled, physically dependent, mentally ill and poor people whose lives are marginal, we need new models' and must learn to 'understand that trying to change health policy independent of social policy must inevitably fail our patients and our practices'.[17] For the homeless mentally ill on the streets of New York, however, new models are evidently a scarce commodity and to assist these unfortunate people the authorities have recently introduced an 'aggressive outreach intervention' programme in which psychiatrists take to the streets and are 'empowered to order the police to transport persons meeting the programme's criteria to the emergency room of the psychiatric hospital for further evaluation and, if indicated, hospitalization'. Stern talk of 'aggressive outreach intervention' gives the impression that something is being done and indeed the programme staff took pride in the fact that it appeared to produce 'some public recognition that government officials and mental health professionals cared for these people and were willing to do something about the problem'.[18] Such rhetoric should not, however, blind us as to the essential *passivity* of this style of intervention: in tearing the culprits off the streets nothing has been done to address the structural deficiencies, not least the need for supported housing, that have at the very least exacerbated the difficulties of former mental patients in the community. The British government has not so far felt disposed to authorize a similar programme though there have been worrying indications that it might.[19] The problems of the homeless mentally ill are a special case of the structural impoverishment that enfolds a much wider circle of people with a history of mental illness, but what vexes government agencies is not the invisible demoralization and poverty of people like Ian but those miscreants who have the effrontery to make their poverty persistently *visible* in public places and thereby taunt the 'caring' self-images that authorities are eager to project of themselves.

If we are to avoid reproducing the doctrine of the 'hopeless case' both in the real world of outcomes and in our own perceptions and reflexes, we shall need to proceed from the ethical commitment identified by Manfred Bleuler and attempt to recognize in the former mental patient a 'fellow sufferer and comrade in arms', rather than someone whom 'a pathological heritage or a degenerate brain has rendered inaccessible, inhuman, different or strange'.[20] From this point of view we shall want as far as possible to opt for person- and citizen-centred concepts and approaches, rather than patient- and disorder-centred ones. In so doing, the characteristic erosion of the former mental patient's social identity and sense of worth will have a particular claim on our attention, for as James Glass describes, it is

. . . the self's being in public, its work, its interpersonal relations, and the inevitable politics of persons, institutions and bureaucracies that drive troubled individuals into feelings of failure and hopelessness, particularly if those individuals have already been funnelled through mental hospitals and the professional mental health care network. After such a journey the self experiences itself as so sick that even to think of itself as healthy and worthwhile requires an almost heroic movement from pessimism and dejection to at least some belief in the possibility of transformation. It is the feeling of fragmentation, placelessness, and loss of rights that the chronic patient strives to escape.[21]

Proposals to put citizen- and person-centred concerns at the top of the agenda have, however, recently met with a frosty reception. According to Kathleen Jones, for example, the 'present disorganization and lack of focus' in mental health services is to be explained by the influence of the ideology of 'normalization' which consists, so she tells us, 'of the conviction that if people with handicaps are treated like everyone else, their handicap will cease to be of importance to them and to society'.[22] The trouble with 'normalization',

Jones claims, is that it pays insufficient heed to the disabilities of people with mental illness and their need for specialized support. As a result

an attitude which has its origin in a desire to improve conditions is very easily twisted into an excuse for ignoring real needs: public services assume that no special provision is necessary for chronic patients discharged from hospital because 'they are the same as anyone else, aren't they?', and provided they have a roof over their heads, and a pittance to live on, they can get on with the rich potential of community life for themselves.[23]

Now, while it is not of course to be denied that practices of the type Jones derides exist, it can hardly be claimed, as Jones appears to want to, that they are at all *representative*. Indeed, much more typical is the case we described of the former mental patients in Bath under threat of eviction from their homes. And what we found there was a bold experiment by the local health authority to combine specialized structured support with conditions of ordinary community living, now undercut by a judiciary which has declared that these ostensible private citizens are in reality mental patients. Far from being told that they were just the same as everyone else, these people were being told that because of their disabilities they could not be accorded the rights and recognitions enjoyed by most other members of the community. Those who scorn normalization are those who want to unmask the mental patient behind the façade of the ordinary person and retrieve him for mental patienthood. Jones in her insistence on the deficiencies of former mental patients lends support to those who, like the Master of the Rolls, appear to want to challenge the presumptions of such people to aspire to become something other than mental patients, and return them to their rightful place as second-class citizens, permanent denizens of some hospital annexe.

The issue is not to dispute 'difference', and the need for specialized support and refuge, but to locate approaches to these within a more aggressive challenge to the pauperization of mental patient lives and to the prevailing attitudes that diminish and degrade them. The argument of normalization theorists is not that there is not a real difference to be identified but that this difference need not signal the enfolding of the subject in a web of psychiatric domestication.[24] As Jonathan Miller put it recently, research has repeatedly shown that 'the destiny of people who are assigned the role of mental patient depends on the degree to which those around them recognize and respect how normal they are, rather than how ill they are'.[25] If we have learned that psychiatric disabilities persist even after the patient has left the asylum, we have surely also learned that the problems of disability and demoralization cannot simply be dealt with in narrow technical terms. The real dispute is not between those who think chronic mental illness has been left behind in the asylum and those who recognize it for what it is, but between those who want to improve the social prospects of people with long-term mental illness, to reclaim them not for mental patienthood but for citizenship, and those who settle for a highly restricted vision of the 'place' of people with mental illness in social life in which, like Ian, they must be 'content to be on the sick and cope and manage' as best they can. If we are to take the concerns of someone like Ian seriously, we must attempt to increase the opportunities and power of people with long-term mental illness and assert a strategic direction for the elimination of poverty that looks beyond social-security benefits and attempts to foster the conditions in which they and other disadvantaged groups can be helped to play valued and productive roles.[26]

Mention of new opportunities and power for people with long-term mental illness is, however, precisely what alarms some established hierarchies. As we have seen, it would be mistaken to account for the instabilities and ambiguities consequent upon the re-entry into social life of a group of people who had previously been excluded from it, solely by reference to governmental failures to provide adequate resources for the implementation of the new policies. It needs to be recognized also that some such instabilities and ambiguities are an inevitable, and wholly necessary, consequence of the attempt to overturn traditional ways of disposing of the mentally ill. Deinstitutionalization implicates rather more than the administrative substitution of one locus of care for another, and invites also a drastic reshaping of the ways in which we think about, describe and, in particular, relate to people with a history of mental illness. Those who appear determined to show that community-care policies have failed are frequently those who find the challenges of a more egalitarian mental health culture distasteful and threatening. Consider for example the antics of SANE

(Schizophrenia: A National Emergency), a pressure group which has lobbied extensively against the closures of mental hospitals. In 1989 travellers in the south of England were treated to the display in railway stations and bus shelters of a number of large posters, each of them portraying a thin, elongated and slightly distorted face, with captions down the centre such as:

> HE THINKS HE'S JESUS
> YOU THINK HE'S A KILLER
> THEY THINK HE'S FINE

or

> HE HEARS VOICES
> YOU HEAR LIES
> THEY HEAR NOTHING

And under each of them the slogan 'STOP THE MADNESS'. It does not require a very astute student of semiotics to discern that what is being established here is a view of the person with schizophrenia as irretrievably mad and dangerous, a view that plays on popular fears of mental illness in order to put in question the wisdom of attempts to resettle the mentally ill in the community. On the logic of this campaign, a social policy of community psychiatric care can scarcely claim much rational basis in the face of such an intractable malady.

Critics of this display remonstrated on the grounds that, among other things, SANE had presented a travesty of people who have experienced a schizophrenic illness, and they tried instead to assert a more positive approach that stressed the ordinary human qualities of such people.[27] These criticisms are, of course, well-founded but they perhaps betrayed a rather naïve understanding of the motives behind the campaign. For the irony is that the sorts of people who promote campaigns like this recognize all too well the implications of the shift in perspective from the mental patient to the person that policies of deinstitutionalization have introduced, and are bent upon eschewing the changes and complications of relationship that must follow from them. One of the dangers of the current moment, it might be said, is that former mental patients are becoming 'too much like us'. From this point of view, representations of the schizophrenic as a malign or alien character help to re-establish the distance that has been eroded and to reassert a more traditional scheme of things. This may also help us understand why the image of the homeless mental patient has come to figure so largely in attacks on community-care policies. Far from being an affront, the 'discovery' of the destitute mental patient is something of a relief. By contrast with the *arrivistes* of the user and self-advocacy movements, the homeless mentally ill are displaced fragments from a familiar dramatic script that seem to beckon the restoration of an older psychiatric order.

It is certainly encouraging to discover that SANE has now embarked upon some rather more promising projects – for example it has recently established a national telephone helpline for the families of people with schizophrenia – but the drift of its proclamations tends to favour technical above social solutions to the problems of severe mental illness. 'Never in the history of research into the workings of the brain,' we learn, 'has there been such hope that the cause or causes of this illness will soon be discovered. What is known is that schizophrenia is most likely to be a biochemical disorder of the brain.'[28] Alas, what is actually known is rather more complicated than the writer suggests and the riposte to this type of thinking has recently been forcefully delivered in an address by the President of the Royal College of Psychiatrists. If psychiatrists try to sell what has been termed 'mindless' psychiatry to the public, J. L. T. Birley suggests, they do both their patients and themselves a disservice. The attempt to disguise mental illness as 'just like any other sort of illness' is, as he remarks, the product of a long history of over-simplification and he believes that his colleagues should now 'abandon the approach of promoting psychiatry as a special form of physical illness'. What especially concerns him is that those who prosecute these misconceptions may aggravate the devaluation of people with mental illness and obstruct their endeavours to transcend their condition as a 'submerged and stigmatized group'. Appositely, Birley explicitly links his worries about devaluation with the history of 'deadly compassion' that we discussed earlier, not because he thinks that the history is likely to repeat itself but because in an economic and demographic climate in which in all probability there will be increased competition for scarce health resources, hard choices will have to be made and people with long-term mental illness are therefore going to need all the support and recognition as integral members of the community that they can get.[29] Historically, we have tended to see people with mental illness as secondary sorts of people and to debate rival schemes for dealing with such secondary people. If we are to protect the interests of these vulnerable citizens in the future, however, we are going to require something rather more challenging than the renewal of a tradition of care conferred by those who are persons in the full sense upon those who are not.

Grounds for Hope?

Are we able, I asked at the beginning of this book, to give people with mental illness something to hope for? In attempting to surmount the legacy of the Victorian asylum we are trying to bring people with mental illness back from the heath. As Michael Ignatieff says, the heath is among other things '. . . the vast grey space of state confinement. On the wards of psychiatric hospitals, the attendants shovel gruel into the mouths of vacant or unwilling patients; in the dispensaries, the drug trays are prepared . . . Needs are met, but souls are dishonoured. Natural man – the "poor, bare, forked animal" – is maintained; the social man wastes away.'[30]

But can our social arrangements satisfy the needs of people with mental illness, provide the conditions in which they do not simply survive but flourish? The irony of the history of deinstitutionalization is, as we have seen, that the social man may waste away still further and we must face the possibility that by investing the project of closing the asylum with the hope of creating a more promising set of career prospects for people with mental illness, we shall find that these historical hopes of ours are mere fellow-travellers on a vehicle that is bound elsewhere. The real question, I believe, is about the grounding of hope. These hopes are certainly clinically well enough grounded, but as to whether they are politically securely grounded, grounded that is in an accurate recognition of the type of outcome that is at all likely within the antagonistic processes of a modern society, is quite a different question.[31]

'According to our present-day concept,' writes Manfred Bleuler, 'people with schizophrenia founder under the same difficulties with which all of us struggle all our lives.'[32] But that is actually rather an ancient concept and Manfred Bleuler himself speaks from his own religious convictions. Modern societies have, however, to a considerable extent lost contact with the moral sources through which we are 'moved by a strong sense that human beings are eminently *worth* helping or treating with justice, a sense of their dignity or value'. The modern cultural predicament which attracted Nietzsche's scorn is one in which 'morality can only be powered negatively, where there can be no such thing as beneficence powered by an affirmation of the recipient as a being of value'.[33] From this point of view, those who declare that people with mental illness are *in* the community but not an integral part *of* the community may know something which those of us who entertain communal hopes are prone to overlook. They have glimpsed 'a ferocious law which states: "to him that has, will be given; from him that has not will be taken away"'. They know that these former asylum inmates are 'only here on a visit, that in a few weeks nothing will remain of them but a handful of ashes in some nearby field and a crossed-out number on a register', and that they will have died in solitude or disappeared, 'without leaving a trace in anyone's memory'.[34] In the grounds of Friern Hospital, adjacent to the field where 2,696 asylum inmates were buried from 1851 to 1873, there stands a memorial to the unknown pauper lunatic.[35] It remains an open question as to whether it will be thought fitting to erect a memorial to the unknown community mental patient of the era of deinstitutionalization.

7 Are 'the Mad' Still with Us?

Asylum Heritage

Time to change tense: closing, closing . . . closed. By the end of 1997, eighty-four out of a total of 121 large mental hospitals open in 1986 will have closed; another fourteen are due to close by the millenium, a small number have not finalized their plans, and eighteen do not intend to close this century. Those that have closed since 1991 include Claybury (at the time of its opening the fifth London County Council pauper lunatic asylum); Friern (former Colney Hatch asylum, the second Middlesex county pauper lunatic asylum); Cane Hill (the third Surrey county pauper lunatic asylum); Central, at Hatton in Warwick (former Warwick county lunatic asylum); Glenside in Bristol; Horton in Epsom (a war hospital during both World Wars); Long Grove, also in Epsom; Middlewood, near Sheffield; Netherne in Surrey, a former London County Council asylum; Roundway in Devizes (former Wiltshire county asylum); Rubery Hill in Birmingham; Stanley Royd in Wakefield (former West Riding asylum); Storthes Hall, Kirkburton, West Yorkshire; and Whittingham in Lancashire (the third Lancashire county asylum). Those in the process of closing include: All Saints, Birmingham (former Winson Green asylum); Bexley in Kent, another London County Countil asylum; Fulbourn in Cambridge; High Royds, the former Menston asylum, in the West Riding; Lancaster Moor (former Lancashire county pauper lunatic asylum); Napsbury, near St Albans, the former county of Middlesex asylum (also a former war hospital); Severalls in Colchester; and Winterton (former Durham county pauper lunatic asylum).[1]

'Not since the Beeching Axe fell on the railways', proclaims Marcus Binney, 'has so large a slice of the nation's public architectural heritage been made so precipitously redundant.'[2] The celebrated Victorian architect Sir George Gilbert Scott, who designed the Albert Memorial and St Pancras Station, early on in his career was progenitor of a number of asylums, for example the Somerset and Bath county asylum, near Wells. And there were other architects who fashioned distinguished careers around the design of asylums, notably G. T. Hine, who designed Claybury, served as consulting architect to the Commissioners in Lunacy, and had a hand in the design or refurbishment of upward of twenty institutions. Yet today we are inclined to view with ambivalence, if not disdain, expressions of aesthetic rapture over the spectacle of these magnificent estates in Victorian lunacy, with their clock-towers, ballrooms, lodges, and in many instances elaborately landscaped grounds, preferring to regard them as the grandiose creations of a society subtended by the Poor Law, a legacy which we have now happily transcended. And it is such disaffection, combined with managerialist apologetics, the eagerness of health authorities to shed the load of the past, avaricious developers, the inadequate planning restrictions of some councils, and brute ignorance of the achievements of nineteenth-century lunacy reform, that in the judgement of attentive conservation groups have resulted in the neglect and sometimes demolition of the architectural legacy of the Victorian asylum, where a programme of sensitive conversion would have been entirely feasible.[3] In some rare but lucky instances, the listed building has been acquired by a housing association for conversion into a low-cost housing scheme; at least two asylum complexes have been absorbed into universities or colleges of higher education; there are plans to convert some into supermarkets, whilst others have been been turned over to developers; in one case part of the site is derelict but used for dog training; another hospital has been standing empty for at least five years awaiting settlement of a dispute between the health authority and the local council over its future, boarded up and deteriorating, a likely prey for vandals. An emerging pattern seems to be that a few listed buildings are retained – the clocktower and the chapel, for example – but those around them are razed.

The Mental Hospital Culture

There can be no doubting the finality of what has taken place. Since Enoch Powell delivered his famous speech, the prolonged interlude between the intimation and the act, during which it was possible to entertain alternative prospects and dilute the severity of what was threatened ('it is our duty to err on the side of ruthlessness'), has been terminated. Still, it would be misleading to conclude that the mental hospital as such has now been vanquished by reformist zeal. Upward of fifty of the large mental hospitals that are closing, or have closed, plan to retain some mental health units on site, though the main building may have been demolished or converted for alternative use. The mental hospital that remained in 1993 was rather different from the institution that it had been in 1986: the average size had reduced from 468 to 223 patients; the proportion of inmates over sixty-five had fallen from 59 per cent to 48 per cent; and there had been a dramatic decline in the average length of stay, down to seventy-six days from a high of 162.[4] These changes are part of a general trend. Though there are certainly far fewer in-patient places for mental illness than there were in the 1950s, the belief that there has been a decline in the availability of asylum for the mentally ill in Britain, James Raftery has argued recently, is largely a myth, and in the post-war period there has in fact been a dramatic increase in the proportion of the population admitted to in-patient psychiatric units.[5] Fewer beds, more people, hence shorter periods of stay.

By and large, the asylum that has closed is the one where people stayed a long time, or came to live permanently. The institutions listed above were among the centrepieces of the Victorian asylum landscape: hierarchical, enclosed, largely self-sufficient communities of mental patients, on whose labour the asylum very largely depended, with staff, one generation from a family often succeeding another in the job, presided over by a medical superintendent who lived in commodious style, in a large house with open fires, with patient labour to fetch and carry coal for him. As David Clark, himself the reforming medical superintendent of one of the old county asylums in the 1950s and 1960s, who succeeded both in transforming the institution and hastening the abolition of his own post, has remarked about English mental hospitals in the period between the wars: 'Everyone knew how mental hospitals should be – custodial but humane – an enclosed world where nothing changed from generation to generation, where long-stay patients and staff grew old together watching cricket, enjoying social events such as balls and dances and regarding innovations with distaste.'[6] However, the placid routine of asylum existence was invariably punctuated by escapes. So, for example, the medical superintendent of Claybury told his committee in 1918 that he regretted to have to report that patient William Stevens:

while on a shopping party to the village at 3.20pm. on the 22 May, effected his escape and got clean away. Attendant Costar and Temporary Attendant Hudgell were in charge of the party, which consisted of 11 patients and 2 attendants . . . This escape should, undoubtedly, never have occurred had the rules of the walking party been properly observed. I find that attendants have been allowing their patients to scatter unnecessarily, and have been permitting them to take meals at 'The Village Rest'. I have severely reprimanded Attendant Costar, and rules are now appended to the walking list as reminder to attendants . . .[7]

However, walking parties continued to present problems, for later in the year the acting medical superintendent reports that 'while on a Boundary Walk consisting of 90 patients and 5 attendants, Benjamin Godfrey and John Smith hid behind a hedge and succeeded in effecting their escape'. The medical superintendent thinks that these boundary walks in such large numbers are 'unwieldy', furthermore he has heard that they are unpopular with the patients, and he proposes that the size of the walking party be reduced to fifty, in the charge of four attendants.[8]

Mental hospital admission wards were often attractive, with flowers, curtains and cooperative patients, and the visitor walked through the main door of the asylum along 'shining floors and spotless corridors'. As David Clark describes, it was only when the visitor 'penetrated further, into the back corridors, the airing courts and the wards that the vast mass of human hopelessness became apparent'. There were, in every mental hospital:

the 'back wards', filled with people for whom hope had been abandoned – the 'chronics', the 'back ward patients', the incurables and the intractables . . . Anyone who came to work in a mental hospital – nurse, doctor or orderly – had in due course to come to terms with the back wards. They learned to tolerate the squalor, smell and brutality and hopelessness – or, if they could not, left the asylum service.[9]

Of course, the unmaking or unpicking of this social and therapeutic order has been happening gradually for a good while, at least since the Mental Health Act of 1930. In the 1920s, at Colney Hatch, there was already talk of open-door wards and of unblocking ground-floor windows. In March 1922 the medical superintendent reported that the 'experiment of serving tea in a household manner in the wards' had been tried on one female ward and one male ward, and had been 'entirely successful and much appreciated by the patients'.[10] Considering a proposal in the following year that patients be given lockers to store their private belongings, the deputy medical superintendent reckoned that about one in three of the inmates would be fit to have one, and would appreciate its possession.[11]

Arguably, there has throughout the history of the asylum always been a counter-movement to that which turned mental patients into permanent cases. Historians have started to turn their attention to the process of 'casting out', examining the pressures and circumstances that led families to decide to commit their relatives to the asylum – but there was evidently also a process of 'bringing back', initiated by relatives themselves.[12] In 1923 the medical superintendent of Hanwell asylum noted that of the seventy-three applications by relatives for patients to be discharged under the terms of the 1890 Lunacy Act, forty-four had been successful, though he was inclined to think that in many of these cases either the home circumstances or the relatives themselves were inadequate to cope with the patient. Thirteen of the forty-four were men:

Female relatives took out 6 elderly men to nurse them at home; mothers (in one case an aunt) took out 4 weak-minded sons; a son took out his father who is a drunkard & a gambler; a sister took out an elderly imbecile; two parents, both having been insane, took out a weak-minded son . . .

Female discharges, the medical superintendent felt, presented a different problem to the men:

Women are anxious to have their male folk at home and nurse them there. The male wants his wife at home to look after the house and children . . . Thus only one man took his wife out to look after her, whereas 11 took them out for housekeeping reasons and one to get her back to France if possible. Mothers took out weak-minded daughters in 5 instances, 5 elderly women were taken out to be nursed at home by relatives, 3 patients, young & insane, were removed by their sisters, 4 middle-aged women were removed by a son or a daughter, and one very doubtful case was the last, an amorous imbecile aged 39, who was allowed out on the undertaking of her former mistress, a hairdresser.[13]

Though brutality certainly existed, it would be hugely disobliging towards the achievements of Victorian lunacy reform to contend that the universe of the asylum was devoid of compassion, and it is unlikely that we shall find in sentiments such as this the measure of the distinction from contemporary attitudes and approaches. Writing about the history of a mental hospital, the attitudes of the staff who had worked there, and the sensibilities that had animated it, Diana Gittins fastens on the real break with the past when she explains that 'many staff seemed to genuinely love the patients, though certainly never as equals. They were very much regarded as "other" . . .'. Many of the staff modelled their conception of the hospital on the analogy of the family, in which the patients were invariably the children. The universe of boundary walks and amorous imbeciles did not necessarily lack for compassion, but it was certainly an exclusionary universe in which mental patients were 'not like us', and it is this aspect which those who have grown up under the Welfare State with its commitment to equality are inclined to find most repugnant. As Diana Gittins explains further, the hospital she studied apparently stopped feeling like a family when the railings came down and the message of reform was received that 'patients were not, in fact, like children at all, but like everyone else'.[14] This, in essence, is the message that, for good and ill perhaps, has fuelled the enthusiasm for the closure of asylums, and has energized the inclusionary counter-visions of contemporary mental health policies which are intent upon affirming 'the humanity and worth of people with severe mental illness, and their rights as citizens'.[15]

Former Long-Stay Patients in the Community

So what has been happening to some of the people who were formerly long-stay residents in large mental hospitals which have now closed? The research team which is carrying out an evaluation of the resettlement of patients from Friern and Claybury hospitals is continuing to report its findings. Data are now available for the five-year follow-up of four cohorts of former long-stay patients: not a single patient was imprisoned over the period, and there were very few reported assaults, none on strangers; positive psychiatric symptoms did not alter appreciably but negative symptoms – those most amenable to social influence – declined significantly. The residents greatly appreciated the freedom in the community homes, and 80 per cent wanted to stay there. Out of a total of 550 patients from Friern, seventy-two were considered too disturbed to be relocated in the standard community homes, and instead were placed in highly staffed facilities (a staff–patient ratio of 1.7: 1), mostly on hospital sites. Inevitably, these were by far the most costly of the long-stay patients and the mean total cost of care for this group (cohort eight) was £913 per week, compared with £322 per week for the most independent members of the long-stay group (cohort one). Because of the complex mix of factors that have to be taken into account, the comparison of community and hospital-based costs must be treated with caution, but Martin Knapp and his colleagues have proposed a figure of £595.24 to reflect the weekly cost of care in Friern hospital (based on 1985/6 figures inflated to 1994/5 prices), compared with £665.26 per week averaged over all the former Friern long-stay patients now living in the community. As they reasonably claim, given the improvements in mental health and quality of life that have demonstrably taken place in this group, this represents value for money.[16]

Overall, the resettlement programme has worked well, and exemplifies an approach to hospital closure that is accompanied by the reprovision of care and services in the community. However, 15 per cent of the former long-stay patients had to be readmitted to hospital during the first year, putting increased pressure on acute beds in the district general hospitals. The reprovision of admission facilities was seen to be the main area of difficulty, and it has been suggested that increased provision of community rehabilitation units and a wider range of sheltered accommodation might obviate some of the crisis admissions. Knapp and his colleagues were careful to stress that their findings show that:

the relocation of care from Friern and Claybury has not eliminated the need for hospitals and the services they provide. There is a continuing need for clinical, social and other support provided by in-patient, day-patient and out-patient facilities. To provide adequate and appropriate community-based care for people with high support needs, it is vital that all services which long-stay hospitals provide are relocated appropriately, in sufficient number, and that they can be accessed when needed . . .[17]

The 'Person with Mental Health Problems'

As we have seen, contemporary mental health policy is based on the recognition that to conscript people with mental illness as full-time mental patients is for the most part unnecessary and damaging. The permanence and division of 'mental patienthood' has to a large extent yielded to identities that are altogether more provisional and negotiable. In the contemporary idiom, the former mental patient or sufferer from mental illness may be reconstrued as a 'person with mental health problems'. Self-ascriptions such as these are entirely appropriate to a culture in which, as Alan Ryan has remarked, there is a growing conviction that the Welfare State is broken. As Ryan goes on to say, this conviction is based not only on scruples about the cost of the Welfare State but also on the assessment that in actuality 'the "beneficiaries" of the Welfare State are really its victims: they have been turned from self-sufficient members of society, able and willing to meet their duties to themselves and everyone else, into clients, "cases" and "problems"'.[18] As one former mental patient put it:

'If we are to become part of the community we need to be there as people in our own right with skills and failings, not as the local schizophrenic. I don't want to be a schizophrenic "doing well": "Isn't he good, even though he's had a mental illness?" I just want my illness to be forgotten about. I'm not proud of it, it's a bloody nuisance. I hate being called a schizophrenic.'

Needless to say, the shift of focus from the 'mental patient' to the 'person' has generated complications and ambiguities. Often enough, these ambiguities reflect genuine uncertainties and dilemmas arising from the enormous diversity of conditions and circumstances that are assembled under banners like 'people with severe mental illness' and 'people with mental health problems'. For example, a report by the Mental Health Foundation estimates that there are about 300,000 people with severe mental illness in England and Wales, but then says that it is difficult to provide a definition of what is meant by severe mental illness. 'The principal problem with setting a precise definition is the evolving nature of mental illness: people can move in and out of the condition with some rapidity and it is not easy to pin down the point at which they do so.'[19] So when the report talks about people with severe mental illness, it does not necessarily mean people who are *actively* mentally ill. Many of them are people who have been ill in the past and whose lives have been affected by their illness, and who may perhaps become ill again in the future, yet would not necessarily consider themselves, or be considered by others, to be suffering from mental illness at the present. In brief, many 'people with severe mental illness' can, quite reasonably, be construed as 'people with mental health problems' of whose illness one can, over long periods of time, become forgetful.

Well, But Still Mentally Ill

Recently, the question of when a person can properly be said to be suffering from a mental illness has been examined by committees, which have inquired into the circumstances surrounding a number of tragic incidents involving people with a history of severe mental illness. Perhaps the most searching of these is the report of the inquiry into the tragic killing of an occupational therapist by Andrew Robinson, a patient with a long history of schizophrenic illness.[20] Andrew Robinson had a history of violence; he had been psychotic and had at one point threatened a woman with a shotgun. Moreover, when he was ill he frequently produced quite horrific sadistic and homicidal ideation, directed mainly against women. From quite an early stage in his career as a mental patient, it was apparent that Andrew was always liable to relapse and become floridly psychotic a few weeks after coming off medication. Andrew was himself reluctant to stay on medication, not least because he was troubled by side-effects and upset by the effect of the medication on his potency.

The committee concluded that, in the light of the serious risks he posed to others, Andrew's qualms about side-effects were scarcely a primary consideration. He was demonstrably suffering from an underlying disorder which, if left untreated, would render him dangerous. As a result, the committee argued, even when asymptomatic, this individual could be said, both in a clinical and more controversially in a legal sense, to be 'suffering from mental illness'. In his case, the episodic model of mental illness, in which periods of illness are followed by periods of relative 'wellness' where the former patient can be regarded as a rational agent, does not stand up.

In periods of remission, Andrew Robinson was, it would appear, an exceedingly intelligent and charming person, but those mental health professionals who at numerous points along the way permitted themselves to be swayed by him – there are veiled allusions to 'unscheduled nocturnal conversations' in 'dark corners' between Andrew and a female doctor – and to become forgetful of his illness, evidently (with the benefit of hindsight, of course) did so mistakenly. In these and other exchanges, the patient and the professionals colluded in entertaining the idea that the patient's future life might not be entirely bound by his psychiatric disorder, that there might after all be something else to hope for. Instead, Andrew should have been told that he would be on medication 'indefinitely'. 'We think it would have been preferable to face the unpalatable truth from the outset, so that Andrew would come to terms with the reality of his disorder and the permanent impact it was going to have on his life.'[21] In hospital or outside of it, Andrew Robinson should always have been dealt with as a patient whose life was to a large extent defined by his illness, and there should never have been any supposition – in the minds of professionals or of the patient – of an alternative course.

In essence, it is being argued here that there is a small minority of people who, even when apparently 'well', are none the less still 'suffering from mental illness'. Such people should not be cast as 'people with mental health problems' who can legitimately enter into negotiations with doctors and others over how they should be labelled and treated. Professionals, it is implied, have been uncritically partial towards the 'person' perspective and the humanization of the mental patient, and have either failed to detect signs of danger or have overlooked them and failed to communicate relevant information to other agencies, in the belief that to do so might stigmatize the patient or breach confidentiality. In the view of Louis Blom-Cooper and his colleagues, the 1983 Mental Health Act is irretrievably flawed, mainly because it accords a central role to the psychiatric hospital in the delivery of mental health care, and hence fails to provide the sorts of capabilities that are needed to deal with problems in a care system in which the community is the primary site of care. The authors sketch in outline some of the community-based principles on which a new mental health act should be constructed, including powers of compulsory care at designated sites in the community.

The Control of Mental Patients in the Community

Largely in response to this and other reports, the government hatched proposals for a power of supervised discharge from psychiatric hospitals which became law in April 1996 as the Mental Health (Patients in the Community) Act. The Act provides not for the compulsory treatment but for the compulsory supervision of patients in the community, and unlike the existing provisions for guardianship under the 1983 Mental Health Act which are social services led, the new Act is health led. According to the Minister:

'We are not talking about managing someone who is in the community, but about a decision to discharge someone from hospital, which must be made by the health services and the health authority. The care required should be based on a health judgement and, therefore, health management. That is right and it makes sense to the public'.[22]

Most importantly, the Act includes a power to take and convey, whereby patients who fail to adhere to the terms of the agreed treatment plan can be taken and conveyed 'to any place where the patient is required to reside or to attend for the purpose of medical treatment, occupation, education or treatment'.[23] We have only to sketch out the rudiments of the Act to recognize it as a compromise: it shies away from the vexed issue of compulsory treatment in the community, but at the same time provides for powers of arrest – some have argued to no apparent purpose. One psychiatrist claims that it 'unreasonably restricts civil rights', and that 'a highly detrimental therapeutic effect is likely to arise from community psychiatric nurses forcing unwilling patients into their cars and taking them to day centres or hospitals where they are then asked to take treatment that they have (presumably) already refused . . .'. Actions of this type 'are inconsistent with properly exercised assertive care, which rests on painstaking and careful building of a relationship with the patient'.[24] According to the Minister, the Act is unlikely to apply to more than about twenty people in each health district, but fears have been expressed that the net will be cast more widely.

Supervised discharge orders may perhaps be viewed as a temporary measure pending a fuller debate over the reform of the Mental Health Act, which will once again need to address the question of the compatibility of compulsion with care in the community.[25] Regardless of the disquiet over the existing legal framework, there is growing acceptance that in order to maintain public support for an inclusionary vision of mental health policy, there is the need for a more nuanced, discriminating, and at times hard-headed approach to community mental health care that is capable of recognizing and acknowledging its own limitations. The 'person with mental health problems' is a welcome product of a far less punitive mental health culture, yet it should be obvious at the same time that we shall continue to stand in need of concepts and theories of mental illness. As the Ritchie Report puts it, if the needs of that small group who are judged to need special supervision are not met, 'care in the community will be discredited and may be perceived as a policy which has failed'.[26] Though debate about the legal options will continue, important reforms are proceeding in any case, notably in the improvement of measures of risk assessment and procedures for the management of violence.[27]

Public Doubts

But how committed in any case is public opinion in Britain to an inclusive vision of mental health policy? Quite apart from the recent spate of alarms, there are reasons to be sceptical about the depth and extent of public commitment to reform. Public feeling has certainly been stirred in the past by revelation of abuses in mental hospitals, and the principle of a community- rather than hospital-based existence for people with mental illness appears to have attracted widespread support. David Clark writes of the changes that he and his team brought about at Fulbourn hospital in the 1950s and 1960s: 'All this happened at a time when mental hospitals were on the brink of change because English society as a whole wanted authoritarian institutions to become more liberal.'[28] Yet in recent years it is far from obvious that public thinking about people with mental illness has kept pace with the shifts that have taken place among various sections of the professional community and among former mental patients themselves. A commitment to equality in principle, perhaps, but with some measure of reserve. In certain respects, former mental patients are still under suspicion: they cannot always be trusted with children; they are unreliable employees, and so forth. Journalists continue to speak of 'the mentally ill' as of another caste, and whilst policy-makers may have decided that mental patients and former mental patients are not like children and are like everyone else, there is a lurking sense that that is still what they are: difficult children. Public tolerance and sympathy for the mentally ill is genuine but it lacks solidity, and provides only a very shaky foundation on which to generate support for programmes that declare an interest in securing a better deal for former mental patients in social life, attending to their rights, and transforming their social relationships. And, inevitably, the insolidities of public feeling and perception are likely to be sorely tested by ill winds bringing news of tragic incidents.[29]

The 'Mentally Disordered Offender'

To illustrate some of these instabilities, we may consider briefly the sorts of problems that bring people with a history of severe mental illness into the criminal justice system. Some recent research suggests that the belief that 'there is an invisible army of the mad tramping daily through our courts' is not supported by the evidence.[30] For example, individuals considered to be psychotic and urgently in need of treatment amounted to only 20 per cent of the mentally disordered offenders who appeared at a magistrates' court, and most of these were obvious from the point of their detention and so could readily be assessed by a court-based psychiatric team, and transferred to hospital where appropriate. At the same time, there was another group of offenders, many of them people with a history of psychotic illness, exhibiting mildly psychotic behaviour that did not necessarily require hospitalization. Some of these were persistent petty offenders, who though numerically not especially significant, were highly visible and time-consuming in virtue of the baggage of seemingly intractable problems that they carried with them, a 'tight bundle of multiple social need', most of them receiving inadequate support from mental health and social services.

So, for example, the majority of offenders with mental health problems did not have permanent accommodation, and compared with the remainder of the offenders were twice as likely to be living in temporary accommodation or a hostel, and three times as likely to have no fixed abode. Moreover, some of the accommodation described as 'permanent' was most precarious, and the referrals requiring most support were often 'psychotic individuals living without electricity or hot water because of unpaid bills, and with virtually no furniture'. In some cases, the instability in accommodation was related to the offence – for example loss of accommodation due to personal violence, threats or damage in the home. Other research has described the difficulties that some people with severe mental illness experience in coping with housing allocation procedures, and there is evidently need for enhanced support, not simply in securing appropriate stable accommodation but in sustaining a tenancy and minimizing the risk of breakdown and eviction through rent arrears or disputes with neighbours.

Such is the force of the stereotypical association of mental illness with violence that a violent act committed by a mentally disordered person is inevitably more 'visible' and felt to be more provocative than a similar act committed by a non mentally disordered person. As Burney and Pearson describe, when a mentally disordered person 'actually commits a violent act, he or she comes to embody this fearful stereotype. Stereotypes of violence by the mentally ill imply "unpredictability" (the "maniac" running "amok" or going "berserk") and hence are less likely to be dealt with in a confident way by either the public or professionals.' All efforts to provide practical assistance to mentally disordered offenders will 'on some occasions run headlong into this set of powerfully charged emotions', the more so if the offender is black. The conduct of black mentally disordered offenders, especially where a violent act is involved, assumes a still higher visibility, and 'while the "violent" black mentally disordered offender is hardly a big problem in numerical terms, this represents a tight concentration of high-profile problems'. Perhaps, the authors conclude, 'it is out of such acorns that the mighty oaks of stereotypical judgements grow'. Though a small minority of mentally ill offenders are acutely psychotic and are in need of immediate access to a bed in a psychiatric facility, the solutions for the great majority lie in 'local support of a low-key nature provided by a combination of health, housing and social services at ground level', and it is the creation of properly resourced structures like these that 'will prevent more mentally disturbed people from acquiring the role and status of "disordered offender"'.

The Experience of the Public Self

Lack of resources coupled with personal peculiarities frequently precipitate edgy encounters between former mental patients and bureaucratic systems of one kind or another, in which ex-patients are put in the position of having to account for themselves. For the person who is already experiencing enormous difficulties in establishing himself in a social world and in placing sufficient trust in a social setting to be able to relinquish a delusional system of reference, such encounters may serve only to confirm the humiliation that the individual already feels. James Glass has drawn attention to the importance of taking account of the vicissitudes of the individual's dealings in the public sphere, and of ministering to the 'public self of the chronically disturbed'.[31] If the former mental patient is to survive, even perhaps thrive, there need to exist some conditions at least in which the experience of the public self can become a source or focus of relative satisfaction, rather than a perpetual nullity or threat. The language of disease, James Glass writes, 'the medical language that exercises such a powerful hold over the patient's sense of identity and liberty, reinforces the self's knowledge of its own separateness, its essential and abiding alienation from the species, from community . . .'. In considering the recovery of the former mental patient's 'place' in society, it might, he proposes, 'be productive to think of place in a political language – the language of community and civility, productive activity and collaboration – and not only in medical language and the paradigm of disease and hospitalization'.[32] This is a useful distinction in redressing the balance, yet it needs to be recognized at the same time that, for some former patients at least, it may be sufficient to resume their 'place' – at the table, at the bar – rather than join a group or an association. So, for example, an ethnographic study of former mental patients by Ellen Corin has shown that the ability to avoid rehospitalization is strongly associated with a certain way of moving in urban space, in which former patients make use of various kinds of public space such as bars and cafés as 'mediating spaces' that 'allow them to stay simultaneously "within" and "outside" the social field, to remain "at a distance" while staying in touch with others'.[33]

The Care of 'the Mad'?

Largely because the fortunes of people with mental illness are so heavily determined by more pervasive features of the social fabric – especially, as we have seen, the existence of poverty – it is easy to see the whole problem as intractable and to lose cognizance of what has been achieved.[34] The volatile temper of current opinion towards the mentally ill in the community is illustrated in a recent article by a psychiatrist, writing in the *British Medical Journal*.[35] According to Simon Wessely, over the past few years government policy and influential sections of the psychiatric profession have 'united to promote the concentration of resources on what has become known as "severe mental illness"'. Wessely goes on to attack 'the obsession with severe mental illness' and the 'increasing emphasis on the care of the long-term psychotic patient' at the expense of other areas of potential psychiatric concern. 'The increasing equation of psychiatry with psychosis – and only psychosis – marks a return to the world of Victorian psychiatry.' The great asylums may have been abolished but psychiatry is reverting to 'the days of alienism: in Victorian terms, the care of "the mad"'.

The care of 'the mad'? At first reading, these are astonishing remarks that appear to telescope seven decades or more and to obliterate in a single swipe not only the significant markers of mental health legislation, but equally the achievements of psychiatry (and particularly of social psychiatry) in assisting former mental patients along the bumpy road towards more independent and dignified life-situations. The term 'lunatic' was, of course, formally abolished in 1930, when the stigma of pauperism was at least moderated, and the pauper lunatic became a 'rate-aided person'; and 'madness' disappeared with the Mental Health Act of 1959 in which the 'person of unsound mind' was replaced by the softer attribute of 'mental disorder'. As a sociologist explains, 'these changes were justified on the basis that the old terms of madness, insanity and lunacy did not correspond to the changed perception of the mentally ill in a more tolerant society'. And the changes in terminology were accompanied by major changes in policy towards the mentally ill: 'the new era of liberalism and humanitarianism would be marked by the disappearance of the asylum and the end of insanity as it had been understood'.[36] Much of the argument and analysis in this book is built on the belief that these various changes do indeed amount to something. Some, at least, of those who once took tea in a household manner on mental hospital wards have become householders in their own right, either singly or in homes shared with others, and for all the fits and starts, burps and stutters of mental health policy, there have been limited but still significant changes in the life-chances of people with severe mental illness, in their position in social life, and in the perceptions that are commonly held of them.[37]

But we can see where Wessely is coming from. From the angle of a scientific and technical culture with a repair-shop mentality, eager to circumscribe and produce neat solutions to human problems, the long-term mentally ill have failed lamentably as patients – they hang around, some of them, in their brokenness, and to make matters worse, messy social conditions seem to cling to their persons. It is understandable that some people should feel that the mad *are* still with us. But psychiatrists, among others, have helped to stimulate unrealistic expectations in the public mind, and they are partly to blame if these are now frustrated. As the historian of American psychiatry, Gerald Grob, asserts, for 'too long mental health policies have embodied an elusive dream of magical cures that would eliminate age-old maladies', largely because 'psychiatrists and other professionals have justified their raison d'être in terms of cure and overstated their ability to intervene effectively'.[38] To a large extent, it is magical thinking that spawns the rhetoric about the 'failure' of community care. As we have seen, there is plenty of promise, plenty to build upon; yet even so, the mentally ill are still a vulnerable group in our society, not least under the pressure of competing priorities. Most people with a history of severe mental illness lead humdrum, unexceptional lives, but for the television producer, exercised by the requirement to stimulate jaded audiences, and the charity fundraiser, always on the lookout for a new recipe to tempt philanthropic palates, the ordinariness of the lives of former mental patients is something of an embarrassment.

The realization that came to David Clark in the 1970s is as valid for the former mental patient in the community as for the patient in the asylum. The forces that changed patients for better or for worse, David Clark was led to acknowledge, were 'social rather than medical. It was the environment, its messages of fear, or hope, or recovery, rather than the pills they were given which determined how they recovered'.[39] We have surely learned what may happen when the messages from the environment are discouraging, when people in positions of authority once again start to talk about 'the mad' and to question the value of people with severe mental illness and the resources that are being spent on them.[40] That is why an obsession with severe mental illness should not be a matter of personal latitude but of urgent social obligation; and hence why we should feel obliged to continue to tackle the issue on several fronts simultaneously; it is a problem of control and public protection, certainly, but also of public education, and in the broadest sense of social rights and resources.[41]

Notes

Introduction

1. For discussion of Joseph, see Barham, 1984.
2. Sheppard, 1872.
3. Bennett and Morris, 1983, p. 5. For discussion of the conflictual and sometimes peculiar meanings of deinstitutionalization, see Bachrach, 1989.
4. Sheppard, 1872.
5. Talbott, 1979.
6. Powell, 1961.
7. Social Services Committee, 1985.
8. 'Asylum closures to be hastened, says minister', *Guardian*, 13 November 1990; Secretary of State for Health, 1991.
9. Porter, 1987a, p. 35.
10. ibid., p. 25.
11. See, for example, Lewis *et al.*, 1989; Shadish *et al.*, 1989.
12. On women and mental illness, see Bachrach and Nadelson, 1988.

1. Exodus

1. See Martin, 1984.
2. Wynter, A., *Lunatic Asylums*, reprinted from the *Quarterly Review*, 1857, in *Curiosities of Civilization*, 1860, quoted in Hunter and Macalpine, 1974, p. 136.
3. Commissioners in Lunacy, 1865, quoted in Hunter and Macalpine, 1974, p. 137.
4. Goffman, 1961.
5. See Scull, 1979 and 1984a; also Barham, 1993.
6. Bott, 1976, p. 102. For the history of mental health policy in Britain in this period, see also Jones, 1972 and 1988.

7. Bott, 1976, p. 105.
8. ibid.
9. ibid., p. 97.
10. ibid., p. 132.
11. ibid., p. 133.
12. Martin, 1962, p. 2.
13. ibid., p. 4.
14. ibid., p. 6.
15. ibid., p. 15.
16. Bott, 1976, p. 133.
17. ibid.
18. Martin, 1962, p. 13.
19. Bott, 1976, p. 129.
20. ibid., p. 135.
21. ibid., p. 110.
22. Powell, 1961.
23. Jones, 1988, p. 81.
24. Bennett and Morris, 1983, p. 9.
25. Tooth and Brooke, 1961; and, for comment, Bennett and Morris, 1983.
26. See Bennett and Morris, 1983.
27. Bott, 1976, p. 116.
28. Bennett and Morris, 1983, p. 10.
29. Busfield, 1986, p. 343.
30. Bleuler, 1978a, p. 441.
31. Sir Keith Joseph, 1971, quoted in Jones, 1988, p. 35.
32. Jones, 1988, p. 35.
33. ibid., p. 83.
34. DHSS, 1975.
35. e.g., Mann and Cree, 1976.
36. Bennett and Morris, 1983, p. 18.
37. Recent discussions in Ramon, 1988; Thornicroft and Bebbington, 1989.
38. Audit Commission, 1986; Social Services Committee, 1985.
39. MacCarthy, 1988, p. 212.
40. Groves, 1990, p. 1061.
41. Wing, 1991, p. 15.
42. Thornicroft and Bebbington, 1989.
43. Social Services Committee, 1985, vol. I, p. xix.

44. National Schizophrenia Fellowship, 1988.
45. Robin Cook, House of Commons, 26 June 1989.
46. Social Services Committee, 1985, vol. I, pp. xv–xvi.
47. DHSS, 1980.
48. Wing, 1991, p. 15.
49. See Thornicroft, 1989.
50. Team for the Assessment of Psychiatric Services (TAPS), 1989 and 1990. An evaluation of the closure of Cane Hill Hospital is also being undertaken by the South-east Thames Region and other regionally funded evaluations are due to start in the near future (Lindesay and Clifford, 1989).
51. National Unit for Psychiatric Research and Development (NUPRD), 1989a.
52. NUPRD, 1989b, p. 96.
53. Department of Health, 1990; Knapp *et al.*, 1991; Renshaw *et al.*, 1988.
54. PSSRU, 1990, p. 2.
55. ibid., p. 8.
56. ibid., p. 7.
57. ibid., p. 9.
58. Dayson, 1989, p. 35.
59. ibid., p. 40.
60. Bachrach, 1980.
61. On Torbay, see Beardshaw and Morgan, 1990; on the Worcester Development Project, Hall and Brockington, 1991, and Milner and Hassall, 1990/91.
62. Tansella, 1991.
63. Hatch and Nissel, 1989. On the housing problems of people leaving psychiatric care in London, see also Kay and Legg, 1986.
64. Melzer and Hale, 1989.
65. ibid., pp. 66–7.
66. ibid., p. 64.
67. Patrick *et al.*, 1989.
68. Holloway *et al.*, 1988.
69. Patrick *et al.*, 1989, p. 23.
70. For the argument that the norms used in planning psychiatric services should take explicit account of the extent of local social and economic deprivation, see Hirsch, 1988; Wing, 1991.
71. Recent discussions of ethnic minorities and the mental health

system include Dunn and Fahy, 1990; Fernando, 1988 and 1989; Harrison *et al.*, 1988; Littlewood, 1990.

72. Jones, 1979, p. 560.
73. Jones, 1988, p. 81.
74. Martin, 1962, pp. 4–5.
75. Haslam, 1984, p. 97.
76. Weller, M., Letter, *Guardian*, 21 March 1990.
77. Scottish Home and Health Department, 1989.
78. Kendell, 1989. And for a lively riposte, see Turner, 1989.
79. National Schizophrenia Fellowship, 1989.

2. 'Get Back to Your Ward'

1. Laurance, J., 'The patients who choose loneliness', *Sunday Correspondent*, 17 September 1989.
2. Lovett, A., and Turner, T., Letter, *Sunday Correspondent*, 24 September 1989.
3. Department of Social Security, 1990.
4. Goldie, 1988.
5. Bott, 1976, p. 117.
6. Beeforth *et al.*, 1990, p. 6.
7. Jones in Jones and Fowles, 1984, p. 168.
8. Social Services Committee, 1985, vol. I, p. xviii.
9. Wing, 1982.
10. Some of the material discussed here is reported in more detail in Barham and Hayward, 1995.
11. For an attempt in The Netherlands to develop such a solution, see Wiersma *et al.*, 1989.
12. For discussion see Mangen, 1988.
13. Jones, 1978, p. 328.
14. Mangen, 1988.
15. ibid., p. 75.
16. Goldie, 1988, p. 25.
17. ibid., pp. 28–9.
18. Mangen, 1988, p. 73.
19. ibid., p. 74.
20. MacCarthy *et al.*, 1986, p. 436.
21. Goldie, 1988, p. 4.
22. Bennett and Morris, 1983, p. 17.

23. Segal and Baumohl, 1985, p. 112.
24. Martin, 1962, p. 16.
25. Davis, 1988, p. 35.

3. The Asylum and the Dehumanization of the Insane

1. Foucault, 1972. For critical reassessments of Foucault's *Histoire de la folie*, see *History of the Human Sciences*, 3, nos. 1 and 3, 1990.
2. Parry-Jones, 1971; Porter, 1987b.
3. Scull, 1979 and 1981.
4. Digby, 1985, pp. 55–6.
5. ibid., p. 64.
6. Sir William Ellis, 1838, quoted in Scull, 1989, p. 226.
7. Scull, 1989, pp. 228–31.
8. Cochrane, 1988, p. 251.
9. Porter, 1987a, p. 20.
10. Porter, 1985, pp. 21–2.
11. Walton, 1985, p. 135.
12. Hare, 1983.
13. Scull, 1984b.
14. William Ley, Littlemore Asylum Annual Report, 1855.
15. Busfield, 1986, p. 265.
16. Walton, 1985, p. 141.
17. Metropolitan Commissioners in Lunacy, 1844, quoted in Busfield, 1986, p. 271.
18. Walton, 1985, p. 143.
19. Cochrane, 1988, p. 263.
20. Granville, House of Commons, 1877, quoted in Scull, 1984b.
21. Maudsley, 1871a.
22. Maudsley, 1871b.
23. Scull, 1984a, p. 130.
24. Quoted in Jones, 1971, pp. 274–5.
25. Maudsley, 1877, quoted in Hare, 1983.
26. Bucknill, 1880, pp. 3–4, quoted in Scull, 1979, p. 253.
27. Walton, 1985, p. 133.
28. Johnstone, 1909. For discussion, see Barham, 1993.
29. Knowles-Stansfield, 1914.
30. Bleuler, 1978a, p. 447.

31. ibid., p. 417.
32. Porter, R., 'Hearing the Mad', unpublished paper, European Congress on the History of Psychiatry, The Netherlands, October 1990.
33. Bauman, 1989, pp. 28–9.
34. ibid., p. 184.
35. Ibid., p. 191.
36. Lifton, 1986, p. 47.
37. Marrus, 1987, pp. 51–2, 213 n. 59.
38. Rydzinski, Z., 'The extermination of the mentally ill in Poland during the years of German occupation', unpublished paper, 1989.
39. Dörner, 1989, pp. 56–7.
40. Lafont, 1987.
41. Dörner, 1989, p. 60.
42. Burleigh, 1990, p. 14.
43. Levi, 1987, pp. 111–12.
44. Dörner, 1989, p. 8.
45. ibid., p. 49.
46. ibid., pp. 58–9.
47. Lifton, 1986, pp. 82–3.
48. ibid., 112–13.
49. Schröder, S., 'The Bürgerhospital, Stuttgart', unpublished paper, European Congress on the History of Psychiatry, The Netherlands, October 1990.
50. Lifton, 1986, p. 95.
51. See Dörner, 1989, p. 124.

4. Broken and Flawed Individuals

1. Bleuler, 1978b, pp. 663–4.
2. Marx, *Capital*, London, Lawrence & Wishart, 1960, pp. 643–4, quoted in Warner, 1985, p. 135.
3. Warner, 1985, p. 137.
4. Levi, 1987, chapter 9.
5. Warner, 1985, pp. 180, 188–9.
6. Scull, 1984a.
7. Warner, 1989, p. 23.
8. Warner, 1985, p. 99.

9. ibid., pp. 257–8.
10. Barrett, 1988, p. 373.
11. ibid., p. 374.
12. Alexander and Selesnick, 1966.
13. Barrett, 1988, p. 376.
14. ibid., p. 375.
15. Harding, 1987, p. 1227.
16. Eisenberg, 1988, pp. 4–5. On course and outcome in schizophrenia see, *inter alia*, Barham and Hayward, 1990; Bleuler, 1978a; Ciompi, 1980a and 1980b; Harding *et al.*, 1987b; and WHO, 1979.
17. Eisenberg, 1988, p. 5.
18. Warner, 1985, pp. 180–81.
19. Rutter, 1977.
20. Warner, 1985, p. 132.
21. Estroff, 1987, p. 5.
22. Ciompi, 1980a; Harding *et al.*, 1987a.
23. Estroff, 1989, p. 191.
24. Wing, 1989b, pp. 173–4.
25. ibid., p. 174.
26. Zubin *et al.*, 1983, p. 557.
27. Zubin, 1985, p. 466.
28. ibid., p. 467.
29. Strauss, 1989, p. 182.
30. ibid., p. 184.
31. Lally, 1989, p. 262.
32. ibid., p. 263.
33. Estroff, 1989, p. 191.
34. ibid., p. 194.
35. Wing, 1989a, p. 13.
36. Strauss *et al.*, 1989, p. 131.
37. Warner, 1985, pp. 299–300.
38. ibid., p. 133.
39. ibid., p. 186. For evidence in favour of this hypothesis, see Doherty, 1975, and for a discussion of 'insight', Greenfeld *et al.*, 1989.
40. Warner, 1985, p. 300.

5. Citizens and Paupers

1. For the concept of the 'abstract individual' see Lukes, 1973.
2. Lewis *et al.*, 1989, pp. 173–4.
3. Jodelet, 1991, pp. 115, 104.
4. Freeman and Roesch, 1989, p. 113.
5. Gunn *et al.*, 1991.
6. Verdun-Jones, 1989; Butler Report, 1975.
7. Gunn *et al.*, 1991.
8. Verdun-Jones, 1989, pp. 3, 20 and 22.
9. Shah, 1989, p. 240.
10. Groves, 1990, p. 1188.
11. Seebohm Report, 1968, p. 147. For discussion see Bulmer, 1987.
12. Social Services Committee, 1985, vol. I, p. lxvi.
13. Groves, 1990, p. 1188. For evidence of homelessness among former long-stay patients, see Garety and Toms, 1990.
14. Social Services Committee, 1985, vol. II, p. 219.
15. Shepherd, 1990a, pp. 14–15.
16. For example, a report on Bloomsbury Health Authority, *Guardian*, 8 March 1990.
17. Torrey, 1989, p. 34. See also Dear and Wolch, 1987; Durham, 1989.
18. Torrey, 1989, pp. 204–5.
19. ibid., p. 10; Pepper, B., 'Comprehensive care-systems: a review of the American experience', unpublished paper, symposium on 'The care of the chronic mentally ill', Section of Psychiatry, Royal Society of Medicine, May 1990.
20. Szasz, 1985.
21. Susser *et al.*, 1989.
22. Torrey, 1989, p. 15.
23. Grimshaw, 1989, p. 130.
24. ibid., p. 134.
25. ibid., p. 135.
26. ibid., p. 138.
27. Scull, 1984a; Eyles, 1988.
28. Porter, 1987c, p. 279.
29. *Community Care*, 4 October 1990.
30. Law Report, *Guardian*, 9 November 1990, Court of Appeal

C & G Homes Ltd *v.* Secretary of State for Health, before Lord Donaldson of Lymington, Master of the Rolls, Lord Justice Nourse and Lord Justice Russell, 5 November 1990.

31. ibid.
32. Melanie Phillips, 'When caring communities are hard to find', *Guardian*, 9 November 1990.
33. Mind, 1989, p. 13.
34. Ignatieff, 1989; for a stimulating discussion of the changing welfare culture see Heginbotham, 1990a.
35. Bennett, 1978, and also 1983.
36. Levi, 1987, p. 96.
37. Dahrendorf, 1988.
38. Lindow, 1990, p. 10.
39. Campbell, 1990a, p. 71.
40. See Hervey, 1986, and Porter, 1987a.
41. Campbell, 1990a, p. 69.
42. ibid.
43. Sedgwick, 1982.
44. WHO, 1989.
45. Towell and Kingsley, 1989, p. 171. For stimulating discussions of service innovation see in particular Milroy and Hennelly, 1987 and 1989; also Brackx and Grimshaw, 1989; Braisby *et al.*, 1988; Lavender and Holloway, 1988; Mind, 1987; Patmore, 1987; and Ramon, 1988.
46. O'Callaghan, 1990, pp. 81–2.
47. Lewis *et al.*, 1989, p. 178.
48. Bachrach, L., 'Deinstitutionalisation', unpublished paper, Schizophrenia 1990 International Conference, Vancouver, British Columbia, July 1990.
49. Wisconsin Department of Health and Social Services, 1985, quoted in Mosher and Burti, 1989, pp. 330–32.
50. Estroff, 1981, p. 38.
51. ibid., pp. 234–5.
52. ibid., p. 174.
53. Mosher and Burti, 1989, pp. 333, 344.
54. ibid., pp. 345–6.
55. Scott-Moncrieff, 1988, p. 221.
56. ibid.
57. Cavadino, 1990.

58. Leff, 1990.
59. Campbell, 1990b.
60. Scott-Moncrieff, 1988, p. 222.
61. ibid.
62. Kleinman *et al.*, 1989.
63. McClelland, in McClelland *et al.*, 1989.
64. Jolley *et al.*, 1989.
65. Bott, 1976, p. 118.
66. ibid., pp. 118–19.
67. ibid.
68. ibid., p. 119.
69. See, e.g., Braginsky *et al.*, 1969, and Goffman, 1961.
70. Bott, 1976, p. 120.
71. Miguel Cervantes, *Don Quixote*, part II, chapter 18.
72. Brown *et al.*, 1962. For a recent review of the literature on the family care of people with mental illness see Perring *et al.*, 1990, and for educational strategies to support relatives Berkowitz *et al.*, 1990.
73. Bean, 1986, p. 129; Percy Commission, 1957.
74. Bean, 1986, p. 149. For discussion of paternalism and civil commitment see Campbell and Heginbotham, 1991.
75. ibid., p. 176.
76. 'Police are praised for help to the mentally ill', *Independent*, 9 April 1990.
77. Hunter and Judge, 1988, p. 8.
78. ibid., p. 14. For discussion of case management see Shepherd, 1990b; Thornicroft, 1990; Holloway *et al.*, 1991.
79. Groves, 1990, p. 1062.
80. T. Hammond, personal communication, January 1992.
81. NCVO, 1989.
82. Smith, 1989, p. 6.
83. ibid., p. 7.
84. Pollitt, 1990, p. 1. On users working with purchasing authorities, see Ingrid Barker 'Agents for change', *Open Mind*, 53, Oct./Nov. 1991.
85. For a critical assessment see Pfeffer and Coote, 1991, and for a promising approach to quality assurance Richards and Heginbotham, 1990.
86. Pollitt, 1990.

87. Heginbotham, 1990b.
88. Groves, 1990, p. 924.
89. ibid., p. 1129.
90. ibid., p. 1187.
91. Thornicroft and Strathdee, 1991.
92. Hawker and Ritchie, 1990, p. 2.

6. 'Give Us Some Hope!'

1. Bott, 1976, p. 129.
2. Introduction to Bynum *et al.*, 1988, p. 3.
3. ibid., p. 7.
4. See Bynum *et al.*, vols. I and II, 1985; vol. III, 1988.
5. Crepet, 1990.
6. Crepet and Pirella, 1985, p. 165.
7. Mollica, 1985, p. 34.
8. WHO, 1985.
9. On the semantics of deinstitutionalization see Bachrach, 1989, and for a more political understanding Giannicheda, 1988.
10. Johnstone *et al.*, 1991.
11. Thornicroft and Strathdee, 1991.
12. Patmore and Weaver, 1991.
13. HRH The Prince of Wales, 1991.
14. National Schizophrenia Fellowship, Annual Review, 1990/91.
15. Dickens, 1966, pp. 259–60.
16. Warner, 1991, p. 15. See also Warner *et al.*, 1989.
17. Astrachan and Scherl, 1991.
18. Marcos *et al.*, 1990.
19. 'Ministers act on mental care', *Independent*, 20 January 1992.
20. Bleuler, 1978a, p. 502.
21. Glass, 1989, p. 215.
22. Jones, 1988, pp. 130, 90.
23. ibid., p. 94.
24. See, for example, the useful discussions of normalization theory and its applications in Ramon, ed., 1991, and Wainwright *et al.*, 1988.
25. Jonathan Miller, *Madness*, BBC 2, 3 November 1991.
26. David Piachaud, 'The god that failed', *Guardian*, 31 July 1991.
27. For a sensitive discussion of the curious advertising practices

of charities for people with disabilities see Scott-Parker, 1989.

28. Marjorie Wallace, SANE charity profile, *The Big Issue*, October 1991.

29. Birley, 1991.

30. Ignatieff, 1984, pp. 50–51.

31. On the core antagonisms of modern societies see Dahrendorf, 1988.

32. Bleuler, 1978a, p. 502.

33. Taylor, 1989, pp. 515–16.

34. Levi, 1987, pp. 94–5.

35. Hunter and Macalpine, 1974, p. 69.

7. Are 'the Mad' Still with Us?

1. These figures are indicative only, since inevitably the timing of closures is open to some revision. See Davidge *et al.*, 1993, 1994; SAVE, 1995.

2. SAVE, 1995, p. 1.

3. Emma Phillips of SAVE Britain's Heritage has produced an excellent guide to the asylum scene, SAVE, 1995. On the history of asylum architecture, see Taylor, 1991.

4. Davidge *et al.*, 1993, 1994.

5. Raftery, 1996.

6. Clark, 1996, p. 192. David Clark's book, at once a personal biography and the biography of a mental hospital, is undoubtedly the best account of English mental hospital culture, both traditional and reformed, in the twentieth century. Another excellent study is Crammer, 1990. As they close, histories of individual hospitals are starting to appear, e.g. Valentine, 1996.

7. Greater London Record Office (GLRO), LCC/MIN/949.

8. Ibid.

9. Clark, 1996, pp. 33, 35.

10. GLRO, H12/CH/A/8/1.

11. GLRO, H12/CH/A/8/3.

12. See Wright, 1997, for a critical re-examination of the social role of asylums, and our understanding of confinement, in the nineteenth century.

13. GLRO, H11/HLL/A7/7/1.

14. Gittins, 1996.

15. Mental Health Foundation, 1994, p. 17
16. Team for the Assessment of Psychiatric Services (TAPS), 1995 and 1996. An overview of the TAPS research project will appear in Leff, 1997.
17. TAPS, 1995.
18. Alan Ryan, review of 'The Principle of Duty' by David Selbourne, *London Review of Books*, 24 November 1994.
19. Mental Health Foundation, 1994, p. 15. For more detailed discussion of this issue, and practical proposals, see Powell and Slade, 1996.
20. Blom-Cooper *et al.*, 1995. A slightly more detailed discussion of this and other reports, and the issues they raise, is in Barham and Hayward, 1995.
21. Blom-Cooper *et al.*, 1995, p. 186.
22. Mental Health (Patients in the Community) Bill, Standing Committee F, 4 July 1995, House of Commons Official Report, London, HMSO.
23. Mental Health (Patients in the Community) Act 1995, London, HMSO.
24. Eastman, 1995.
25. On the debate over the Mental Health Act, see Eastman, 1994.
26. HMSO, 1994, p. 115, para 47.0.3.
27. See Eastman, 1996; Vinestock, 1996. On refining criteria to identify 'at risk' groups, see Powell and Slade, 1996.
28. Clark, 1996, p. 239.
29. The *Sun* reported the government's decision to increase provision of 24-hour nursed care for people with severe and enduring mental illness under the heading: 'WE'LL LOCK UP 5,000 PSYCHOS': 'Thousands of dangerous mental patients are to be kept off the streets in a huge shake-up of the controversial care in the community policy' (21 February 1996). In one of their admirable fact sheets, the National Schizophrenia Fellowship (1996) summarize succinctly what is known about the association between schizophrenia (and severe mental illness more generally) and violence: 'Despite the images often portrayed in the media, violence towards others is uncommon in schizophrenia. Homicide is rare, with suicide and self-harm being far more prevalent ... most people with schizophrenia are not violent and are in fact more withdrawn and less aggressive than the general population.

Many crimes of violence against people with schizophrenia are not reported and it could be argued that a person with a mental illness such as schizophrenia is far more likely to be on the receiving end of violence than to be the perpetrator.' For an illuminating attempt to put some of the incidents which have attracted public attention in a wider context, see also Bennett, 1995 and 1996. Fiona Carr (*NSF Today*, winter 1996, p. 8) also cites evidence to suggest that accusations of rape made by women with mental illness are not reaching court because the Crown Prosecution Service questions their capacity 'to testify or to understand what was happening at the time of the attack'.

30. Burney and Pearson, 1995. The quotations that follow are taken from this paper.
31. Glass, 1989, p. 212.
32. Ibid., p. 214.
33. Corin, 1990.
34. A recent and accessible discussion of poverty is the Report of the Channel 4 Commission on Poverty (Channel 4, 1996), in which the members of the commission venture a comparison between approaches to poverty in Britain and the Netherlands that is highly germane to the marginalized position of people with long-term mental illness:

'We find much to recommend in the Netherlands interpretation of poverty – that it is not just about money, but about how lack of money brings isolation and exclusion from the rest of society and mainstream life. Recognising this, they are looking at ways to engage the jobless in society and increase social activity . . . In the Netherlands there exists a political culture based more on compromise and negotiation, and less on the oppositional politics that we have here in Britain . . . There is more consensus in politics; there is a greater willingness for the public and private sectors to work in partnership; there is a greater sense of collective solidarity across income groups . . .'

So what has been achieved? A solid collection of papers on the state of the art in the commissioning of mental health services, and on the refinement of the 'contract culture', with contributions from planners, researchers, clinicians, and users of psychiatric services, is Thornicroft and Strathdee, 1996. A valuable collection that explores many of the issues touched on in this book is Heller *et al.*, 1996. The government proposes to introduce a patient's charter on mental health. Guidelines for a local charter have already been published, see Department of Health, 1994.

35. Wessely, 1996.
36. Armstrong, 1980.
37. Porter, 1996, delivers a wide-ranging account of the ups and downs of psychiatric fortunes in twentieth-century Britain. Porter manages two cheers for psychiatry. If Wessely turns out to be a trendsetter, we may only be able to raise one. A lively and informative position paper on what it means to be a mentally ill *person* is Young, 1996. Campbell, 1992, offers acerbic reflections based on his personal experience.
38. Grob, 1994, p. 311.
39. Clark, 1996, p. 194. For reflection on recovery and support in social settings, and on ideas of asylum in the community, see the essays in Tomlinson and Carrier, 1996.
40. See especially Burleigh, 1994, for a painstaking analysis of how the fragile bonds that link the mentally ill to their fellow human beings can be violated and sundered. More than any other historical work, Michael Burleigh's study of the murder of the mentally ill in the Third Reich shows that there is real point to ethical reflection on the plight of the mental patient in modern society.
41. On rights and resources, see Eastman, 1994.

References

Alexander, F., and Selesnick, S. (1966), *The History of Psychiatry*, London, Allen & Unwin.

Armstrong, D. (1980), 'Madness and coping', *Sociology of Health & Illness*, 2, pp. 293–316.

Astrachan, B., and Scherl, D. (1991), 'On the care of the poor and the uninsured', *Archives of General Psychiatry*, pp. 48, 481.

Audit Commission for Local Authorities in England and Wales (1986), *Making a Reality of Community Care*, London, HMSO.

Bachrach, L. (1980), 'Overview: model programmes for chronic patients', *American Journal of Psychiatry*, 137, pp. 1023–31.

Bachrach, L. (1989), 'Deinstitutionalisation: a semantic analysis', *Journal of Social Issues*, 45, 3, pp. 161–71.

Bachrach, L., and Nadelson, C., eds. (1988), *Treating Chronically Mentally Ill Women*, Washington D.C., American Psychiatric Press.

Barham, P. (1993), *Schizophrenia and Human Value*, London, Free Association Books (second edition, first published by Basil Blackwell, 1984).

Barham, P., and Hayward, R. (1990), 'Schizophrenia as a life-process', in Bentall, R., ed., *Reconstructing Schizophrenia*, London, Routledge.

Barham, P. and Hayward, R. (1995), *Relocating Madness: from the Mental Patient to the Person*, London, Free Association Books (second edition, first published by Routledge, 1991).

Barker, I., and Peck, E. (1987), *Power in Strange Places: User Empowerment in Mental Health Services*, London, Good Practices in Mental Health.

Barrett, R. (1988), 'Interpretations of schizophrenia', *Culture, Medicine & Psychiatry*, 12, pp. 357–88.

Bauman, Z. (1989), *Modernity and the Holocaust*, Oxford, Polity Press.

Bean, P. (1986), *Mental Disorder and Legal Control*, Cambridge, Cambridge University Press.

Beardshaw, V., and Morgan, E. (1990), *Community Care Works*, London, Mind Publications.

Beeforth, M., Conlan, E., Field, V., Hoser, A., and Bayce, L., eds. (1990), *Whose Service Is It Anyway?*, Research and Development for Psychiatry: 134–8 Borough High Street, London SEI ILB.

Bennett. D. (1978), 'Social forms of psychiatric treatment', in Wing, J., ed., *Schizophrenia: Towards a New Synthesis*, London, Academic Press.

Bennett, D. (1983), 'The historical development of rehabilitation services', in Watts, F., and Bennett, D., eds., *Theory and Practice of Psychiatric Rehabilitation*, Chichester, John Wiley.

Bennet, D. (1995), 'No lion can him fright', *Psychiatric Bulletin*, 19, pp. 565–6.

Bennet, D. (1996), 'Homicide, inquiries and scapegoating', *Psychiatric Bulletin*, 20, pp. 298–300.

Bennett, D., and Morris, I. (1983), 'Deinstitutionalization in the United Kingdom', *International Journal of Mental Health*, 11, 4, pp. 5–23.

Berkowitz, R., Shavit, N., and Leff, J. P. (1990), 'Educating relatives of schizophrenic patients', *Social Psychiatry and Psychiatric Epidemiology*, 25, pp. 216–20.

Birley, J. L. T. (1991), 'Psychiatrists and citizens', *British Journal of Psychiatry*, 159, pp. 1–6.

Bleuler, M. (1978a), *The Schizophrenic Disorders: Long-term Patient and Family Studies*, New Haven, Yale University Press (first published in 1972).

Bleuler, M. (1978b), 'The long-term course of schizophrenic psychoses', in Wynne, L., Cromwell, R., and Matthyse, S., eds., *The Nature of Schizophrenia*, New York, Wiley.

Blom-Cooper, L., Hally, H., and Murphy, E. (1995), *The Falling Shadow: One Patient's Mental Health Care 1978–1993*, London, Duckworth.

Bott, E. (1976), 'Hospital and society', *British Journal of Medical Psychology*, 49, pp. 97–140.

Brackx, A., and Grimshaw, C., eds. (1989), *Mental Health Care in Crisis*, London, Pluto Press.

Braginsky, B., Braginsky, D., and Ring, K. (1969), *Methods of Madness: The Mental Hospitals as a Last Resort*, New York, Holt, Rinehart & Winston.

Braisby, D., Echlin, R., Hill, S., and Smith, S. (1988), *Changing Futures: Housing and Support Services for People Discharged from Psychiatric Hospitals*, London, King's Fund Centre.

Brown, G. W., Monck, E. M., Carstairs, G. M., and Wing, J. K. (1962), 'Influence of family life on the course of schizophrenic illness', *British Journal of Preventive and Social Medicine*, 16, p. 55.

Brugha, T., Wing, J., Brewin, C., MacCarthy, B., Mangen, S., Lesage, A., and Mumford, J. (1988), 'The problems of people in long-term psychiatric day care', *Psychological Medicine*, 18, pp. 443–56.

Bucknill, J. (1880), *The Care of the Insane and Their Legal Control*, London, Macmillan.

Bulmer, M., (1987), *The Social Basis of Community Care*, London, Unwin.

Burleigh, M. (1990), 'Euthanasia and the Third Reich', *History Today*, 40, February, pp. 11–16.

Burleigh, M. (1994), *Death and Deliverance: 'Euthanasia' in Germany 1900–1945*, Cambridge, Cambridge University Press.

Burney, E. and Pearson, G. (1995), 'Mentally Disordered Offenders: Finding a Focus for Diversion', *Howard Journal*, 34, 4, pp. 291–313.

Busfield, J. (1986), *Managing Madness*, London, Hutchinson.

Butler Report (1975), *Report of the Committee on Mentally Abnormal Offenders* (Cmnd 6244), London, HMSO.

Bynum, W. F., Porter, R., and Shepherd, M., eds. (1985), *The Anatomy of Madness*, vol. I, 'People and Ideas', London, Tavistock Publications.

Bynum, W. F., Porter, R., and Shepherd, M., eds. (1985), *The Anatomy of Madness*, vol. II, 'Institutions and Society', London, Tavistock Publications.

Bynum, W. F., Porter, R., and Shepherd, M., eds. (1988), *The Anatomy of Madness*, vol. III, 'The Asylum and its Psychiatry', London, Routledge.

Campbell, A. (1994), 'Dependency: the foundational value in medical ethics', in Fulford, K. W. M., Gillett, G. R., and Soskice, J. M., eds., *Medicine and Moral Reasoning*, Cambridge, Cambridge University Press.

Campbell, P. (1990a), 'Mental health self-advocacy', in Winn, L., ed., *Power to the People: The Key to Responsive Services in Health and Social Care*, London, King's Fund College.

Campbell, P. (1990b), Letter, *Guardian*, 5 January 1990.

Campbell, P. (1992), 'A survivor's view of community psychiatry', *Journal of Mental Health*, 1, pp.117–22.

Campbell, T., and Heginbotham, C. (1991), *Mental Illness: Prejudice, Discrimination and the Law*, Aldershot, Dartmouth.

Cavadino, M. (1990), Letter, *Guardian*, 8 January 1990.

Channel 4 Television (1996), 'The Great, the Good, and the Dispossessed', Report of the Channel 4 Commission on Poverty, London, Channel 4 Television .

Ciompi L. (1980a), 'Ist die chronische Schizophrenie ein Artefakt? Argumente und Gegenargumente', *Fortschritte der Neurologie Psychiatrie* (Stuttgart), 48, pp. 237–48.

Ciompi L. (1980b), 'The natural history of schizophrenia in the long-term', *British Journal of Psychiatry*, 136, pp. 413–20.

Clark, D. H. (1996), *The Story of a Mental Hospital: Fulbourn 1858–1983*, London, Process Press.

Cochrane, D. (1988), '"Humane, economical and medically wise": the LCC as administrators of Victorian lunacy policy', in Bynum, W. F., Porter, R., and Shepherd, M. eds., *The Anatomy of Madness*, vol. III, London, Routledge.

Corin, E. (1990) 'Facts and meaning in psychiatry: an anthropological approach to the lifeworld of schizophrenics', *Culture, Medicine and Psychiatry*, 14, pp. 153–88.

Crammer, J. (1990), *Asylum History*, London, Gaskell.

Crepet, P. (1990), 'A transitional period in psychiatric care in Italy ten years after the reform', *British Journal of Psychiatry*, 156, pp. 27–36.

Crepet, P., and Pirella, A. (1985), 'The transformation of psychiatric care in Italy: methodological premises, current status and future prospects', *International Journal of Mental Health*, 14, pp. 155–73.

Dahrendorf, R. (1988), *The Modern Social Conflict*, London, Weidenfeld & Nicolson.

Davidge, M., Elias, S., Jayes, B., Wood, K., and Yates, J. (1993), 'Survey of English Mental Hospitals, March 1993', Inter-Authority Comparisons & Consultancy, Health Services Management Centre, University of Birmingham.

Davidge, M., Elias, S., Jayes, B., Wood, K., and Yates, J. (1994), 'Survey of English Mental Hospitals, March 1994: Monitoring the Closure of the "Water Towers" ', Inter-Authority Comparisons & Consultancy, Health Services Management Centre, University of Birmingham.

Davis, A. (1988), 'Users' perspectives', in Ramon, S. with Giannicheda, M., eds., *Psychiatry in Transition*, London, Pluto Press.

Dayson, D. (1989), 'The administrative outcome of long-term mental illness in the community', in *Moving Long-stay Patients into the Community: First Results*, Team for the Assessment of Psychiatric Services (TAPS), NE Thames Regional Health Authority.

Dear, M., and Wolch, J. (1987), *Landscapes of Despair: From Deinstitutionalisation to Homelessness*, Oxford, Polity Press.

Department of Health (1990), *Care in the Community: Making It Happen*, London, HMSO.

Department of Health (1991), *The Health of the Nation* (Cmnd 1523), London, HMSO.

Department of Health (1994), 'Guidelines for a local charter for users of mental health services', Mental Health Task Force User Group, NHS Executive. Department of Health, London.

Department of Health and Social Security (DHSS) (1975), *Better Services for the Mentally Ill*, London.

Department of Health and Social Security (DHSS) (1980), Statistical and Research Report Series No. 23, London, HMSO.

Department of Social Security (1990), *Households Below Average Income: A Statistical Analysis 1981–1987*, London, Government Statistical Service.

Dickens, C. (1966), *David Copperfield*, Harmondsworth, Penguin Books, 1966 (first published 1849–50).

Digby, A. (1985), 'Moral treatment at the Retreat, 1796–1846', in Bynum, W. F., Porter, R., and Shepherd, M., eds., *The Anatomy of Madness*, vol. II, London, Tavistock Publications.

Doherty, E. G. (1975), 'Labelling effects in psychiatric hospitalization', *Archives of General Psychiatry*, 32, pp. 562–8.

Dörner, K. (1989), *Tödliches Mitleid*, Gütersloh: Verlag Jakob van Hoddis.

Dunn, J., and Fahy, T., (1990), 'Police admissions to a psychiatric hospital: demographic and clinical differences between ethnic groups', *British Journal of Psychiatry*, 156, pp. 373–8.

Durham, M. (1989), 'The impact of deinstitutionalization on the current treatment of the mentally ill', *International Journal of Law and Psychiatry*, 12, pp. 117–31.

Eastman, N. (1994), 'Mental health law: civil liberties and the principle of reciprocity', *British Medical Journal*, 308, pp. 43–5.

Eastman, N. (1995), 'Anti-therapeutic community mental health law', editiorial, *British Medical Journal*, 310, pp. 1081–2.

Eastman, N. (1996), 'Inquiry into homicides by psychiatric patients: systematic audit should replace mandatory inquiries', *British Medical Journal*, 313, pp. 1069–71.

Eisenberg, L. (1988), 'The social construction of mental illness', *Psychological Medicine*, 18, pp. 1–9.

Estroff, S. (1981), *Making It Crazy*, Berkeley, California: University of California Press (revised paperback edn, 1985).

Estroff, S. (1987) 'No more young adult chronic patients', *Hospital and Community Psychiatry*, 38, 1, p. 5.

Estroff, S. (1989), 'Self, identity and the subjective experiences of schizophrenia', *Schizophrenia Bulletin*, 15, 2, pp. 189–96.

Eyles, J. (1988), 'Mental health services, the restructuring of care and the fiscal crisis of the state: the United Kingdom case study', in Smith, C. J., and Giggs, J., eds., *Location and Stigma*, London, Unwin Hyman.

Fernando, S. (1988), *Race and Culture in Psychiatry*, London, Croom Helm.

Fernando, S. (1989), Letter, *Psychiatric Bulletin*, 13, 10, pp. 573–4

Foucault, M. (1972), *Histoire de la folie à l'âge classique*, Paris, Gallimard (first published 1961).

Freeman, R., and Roesch R. (1989), 'Mental disorder and the criminal justice system: a review', *International Journal of Law and Psychiatry*, 12, pp. 105–15.

Garety, P., and Toms, R. (1990), 'Collected and neglected: are Oxford hostels for the homeless filling up with disabled psychiatric patients?' *British Journal of Psychiatry*, 157, pp. 269–72.

Giannicheda, M. (1988), 'A future of social invisibility', in Ramon, S., with Giannicheda, M., eds., *Psychiatry in Transition*, London, Pluto Press.

Gittins, D. (1996), 'Keep it in the Family', *Health Service Journal*, 25 July, pp. 24–7.

Glass, J. (1989), *Private Terror / Public Life: Psychosis and the Politics of Community*, Ithaca, NY, Cornell University Press.

Goffman, E. (1961), *Asylums*, Harmondsworth, Penguin Books.

Goldie, N. (1988), '"I hated it there but I miss the people": a study of what has happened to a group of ex-long stay patients from Claybury Hospital', London, South Bank Polytechnic, Health & Social Services Research Unit research paper no. 1.

Greenfeld, D., Strauss, J. S., Bowers, M. B., and Mandelkern,n, U (1989), 'Insight and interpretation of illness in recovery from psychosis', *Schizophrenia Bulletin*, 15, pp. 245–52.

Griffiths, Sir R. (1988), *Community Care: Agenda for Action*, London, HMSO.

Grimshaw, C. (1989), 'The Poor Laws revisited', in: Brackx, A., and Grimshaw, C., eds., *Mental Health Care in Crisis*, London, Pluto Press.

Grob, G. (1994), *The Mad among Us: A History of the Care of America's Mentally Ill*, Cambridge, Mass., Harvard University Press.

Groves, T. (1990), 'After the asylums', *British Medical Journal*, 300, pp. 923–4, 999–1001, 1060–62, 1128–30, 1186–8.

Gunn, J., Maden A., and Swinton, M. (1991), 'Treatment needs of prisoners with psychiatric disorders', *British Medical Journal*, pp. 303, 338–40.

Hall, P., and Brockington, I., eds. (1991), *The Closure of Mental Hospitals*, London, Gaskell.

Harding, C. (1987), Letter, *Hospital and Community Psychiatry*, 38, 11, p. 1227.

Harding, C., Rubin, J., and Strauss, J. (1987a), 'Chronicity in schizophrenia: fact, partial fact or artefact?', *Hospital and Community Psychiatry*, 88, 5, pp. 477–86.

Harding, C., Brooks, G., Ashikaga, T., Strauss, J., and Breier, A. (1987b), 'The Vermont longitudinal study of persons with severe mental illness', I and II, *American Journal of Psychiatry*, 144, 6, pp. 718–35.

Hare, E. (1983), 'Was insanity on the increase?', *British Journal of Psychiatry*, 143, pp. 439–55.

Harrison, G., Owens, D., Holton, A., Neilson, D., and Boot, D. (1988), 'A prospective study of severe mental disorder in Afro-Caribbean patients', *Psychological Medicine*, 18, pp. 643–57.

Haslam, M. (1984), 'Psychiatric hospitals and long-stay schizophrenics', *British Journal of Social and Clinical Psychiatry*, December, pp. 96–9.

Hatch, S., and Nissel, C. (1989), 'Is Community Care Working? Report on a Survey of Psychiatric Patients Discharged into Westminster', London, Westminster Association for Mental Health.

Hawker, C., and Ritchie, P. (1990), *Contracting for Community Care: Strategies for Progress*, London, King's Fund Centre.

Heginbotham, C. (1990a), *Return to Community: The Voluntary Ethic and Community Care*, London, NCVO Bedford Square Press.

Heginbotham, C., ed. (1990b), *Caring for People: Local Strategies for Achieving Change in Community Care*, London, King's Fund Centre.

Heller, T., Reynolds, J., Gomm, R., Muston, R., and Pattison, S., eds. (1996), *Mental Health Matters: a Reader*, Macmillan.

Hervey, N. (1986), 'Advocacy or folly: the Alleged Lunatics' Friends Society, 1845–63', *Medical History*, 30, pp. 245–75.

Hirsch, S. (1988), *Psychiatric Beds and Resources: Factors Influencing Bed Use and Service Planning*, London, Gaskell.

HMSO (1994), *Report of the Inquiry into the Care and Treatment of Christopher Clunis*, chaired by Jean Ritchie, London, HMSO.

Holloway, F., Davies, G., Silverman, M., and Wainwright, T. (1983), 'How many beds? A survey of needs for treatment and care in an out-patient unit', *Bulletin of the Royal College of Psychiatrists*, 12, pp. 91–4.

Holloway F., McLean E., and Robertson, J. (1991), 'Case management', *British Journal of Psychiatry*, pp. 159, 142–8.

Hunter, D., and Judge, K. (1988), *Griffiths and Community Care*, London, King's Fund Institute.

Hunter, R., and Macalpine, I. (1974), *Psychiatry for the Poor*, London, Dawsons.

Ignatieff, M. (1984), *The Needs of Strangers*, London, Chatto & Windus.

Ignatieff, M. (1989), 'Citizenship and moral narcissism', *Political Quarterly*, 60, 1, pp. 63–74.

Jodelet, D. (1991), *Madness and Social Representations* (first published in 1989 as *Folies et représentations sociales*, Presses Universitaires de France), Hemel Hempstead, Harvester Wheatsheaf.

Johnstone, E. C., Frith, C. D., Leary, J., and Owens, D. G. (1991), 'Concluding remarks', *Disabilities and Circumstances of Schizophrenic Patients: A Follow-up Study* (*British Journal of Psychiatry*, 159, Supplement 13), pp. 43–6.

Johnstone, T. (1909), 'The case for dementia praecox', *Journal of Mental Science*, 55, pp. 64–91.

Jolley, A., Hirsch, S., and Manchanda, R. (1989), 'Trial of brief intermittent neuroleptic prophylaxis for selected schizophrenic out-patients: clinical outcome at one year', *British Medical Journal*, 289, pp. 985–90.

Jones, G. (1971), *Outcast London*, Harmondsworth, Penguin Books.

Jones, K. (1972), *A History of the Mental Health Services*, London, Routledge & Kegan Paul.

Jones, K. (1978), 'Society looks at the psychiatrist', *British Journal of Psychiatry*, 132, pp. 321–32.

Jones, K. (1979), 'Deinstitutionalization in context', *Milbank Memorial Fund Quarterly/Health and Society*, 57, 4, pp. 552–69.

Jones, K. (1988), *Experience in Mental Health*, London, Sage Publications.

Jones, K., and Fowles, A. (1984), *Ideas on Institutions*, London, Routledge & Kegan Paul.

Kay, A., and Legg, C. (1986), *Discharged to the Community: A Review of Housing and Support in London for People Leaving Psychiatric Care*, London, Good Practices in Mental Health.

Kendell, R. E. (1989), 'The future of Britain's mental hospitals', *British Medical Journal*, 299, pp. 1237–8.

Kleinman, I., Schacter, D., and Koritar, E. (1989), 'Informed consent and tardive dyskinesia', *American Journal of Psychiatry*, 146, 7, pp. 902–4.

Knapp, M., Cambridge, P., Thomason, C., Allen, C., Beecham, J., and Darton, R. (1991), *Care in the Community: Evaluating a Demonstration Programme*, Aldershot, Gower.

Knowles-Stansfield, T. (1914), 'The villa or colony system for the care and treatment of cases of mental disease', *Journal of Mental Science*, 60, pp. 30–39.

Lafont, M. (1987), *L'Extermination douce*, France, Ligne, Éditions de l'Arefppi.

Lally, S. (1989), 'Does being in here mean there's something wrong with me?', *Schizophrenia Bulletin*, 15, 2, pp. 253–66.

Lavender, A., and Holloway, F., eds. (1988), *Community Care in Practice*, Chichester, John Wiley.

Leff, J. (1990), Interview, *National Schizophrenia Fellowship Newsletter*, May.

Leff, J., ed. (1997), *Care in the Community: Illusion or Reality?*, Chichester, John Wiley.

Levi, P. (1987), *If This is a Man*, London, Abacus (first published in Italy, 1957).

Lewis, D., Shadish, W., and Lurigio, A. (1989), 'Policies of inclusion and the mentally ill: long-term care in a new environment', *Journal of Social Issues*, 45, pp. 173–86.

Lifton, R. (1986), *The Nazi Doctors*, London, Macmillan.

Lindesay, J., and Clifford, P. (1989) Letter, *British Medical Journal*, 299, p. 1525.

Lindow, V. (1990), 'Participation and power', *Open Mind*, 44, April/May.

Littlewood, R. (1990), Letter, *British Journal of Psychiatry*, 156, pp. 451–2.

Lukes, S. (1973), *Individualism*, Oxford, Basil Blackwell.

MacCarthy, B. (1988), 'The role of relatives', in Lavender, A., and Holloway, F., eds., *Community Care in Practice*, Chichester, John Wiley.

MacCarthy, B., Benson, J., and Brewin, C. (1986), 'Task motivation and problem appraisal in long-term psychiatric patients', *Psychological Medicine*, 16, pp. 431–8.

McClelland, H., Harrison, G., and Soni, S. (1989), 'Brief intermittent neuroleptic prophylaxis for selected schizophrenia out-patients', *British Journal of Psychiatry*, 155, pp. 702–6.

Mangen, S. (1988), 'Dependence or autonomy?' in Ramon, S., with Giannicheda M., eds., *Psychiatry in Transition*, London, Pluto Press.

Mann, S. A., and Cree, N. (1976), '"New" long-stay psychiatric patients: a national sample survey of fifteen mental hospitals in England and Wales 1972/3', *Psychological Medicine*, 6, p. 603.

Marcos, L. R., Cohen, N. L., Nardacci, D., and Brittain, J. (1990), 'Psychiatry takes to the streets: the New York City initiative for the homeless mentally ill', *American Journal of Psychiatry*, 147, pp. 1557–61.

Marrus, M. (1987), *The Holocaust in History*, Harmondsworth, Penguin Books.

Martin, D. (1962), *Adventure in Psychiatry*, Oxford, Bruno Cassirer.

Martin, J. P. (1984), *Hospitals in Trouble*, Oxford, Basil Blackwell.

Maudsley, H. (1871a), 'Insanity and its treatment', *Journal of Mental Science*, 17, pp. 311–14.

Maudsley, H. (1871b), *The Physiology and Pathology of the Mind*, New York, Appleton (first published 1867).

Maudsley, H. (1877), 'The alleged increase of insanity', *Journal of Mental Science*, 23, pp. 45–54.

Melzer, D., and Hale, A. (1989), 'Community care of young people with schizophrenia', in *Towards Informed Action for Health*, London, Directorate of Public Health, West Lambeth Health Authority.

Mental Health Foundation (1994), *Creating Community Care: Report of the Mental Health Foundation Inquiry into Community Care for People with Severe Mental Illness*, London, Mental Health Foundation.

Milner, G., and Hassall, C. (1990/91), 'Worcester Development Project: the closure and replacement of a mental hospital', *Health Trends*, 22, 4, pp. 141–5.

Milroy, A., and Hennelly, R. (1987), 'The North Derbyshire Mental Health Services Project', in Patmore, C., *Living after Mental Illness*, London, Croom Helm.

Milroy, A., and Hennelly, R. (1989), 'Changing our professional ways', in Brackx, A., and Grimshaw, C., eds., *Mental Health Care in Crisis*, London, Pluto Press.

Mind (1989), *Building Better Futures*, London, Mind Publications.

Mollica, R. (1985), 'From Antonio Gramsci to Franco Basaglia: the theory and practice of the Italian psychiatric reform', *International Journal of Mental Health*, 14, pp. 22–41.

Mosher, L., and Burti, R. (1989), *Community Mental Health: Principles and Practice*, New York, Norton.

National Council for Voluntary Organizations (NCVO) (1989), *Contracting In or Out?*, London, NCVO.

National Schizophrenia Fellowship (1988), 'Report on hospital closures', Kingston-upon-Thames, National Schizophrenia Fellowship.

National Schizophrenia Fellowship (1989), *Slipping Through the Net*, Kingston-upon-Thames, National Schizophrenia Fellowship.

National Schizophrenia Fellowship (1996), 'Schizophrenia and Research – UK', Fact Sheet No. 6, Kingston-upon-Thames, National Schizophrenia Fellowship.

National Unit for Psychiatric Research and Development (NUPRD) (1989a), 'Warley Hospital: Patients' Needs Survey', Lewisham Hospital, Lewisham, NUPRD.

National Unit for Psychiatric Research and Development (NUPRD) (1989b), 'Springfield Hospital Long Stay Patients: Assessment of Needs for Care', Lewisham Hospital, Lewisham, NUPRD.

O'Callaghan, M. (1990), 'Community care means never having to say you're sorry', in Sharkey, S., and Barna, S., eds., *Community Care: People Leaving Long-stay Hospitals*, London, Routledge.

Parry-Jones. W. (1971), *The Trade in Lunacy*, London, Routledge.

Patmore, C., ed. (1987), *Living after Mental Illness*, London, Croom Helm.

Patmore, C. and Weaver, T. (1991), *Community Mental Health Teams: Lessons for Planners and Managers*, Good Practices in Mental Health, 380–84 Harrow Rd, London W9 2HU.

Patrick, M., Higgit, A., and Holloway, F. (1989), 'Changes in an inner city psychiatric inpatient service following bed losses: a follow-up of the East Lambeth 1986 Survey', *Health Trends*, 21, pp. 121–3.

Percy Commission (1957), *Royal Commission on the Law Relating to Mental Illness and Mental Deficiency, 1954–7* (Cmnd 169), London, HMSO.

Perring, C., Twigg, J., and Atkin, K., (1990), *Families Caring for People Diagnosed as Mentally Ill: The Literature Re-Examined*, London, HMSO.

Pfeffer, N., and Coote, A. (1991), *Is Quality Good for You?*, London, Institute for Public Policy Research.

Pollitt, C. (1990), 'Consumers and the NHS', *King's Fund News*, 13, 2, p. 1.

Porter, R. (1985), 'The history of institutional psychiatry in Europe', unpublished paper.

Porter, R. (1987a), *A Social History of Madness*, London, Weidenfeld & Nicolson.

Porter, R. (1987b), *Mind-forg'd Manacles*, Harmondsworth, Penguin Books.

Porter, R. (1987c), 'Bedlam and Parnassus: mad people's writings in Georgian England', in Levine, G., ed., *One Culture*, Wisconsin, University of Wisconsin Press.

Porter, R. (1996), 'Two cheers for psychiatry! The social history of mental disorder in twentieth century Britain', in Freeman, H. and Berrios, G., eds., *150 Years of British Psychiatry 1841–1991*, vol. II., *The Aftermath*, London, Athlone.

Powell, E. (1961), Address to the National Association for Mental Health, in *Emerging Patterns for the Mental Health Services and the Public*, London, NAMH.

Powell, R., and Slade, M. (1996), 'Defining severe mental illness', in Thornicroft, G., and Strathdee, G., eds., *Commissioning Mental Health Services*, London, HMSO.

PSSRU (1990), 'Care in the Community: Lessons from a Demonstration Programme', *Care in the Community Newsletter*, 9, Canterbury, University of Kent, Personal Social Services Research Unit.

Raftery, J. (1996), 'The decline of asylum or the poverty of the concept?', in Tomlinson, D., and Carrier, J., eds., *Asylum in the Community*, London, Routledge.

Ramon, S. (1988), 'Community Care in Britain', in Lavender, A., and Holloway, F., eds., *Community Care in Practice*, Chichester, John Wiley.

Ramon, S., ed. (1991), *Beyond Community Care*, Basingstoke, Macmillan.

Ramon S., with Giannicheda, M., eds., (1988), *Psychiatry in Transition*, London, Pluto Press.

Renshaw, J., Hampson, R., Thomason, C., Darton, R., Judge, K., and Knapp, M. (1988), *Care in the Community: The First Steps*, Aldershot, Gower.

Richards, H., and Heginbotham, C. (1990), *The Enquire System: A Workbook on Quality Assurance in Health and Social Care*, London, King's Fund College.

Robertson, J. (1991), contribution to debate 'This House recognizes the continued need for asylum', in: Hall, P., and Brockington, I., eds., *The Closure of Mental Hospitals*, London, Gaskell.

Rutter, D. R. (1977), 'Speech patterning in recently admitted and chronic long-stay schizophrenic patients', *British Journal of Social and Clinical Psychology*, 16, pp. 47–55.

SAVE (1995), 'Mind over Matter: A Study of the Country's Threatened Mental Asylums', SAVE Britain's Heritage, London.

Scottish Home and Health Department (1989), *Mental Hospitals in Focus*, Edinburgh, HMSO.

Scott-Moncrieff, L. (1988), Comments on the discussion document of the Royal College of Psychiatrists regarding Community Treatment Orders, in *Bulletin of the Royal College of Psychiatrists*, 12, pp. 220–23.

Scott-Parker, S. (1989), *'They aren't in the Brief': Advertising People with Disabilities*, London, King's Fund Centre.

Scull, A. (1979), *Museums of Madness*, London, Allen Lane.

Scull, A. (1981), 'Moral treatment reconsidered: some sociological comments on an episode in the history of British psychiatry,' in Scull, A. ed., *Madhouses, Mad-doctors, and Madmen*, London, Athlone Press.

Scull, A. (1984a), *Decarceration*, 2nd edn, Oxford, Polity Press.

Scull, A. (1984b), 'Was insanity increasing? A response to Edward Hare', *British Journal of Psychiatry*, 144, pp. 432–6 (reprinted in Scull, 1989).

Scull, A. (1989), *Social Disorder / Mental Disorder*, London, Routledge.

Sedgwick, P. (1982), *Psychopolitics*, London, Pluto Press.

Seebohm Report (1968), *Report of the Committee on Local Authority and Allied Personal Social Services* (Cmnd 3703), London, HMSO.

Segal, S., and Baumohl, J. (1985), 'The community living-room', *Journal of Contemporary Social Work*, February, pp. 111–16.

Shadish, W., Lurigio, A., and Lewis, D. (1989), 'After deinstitutionalization: the present and future of mental health long-term care policy', *Journal of Social Issues*, 45, pp. 1–15.

Shah, S. (1989), 'Mental disorder and the criminal justice system: some overarching issues', *International Journal of Law and Psychiatry*, 12, pp. 231–44.

Shepherd, G. (1990a), 'Community care: a historical overview', in

Sharkey, S. and Barna, S., eds., *Community Care: People Leaving Long-stay Hospitals*, London, Routledge.

Shepherd, G. (1990b), 'Case management', *Health Trends*, 2, pp. 59–61.

Sheppard, E. (1872), 'On some of the modern teachings of insanity', *Journal of Mental Science*, 17, pp. 499–514.

Smith, H. (1989), 'Collaboration for change', in Towell, D., Kingsley, S., and McAusland, T., eds., *Managing Psychiatric Services in Transition*, London, King's Fund College.

Social Services Committee (1985), *Community Care, with Special Reference to Adult Mentally Ill, and Mentally Handicapped People*, vols I–III, London, HMSO.

Strauss, J., Rakfeldt, J., Harding, C., and Lieberman, P. (1989), 'Psychological and social aspects of negative symptoms', *British Journal of Psychiatry*, 155 (suppl. 7), pp. 128–32.

Strauss, J. (1989), 'Subjective experiences of schizophrenia: towards a new dynamic psychiatry II', *Schizophrenia Bulletin*, 15, 2, pp. 179–88.

Susser E., Struening E. L., and Conover, S. (1989), 'Psychiatric problems in homeless men', *Archives of General Psychiatry*, 46, pp. 845–50.

Szasz, T. (1985), 'A home for the homeless: the half-forgotten heart of mental health services', in Terrington, R., ed., *Towards a Whole Society*, London, Richmond Fellowship Press.

Talbott, J. (1979), 'Deinstitutionalisation: avoiding the errors of the past', *Hospital and Community Psychiatry*, 30, pp. 621–4.

Tansella, M. (1991), 'Community-based psychiatry: long-term patterns of care in South-Verona', *Psychological Medicine*, Monograph Supplement No. 19.

TAPS (1989), *Moving Long-stay Psychiatric Patients into the Community: First Results*, Papers Presented at the Fourth Annual Conference of the Team for the Assessment of Psychiatric Services, NE Thames Regional Health Authority.

TAPS (1990), *Better Out Than In?*, Report of Fifth Annual Conference of the Team for the Assessment of Psychiatric Services, NE Thames Regional Health Authority.

TAPS (1995), Tenth Annual Conference of the Team for the Assessment of Psychiatric Services, Summary of Proceedings, July 1995, TAPS Research Unit, London.

TAPS (1996), Eleventh Annual Conference of the Team for the

Assessment of Psychiatric Services, Summary of Proceedings, July 1996, TAPS Research Unit, London.

Taylor C. (1989), *Sources of the Self*, Cambridge, Cambridge University Press.

Taylor, J. (1991), *Hospital and Asylum Architecture in England 1840–1914*, London, Mansell.

Thornicroft, G. (1989), Letter, *British Medical Journal*, 299, p. 1523.

Thornicroft, G. (1990), 'Case managers for the mentally ill', *Social Psychiatry and Psychiatric Epidemiology*, 25, pp. 141–3.

Thornicroft, G., and Bebbington, P. (1989), 'Deinstitutionalisation – from hospital closure to service development', *British Journal of Psychiatry*, pp. 739–53.

Thornicroft, G., and Strathdee, G. (1991), 'Mental health', *British Medical Journal*, 303, pp. 410–12.

Thornicroft, G. and Strathdee, G., eds. (1996), *Commissioning Mental Health Services*, London, HMSO.

Tomlinson, D., and Carrier, J., eds. (1996), *Asylum in the Community*, London, Routledge.

Tooth, G. C., and Brooke, E. M. (1961), 'Trends in the mental hospital population and their effect on future planning', *Lancet*, 1, p. 710.

Torrey, E. F. (1989), *Nowhere to Go: The Tragic Odyssey of the Homeless Mentally Ill*, NY, Harper & Row.

Towell, D., and Kingsley, S. (1988), 'Changing psychiatric services in Britain', in Ramon, S., with Giannicheda, M., eds., *Psychiatry in Transition*, London, Pluto Press.

Turner, T. (1989), Letter, *British Medical Journal*, 299, pp. 1524–5.

Valentine, R., (1996), *Asylum, Hospital, Haven: A History of Horton Hospital*, Riverside Mental Health Trust, London.

Verdun-Jones, S. (1989), 'Sentencing the partly mad and the partly bad: the case of the Hospital Order in England', *International Journal of Law and Psychiatry*, 12, pp. 1–27.

Vinestock, M. D. (1996), 'Risk assessment: a word to the wise?', *Advances in Psychiatric Treatment*, 2, pp. 3–10.

Wainwright, T., Holloway, F., and Brugha, T. (1988), 'Day care in an inner city', in Lavender, A., and Holloway, F., eds., *Community Care in Practice*, Chichester, John Wiley.

Wales, HRH The Prince of (1991), Lecture as Patron to the Royal

College of Psychiatrists, *British Journal of Psychiatry*, 159, pp. 763–8.

Walton, J. (1985), 'Casting out and bringing back in Victorian England: pauper lunatics 1840–1970', in Bynum, W. F., Porter, R., and Shepherd, M., eds., *The Anatomy of Madness*, vol. II, London, Tavistock Publications.

Warner, R. (1985), *Recovery from Schizophrenia*, London, Routledge.

Warner, R. (1989), 'Deinstitutionalization: how did we get where we are?', *Journal of Social Issues*, 45, 3, pp. 17–30.

Warner, R. (1991), 'Why involve consumers?' *Open Mind*, 51, June/July.

Warner, R., Taylor, D., Powers, M., and Hyman, J. (1989), 'Acceptance of the mental illness label by psychotic patients', *American Journal of Orthopsychiatry*, 59, pp. 398–409.

Wessely, S. (1996), 'The rise of counselling and the return of alienism', *British Medical Journal*, 313, pp. 158–60.

Wiersma, D., Kluiter, H., Nienhuis, F., Ruphan, M., and Giel, R. (1989), *Day Treatment with Community Care as an Alternative to Standard Hospitalization: An Experiment in the Netherlands*, Groningen, University of Groningen, Department of Social Psychiatry.

Wilkinson, G., and Freeman, H., eds. (1986), *The Provision of Mental Health Services in Britain: The Way Ahead*, London, Gaskell.

Wing, J. K. (1982), 'Course and prognosis in schizophrenia', in Wing, J. K., and Wing, L., eds., *Handbook of Psychiatry*, vol. III, Cambridge, Cambridge University Press.

Wing, J. K. (1989a), 'The concept of negative symptoms', *British Journal of Psychiatry*, 155 (suppl. 7), pp. 10–14.

Wing, J. K. (1989b), 'The measurement of "social disablement"', *Social Psychiatry and Psychiatric Epidemiology*, 24, pp. 173–8.

Wing, J. K. (1991), 'Vision and reality', in Hall, P., and Brockington, I., eds., *The Closure of the Mental Hospitals*, London, Gaskell.

World Health Organization (WHO) (1979), *Schizophrenia: An International Follow-up Study*, London, Wiley.

World Health Organization (WHO) (1985), *Mental Health Services in Europe, Ten Years On*, Copenhagen, WHO Regional Office for Europe.

World Health Organization (WHO) (1989), *Consumer Involvement in Mental Health and Rehabilitation Services* (WHO/MNH/MEP, 89, 7), Geneva, Division of Mental Health, WHO.

Wright, D. (1997), 'Getting Out of the Asylum: Understanding the Confinement of the Insane in the Nineteenth Century', *Social History of Medicine*, in press.

Young, R. (1996), 'The moral and molecular in the future of psychiatry', paper presented to the conference on the bicentenary of the founding of The Retreat, York, October 1996 (available from The Retreat, Heslington Road, York YO1 5BN).

Zubin, J. (1985), 'Negative symptoms: are they indigenous to schizophrenia?', *Schizophrenia Bulletin*, 11, 3, pp. 461–9.

Zubin, J., Magaziner, J., and Steinheuer, S. (1983), 'The metamorphosis of schizophrenia: from chronicity to vulnerability', *Psychological Medicine*, 13, pp. 551–71.

Index

READ MORE IN PENGUIN

In every corner of the world, on every subject under the sun, Penguin represents quality and variety – the very best in publishing today.

For complete information about books available from Penguin – including Puffins, Penguin Classics and Arkana – and how to order them, write to us at the appropriate address below. Please note that for copyright reasons the selection of books varies from country to country.

In the United Kingdom: Please write to *Dept. EP, Penguin Books Ltd, Bath Road, Harmondsworth, West Drayton, Middlesex UB7 0DA*

In the United States: Please write to *Consumer Sales, Penguin USA, P.O. Box 999, Dept. 17109, Bergenfield, New Jersey 07621-0120*. VISA and MasterCard holders call 1-800-253-6476 to order Penguin titles

In Canada: Please write to *Penguin Books Canada Ltd, 10 Alcorn Avenue, Suite 300, Toronto, Ontario M4V 3B2*

In Australia: Please write to *Penguin Books Australia Ltd, P.O. Box 257, Ringwood, Victoria 3134*

In New Zealand: Please write to *Penguin Books (NZ) Ltd, Private Bag 102902, North Shore Mail Centre, Auckland 10*

In India: Please write to *Penguin Books India Pvt Ltd, 706 Eros Apartments, 56 Nehru Place, New Delhi 110 019*

In the Netherlands: Please write to *Penguin Books Netherlands bv, Postbus 3507, NL-1001 AH Amsterdam*

In Germany: Please write to *Penguin Books Deutschland GmbH, Metzlerstrasse 26, 60594 Frankfurt am Main*

In Spain: Please write to *Penguin Books S. A., Bravo Murillo 19, 1° B, 28015 Madrid*

In Italy: Please write to *Penguin Italia s.r.l., Via Felice Casati 20, I–20124 Milano*

In France: Please write to *Penguin France S. A., 17 rue Lejeune, F–31000 Toulouse*

In Japan: Please write to *Penguin Books Japan, Ishikiribashi Building, 2–5–4, Suido, Bunkyo-ku, Tokyo 112*

In South Africa: Please write to *Longman Penguin Southern Africa (Pty) Ltd, Private Bag X08, Bertsham 2013*

READ MORE IN PENGUIN

A CHOICE OF NON-FICTION

Citizens Simon Schama

'The most marvellous book I have read about the French Revolution in the last fifty years' – *The Times*. 'He has chronicled the vicissitudes of that world with matchless understanding, wisdom, pity and truth, in the pages of this huge and marvellous book' – *Sunday Times*

1945: The World We Fought For Robert Kee

Robert Kee brings to life the events of this historic year as they unfolded, using references to contemporary newspapers, reports and broadcasts, and presenting the reader with the most vivid, immediate account of the year that changed the world. 'Enthralling ... an entirely realistic revelation about the relationship between war and peace' – *Sunday Times*

Cleared for Take-Off Dirk Bogarde

'It begins with his experiences in the Second World War as an interpreter of reconnaissance photographs ... he witnessed the liberation of Belsen – though about this he says he cannot write. But his awareness of the horrors as well as the dottiness of war is essential to the tone of this affecting and strangely beautiful book' – *Daily Telegraph*

Nine Parts of Desire Geraldine Brooks
The Hidden World of Islamic Women

'She takes us behind the veils and into the homes of women in every corner of the Middle East ... It is in her description of her meetings – like that with Khomeini's widow Khadija, who paints him as a New Man (and one for whom she dyed her hair vamp-red) – that the book excels' – *Observer*. 'Frank, engaging and captivating' – *New Yorker*

Insanely Great Steven Levy

The Apple Macintosh revolutionized the world of personal computing – yet the machinations behind its conception were nothing short of insane. 'One of the great stories of the computing industry ... a cast of astonishing characters' – *Observer*. 'Fascinating edge-of-your-seat story' – *Sunday Times*

READ MORE IN PENGUIN

A CHOICE OF NON-FICTION

Time Out Film Guide Edited by John Pym

The definitive, up-to-the-minute directory of every aspect of world cinema from classics and silent epics to reissues and the latest releases.

Flames in the Field Rita Kramer

During July 1944, four women agents met their deaths at Struthof-Natzweiler concentration camp at the hands of the SS. They were members of the Special Operations Executive, sent to Nazi-occupied France in 1943. *Flames in the Field* reveals that the odds against their survival were weighted even more heavily than they could possibly have contemplated, for their network was penetrated by double agents and security was dangerously lax.

Colored People Henry Louis Gates Jr.

'A wittily drawn portrait of a semi-rural American community, in the years when racial segregation was first coming under legal challenge ... In the most beautiful English ... he recreates a past to which, in every imaginable sense, there is no going back' – *Mail on Sunday*

Naturalist Edward O. Wilson

'His extraordinary drive, encyclopaedic knowledge and insatiable curiosity shine through on virtually every page' – *Sunday Telegraph*. 'There are wonderful accounts of his adventures with snakes, a gigantic ray, butterflies, flies and, of course, ants ... a fascinating insight into a great mind' – *Guardian*

Roots Schmoots Howard Jacobson

'This is no exercise in sentimental journeys. Jacobson writes with a rare wit and the book sparkles with his gritty humour ... he displays a deliciously caustic edge in his analysis of what is wrong, and right, with modern Jewry' – *Mail on Sunday*

READ MORE IN PENGUIN

A CHOICE OF NON-FICTION

Mornings in the Dark Edited by David Parkinson
The Graham Greene Film Reader

Prompted by 'a sense of fun' and 'that dangerous third Martini' at a party in June 1935, Graham Greene volunteered himself as the *Spectator* film critic. 'His film reviews are among the most trenchant, witty and memorable one is ever likely to read' – *Sunday Times*

Real Lives, Half Lives Jeremy Hall

The world has been 'radioactive' for a hundred years – providing countless benefits to medicine and science – but there is a downside to the human mastery of nuclear physics. *Real Lives, Half Lives* uncovers the bizarre and secret stories of people who have been exposed, in one way or another, to radioactivity across the world.

Hidden Lives Margaret Forster

'A memoir of Forster's grandmother and mother which reflects on the changes in women's lives – about sex, family, work – across three generations. It is a moving, evocative account, passionate in its belief in progress, punchy as a detective novel in its story of Forster's search for her grandmother's illegitimate daughter. It also shows how biography can challenge our basic assumptions about which lives have been significant and why' – *Financial Times*

Eating Children Jill Tweedie

'Jill Tweedie re-creates in fascinating detail the scenes and conditions that shaped her, scarred her, broke her up or put her back together ... a remarkable story' – *Vogue*. 'A beautiful and courageous book' – Maya Angelou

The Lost Heart of Asia Colin Thubron

'Thubron's journey takes him through a spectacular, talismanic geography of desert and mountain ... a whole glittering, terrible and romantic history lies abandoned along with thoughts of more prosperous times' – *The Times*

READ MORE IN PENGUIN

A CHOICE OF NON-FICTION

African Nights Kuki Gallmann

Through a tapestry of interwoven true episodes, Kuki Gallmann here evokes the magic that touches all African life. The adventure of a moonlit picnic on a vanishing island; her son's entrancement with chameleons and the mystical visit of a king cobra to his grave; the mysterious compassion of an elephant herd – each event conveys her delight and wonder at the whole fabric of creation.

Far Flung Floyd Keith Floyd

Keith Floyd's culinary odyssey takes him to the far-flung East and the exotic flavours of Malaysia, Hong Kong, Vietnam and Thailand. The irrepressible Floyd as usual spices his recipes with witty stories, wry observation and a generous pinch of gastronomic wisdom.

The Reading Solution Paul Kropp with Wendy Cooling

The Reading Solution makes excellent suggestions for books – both fiction and non-fiction – for readers of all ages that will stimulate a love of reading. Listing hugely enjoyable books from history and humour to thrillers and poetry selections, *The Reading Solution* provides all the help you need to ensure that your child becomes – and stays – a willing, enthusiastic reader.

Lucie Duff Gordon Katherine Frank
A Passage to Egypt

'Lucie Duff Gordon's life is a rich field for a biographer, and Katherine Frank does her justice ... what stays in the mind is a portrait of an exceptional woman, funny, wry, occasionally flamboyant, always generous-spirited, and firmly rooted in the social history of her day' – *The Times Literary Supplement*

The Missing of the Somme Geoff Dyer

'A gentle, patient, loving book. It is about mourning and memory, about how the Great War has been represented – and our sense of it shaped and defined – by different artistic media ... its textures are the very rhythms of memory and consciousness' – *Guardian*

READ MORE IN PENGUIN

A CHOICE OF NON-FICTION

The Pillars of Hercules   Paul Theroux

At the gateway to the Mediterranean lie the two Pillars of Hercules. Beginning his journey in Gibraltar, Paul Theroux travels the long way round – through the ravaged developments of the Costa del Sol, into Corsica and Sicily and beyond – to Morocco's southern pillar. 'A terrific book, full of fun as well as anxiety, of vivid characters and curious experiences' – *The Times*

Where the Girls Are   Susan J. Douglas

In this brilliantly researched and hugely entertaining examination of women and popular culture, Susan J. Douglas demonstrates the ways in which music, TV, books, advertising, news and film have affected women of her generation. Essential reading for cultural critics, feminists and everyone else who has ever ironed their hair or worn a miniskirt.

Journals: 1954–1958   Allen Ginsberg

These pages open with Ginsberg at the age of twenty-eight, penniless, travelling alone and unknown in California. Yet, by July 1958 he was returning from Paris to New York as the poet who, with Jack Kerouac, led and inspired the Beats . . .

The New Spaniards   John Hooper

Spain has become a land of extraordinary paradoxes in which traditional attitudes and contemporary preoccupations exist side by side. The country attracts millions of visitors – yet few see beyond the hotels and resorts of its coastline. John Hooper's fascinating study brings to life the many faces of Spain in the 1990s.

A Tuscan Childhood   Kinta Beevor

Kinta Beevor was five when she fell in love with her parents' castle facing the Carrara mountains. 'The descriptions of the harvesting and preparation of food and wine by the locals could not be bettered . . . alive with vivid characters' – *Observer*